ASPEN PUBLISHERS

2008-2009 Supplement

National Security Law

Fourth Edition

Stephen Dycus
Professor of Law
Vermont Law School

Arthur L. Berney
Professor of Law, Emeritus
Boston College

William C. Banks
Laura J. and L. Douglas Meredith Professor
Syracuse University

Peter Raven-Hansen
Glen Earl Weston Research Professor of Law
George Washington University

Wolters Kluwer
Law & Business

AUSTIN BOSTON CHICAGO NEW YORK THE NETHERLANDS

Aspen Publishers
Attn: Permissions Department
76 Ninth Avenue, 7th Floor
New York, NY 10011-5201

To contact Customer Care, e-mail customer.care@aspenpublishers.com, call 1-800-234-1660, fax 1-800-901-9075, or mail correspondence to:

Aspen Publishers
Attn: Order Department
PO Box 990
Frederick, MD 21705

Printed in the United States of America.

1 2 3 4 5 6 7 8 9 0

ISBN 978-0-7355-7359-8

Library of Congress Cataloging-in-Publication Data

National security law / Stephen Dycus…[et al.]. – 4th ed.
p. cm.
Includes bibliographical references and index.
ISBN 978-0-7355-5614-0 (casebook)
ISBN 978-0-7355-7359-8 (supplement)
1. National security — Law and Legislation — United States. I. Dycus, Stephen.

KF4651.N377 2007
343.73'01 — dc22

2007003759

About Wolters Kluwer Law & Business

Wolters Kluwer Law & Business is a leading provider of research information and workflow solutions in key specialty areas. The strengths of the individual brands of Aspen Publishers, CCH, Kluwer Law International and Loislaw are aligned within Wolters Kluwer Law & Business to provide comprehensive, in-depth solutions and expert-authored content for the legal, professional and education markets.

CCH was founded in 1913 and has served more than four generations of business professionals and their clients. The CCH products in the Wolters Kluwer Law & Business group are highly regarded electronic and print resources for legal, securities, antitrust and trade regulation, government contracting, banking, pension, payroll, employment and labor, and healthcare reimbursement and compliance professionals.

Aspen Publishers is a leading information provider for attorneys, business professionals and law students. Written by preeminent authorities, Aspen products offer analytical and practical information in a range of specialty practice areas from securities law and intellectual property to mergers and acquisitions and pension/benefits. Aspen's trusted legal education resources provide professors and students with high-quality, up-to-date and effective resources for successful instruction and study in all areas of the law.

Kluwer Law International supplies the global business community with comprehensive English-language international legal information. Legal practitioners, corporate counsel and business executives around the world rely on the Kluwer Law International journals, loose-leafs, books and electronic products for authoritative information in many areas of international legal practice.

Loislaw is a premier provider of digitized legal content to small law firm practitioners of various specializations. Loislaw provides attorneys with the ability to quickly and efficiently find the necessary legal information they need, when and where they need it, by facilitating access to primary law as well as state-specific law, records, forms and treatises.

Wolters Kluwer Law & Business, a unit of Wolters Kluwer, is headquartered in New York and Riverwoods, Illinois. Wolters Kluwer is a leading multinational publisher and information services company.

Contents

* * *

Preface

How could a casebook published just a year and a half ago need a supplement that runs more than 300 pages? The answer lies in the recent explosion of National Security Law, reflecting the fact that many of the important questions about separation of powers and civil liberties raised in the wake of 9/11 are only now – seven years later – beginning to be answered. As one wag put it, the terrorism rat is finally beginning to make its way through the judicial snake.

In fact, several of the cases included here were decided just weeks before the completion of this Supplement: *Boumediene v. Bush* and *Munaf v. Geren*, landmark habeas corpus cases in the Supreme Court; *Al-Marri v. Pucciarelli* (4th Cir. en banc), a military detention case; and *United States v. Abu Ali* (4th Cir.), a case involving secret evidence. Certiorari was granted by the Supreme Court in *Iqbal v. Hasty* (2d Cir.), an immigration detention case, on June 16, 2008, and other cases in this Supplement are currently on appeal.

Congress has been busy, too. This Supplement includes edited versions of a Senate Intelligence Committee report on justifications for the Iraq War, published June 5, 2008, and of the FISA Amendments Act of 2008, enacted July 10, 2008.

Finally, just two days before this Supplement was scheduled to go to the printer, the President signed a new executive order, amending Exec. Order No. 12,333, which sets out a charter for the intelligence community. The amended order, too, is excerpted here.

There is no evidence that the pace of change will slacken any time soon. For teachers as well as students, this means that, like practitioners in the field, you will need to be alert to new developments in the law. This is especially true at a time of transition from one presidential administration to the next. By the time you read this, in other words, you will almost surely have to supplement the Supplement.

With all the challenges of trying to stay current, National Security Law remains the most interesting and exciting course we have ever taught, and it engages students like no other. Whether it is offered as a survey course or as a dedicated Counterterrorism Law course, it connects us personally and professionally with what we read on the front page of each day's newspaper. More fundamentally, it provides a unique opportunity to stress the importance of the rule of law and the applicability of sound legal analysis in the life and death decisions that government makes to protect us from terrorists, rogue states, and international criminal gangs.

This Supplement is designed to serve users of both *National Security Law* (4th ed. 2006) and *Counterterrorism Law* (2007). A separate guide containing cross-references to the latter casebook follows this Preface.

As always, we are extremely grateful to our adopters, fellow members of the growing National Security Law Section of the Association of American Law Schools, fellow members of the editorial board of the Journal of National Security Law & Policy, fellow casebook authors (our collaborators in building the field), and our many friends in the national security community. We also wish to thank our research assistants: Sara T. Niazi at George Washington University Law School; and Kimberly Chehardy, Michael Cretella, Eric Goldwarg, and Taylor Neff at Vermont Law School. Thanks are due as well to our copy editor, Julie Nahil, for her help in preparing this Supplement. Finally, we are grateful to Eric Holt, Carmen Corral-Reid, Melody Davies, and Carol McGeehan of Aspen Publishers for their continued encouragement and support.

Stephen Dycus
William C. Banks
Peter Raven-Hansen

July 31, 2008

Conversion Guide for Counterterrorism Law

This Supplement may be adapted for use with *Counterterrorism Law* (2007). Materials herein should be read at the points indicated:

Pages in Counterterrorism Law	**Supplemental Material**	**Page in This Supplement**
Page 155. Insert after Note 6.	*Mayfield v. United States*	31
Page 169. Insert after District Court decision.	*ACLU v. NSA* (6th Cir.)	36
Page 174. Insert after Note 9.	FISA Amendments Act	52
Page 177. Insert after Note 2.	*Warshak v. United States*	69
Page 200. Insert after Note 8.	*Doe v. Gonzales (Doe IV)*	80
Page 238. Insert after Note 10.	*Tabbaa v. Chertoff*	107
Pages 241-242. Replace Exec. Order 12,333 with provisions of amended order.	Amended Exec. Order 12,333	121
Page 310. Insert at bottom.	*Iqbal v. Hasty*	123
Pages 336-346. Substitute for earlier decisions.	*Boumediene v. Bush* (S. Ct.)	133
Page 348. Insert after Note 5.	*Munaf v. Geren*	164
Page 398. Insert after Note 4.	*Al-Marri v. Pucciarelli*	182

Table of Cases

* * *

12

Preemptive War

C. JUSTIFICATIONS FOR THE WAR

Page 315. Add the following material before Notes and Questions.

In June 2008, the Senate Select Committee on Intelligence issued its final report on the relationship between available intelligence and the Bush administration's public statements concerning justifications for the war in Iraq. The report, which runs 172 pages, and which includes fascinating details about the work of the intelligence agencies, is briefly excerpted here.

Senate Select Committee on Intelligence, Report on Whether Public Statements Regarding Iraq by U.S. Government Officials Were Substantiated by Intelligence Information

S. Rep. No. 110- (2008)
available at http://intelligence.senate.gov/080605/phase2a.pdf

I. Scope and Methodology

(U) This report's scope, as agreed to unanimously by the Committee on February 12, 2004, is to assess "whether public statements and reports and testimony regarding Iraq by U.S. Government officials made between the Gulf War period and the commencement of Operation Iraqi Freedom were substantiated by intelligence information."

(U) In order to complete this task, the Committee decided to concentrate its analysis on the statements that were central to the nation's decision to go to war. Specifically, the Committee chose to review five major policy speeches by key Administration officials regarding the threats posed by Iraq, Iraqi weapons of mass destruction programs, Iraqi ties to terrorist groups, and possible consequences of a US invasion of Iraq. . . .

(U) These speeches are the best representations of how the Bush Administration communicated intelligence analysis to the Congress, the American people, and the international community. They are also fairly comprehensive in scope, so evaluations about whether a particular statement in a speech was substantiated can be extrapolated to cover similar statements made at similar times. The Committee believes that these speeches would have been subject to careful review inside the White House and most were also reviewed by the intelligence community. . . .

(U) The Committee selected particular statements from these speeches that pertained to eight categories: nuclear weapons, biological weapons, chemical weapons, weapons of mass destruction (generally), methods of delivery, links to terrorism, regime intent, and assessments about the post-war situation in Iraq. The report is organized along these eight categories . . . .

(U) To conduct this review, the Committee assembled hundreds of intelligence reports produced prior to March 19, 2003 in an effort to understand the state of intelligence analysis at the time of various speeches and statements. . . .

(U) Furthermore, the Committee reviewed only finished analytic intelligence documents, with few exceptions. This did not include intelligence reports "from the field" or less formal communications between intelligence agencies and other parts of the Executive Branch.

(U) The Committee has attempted to note where disagreements existed within the Intelligence Community and where different reporting could substantiate different interpretations. . . .

(U) In addition to examining the question of whether public statements were substantiated by the underlying intelligence, the Committee's review also addressed the extent to which statements were incomplete and where relevant Intelligence Community assessments were not made part of the public discourse. A public statement that selectively uses only that intelligence that supports a particular policy position while ignoring or disregarding intelligence that either weakens or contradicts the position may be accurate on its face but present a slanted picture nonetheless. . . .

II. Nuclear Weapons

- "The Iraqi regime has in fact been very busy enhancing its capabilities in the field of chemical and biological agents. And they continue to pursue the nuclear program they began so many years ago." – *Vice President Richard Cheney, Nashville, Tennessee, August 26, 2002 . . .*

- "But Saddam Hussein has defied all these efforts and continues to develop weapons of mass destruction. The first time we may be completely certain he has a – nuclear weapons is when, God forbids, he uses one." – *President George W. Bush, Address to the United Nations General Assembly, September 12, 2002 . . .*

- "Facing clear evidence of peril we cannot wait for the final proof – the smoking gun – that could come in the form of a mushroom cloud." – *President George W. Bush, Cincinnati, Ohio, October 7, 2002 . . .*

- "The British government has learned that Saddam Hussein recently sought significant quantities of uranium from Africa. Our intelligence sources tell us that he has attempted to purchase high-strength aluminum tubes suitable for nuclear weapons production." – *President George W. Bush, State of the Union Address, January 29, 2003*

- "We have no indication that Saddam Hussein has ever abandoned his nuclear weapons program. On the contrary, we have more than a decade of proof that he remains determined to acquire nuclear weapons." – *Secretary of State Colin Powell, Address to the United Nations Security Council, February 5, 2003 . . .*

(U) In major policy speeches the President, the Vice President and the Secretary of State indicated that the Iraqi government had an active nuclear weapons program. The President and the Secretary of State both indicated that this nuclear weapons program had continued even while international weapons inspectors were in Iraq. . . .

(U) In the late 1990s and early 2000s, the intelligence community produced a number of coordinated assessments regarding possible Iraqi nuclear programs. These assessments consistently concluded that the

International Atomic Energy Agency (IAEA) and the United Nations Special Commission (UNSCO) had destroyed or neutralized Iraq's pre-Gulf War nuclear infrastructure, and that Iraq did not appear to have reconstituted its nuclear weapons program.

(U) These assessments were also consistent in assessing that Iraq had maintained some of the intellectual capital and physical infrastructure necessary for a nuclear weapons program, and that Iraq continued to procure "dual-use" technologies, with both nuclear and non-nuclear potential uses. They agreed that if Iraq decided to restart a nuclear weapons program, with proper foreign assistance it could produce enough fissile material for a nuclear weapon within five to seven years, and that if Iraq in some way acquired adequate fissile material from a foreign source, it could produce a nuclear weapon within one year. . . .

(U) The intelligence community's collective judgment that Iraq did not appear to have reconstituted its nuclear weapons program did not change until the publication of the October 2002 NIE on Iraqi WMD programs . . . . However, some individual agencies shifted their perspectives before this point. In April 2001, the CIA noted that Iraq's attempts to purchase high-strength aluminum tubes and other dual-use equipment suggested that a reconstitution effort might be underway. This judgment was included in several other CIA assessments. In August 2002 the CIA published a paper on Iraqi WMD capabilities . . . which concluded that these procurement activities indicated that the Iraqi government had restarted its nuclear weapons program.

(U) The Defense Intelligence Agency produced several similar assessments in 2002 . . . .

(U) The Department of Energy (DOE) disagreed with the CIA's conclusions regarding the aluminum tubes, and assessed that it was more likely that the tubes were intended for a different use, such as a conventional rocket program. . . .

(U) The Department of State's Bureau of Intelligence and Research (State/INR) disagreed with the CIA that Iraq had restarted a nuclear weapons program, and concurred with the DOE that the aluminum tubes were probably intended for other purposes. . . .

[Most of the analysis of public statements and intelligence concerning an Iraqi nuclear weapons program, along with similar analyses of other WMD programs, delivery systems, and links to terrorists, is omitted here.]

Conclusions

(U) **Conclusion 1**: Statements by the President, Vice President, Secretary of State and the National Security Advisor regarding a possible Iraqi nuclear weapons program were generally substantiated by intelligence community estimates, but did not convey the substantial disagreements that existed in the intelligence community. . . .

(U) **Conclusion 2**: Statements in the major speeches analyzed, as well as additional statements, regarding Iraq's possession of biological agent, weapons, production capability, and use of mobile biological laboratories were substantiated by intelligence information. Intelligence assessments from the late 1990s through early 2003 consistently stated that Iraq retained biological warfare agent and the capability to produce more. . . . Policymakers did not discuss intelligence gaps in Iraq's biological weapons programs, which were explicit in the October 2002 NIE. . . .

(U) **Conclusion 3**: Statements in the major speeches analyzed, as well additional statements, regarding Iraq's possession of chemical weapons were substantiated by intelligence information.

Intelligence assessments . . . stated that Iraq had retained up to 100 metric tons of its chemical weapons stockpile. The October 2002 NIE provided a range of 100 to 500 metric tons of chemical weapons.

(U) **Conclusion 4**: Statements by the President and Vice President prior to the October 2002 National Intelligence Estimate regarding Iraq's chemical weapons production capability and activities did not reflect the intelligence community's uncertainties as to whether such production was ongoing.

The intelligence community assessed that Saddam Hussein wanted to have chemical weapons production capability and that Iraq was seeking to hide such capability in its dual use chemical industry. Intelligence assessments, especially prior to the October 2002 NIE, clearly stated that analysts could not confirm that production was ongoing.

(U) **Conclusion 5**: Statements by the President, Vice President, Secretary of State and Secretary of Defense regarding Iraq's possession of weapons of mass destruction were generally substantiated by intelligence information, though many statements made regarding ongoing production prior to late 2002 reflected a higher level of certainty than the intelligence judgments themselves.

Many senior policymaker statements in early and mid-2002 claimed that there was no doubt that the Iraqi government possessed or was producing weapons of mass destruction. While the intelligence community assessed at this time that the Iraqi regime possessed some chemical and biological munitions, most reports produced prior to fall 2002 cited intelligence gaps regarding production and expressed room for doubt about whether production was ongoing. Prior to late 2002, the intelligence community did not collectively assess with any certainty that Iraq was actively producing any weapons of mass destruction. . . .

(U) **Conclusion 10**: Statements in the major speeches analyzed, as well additional statements, regarding Iraq's support for terrorist groups other than al-Qa'ida were substantiated by intelligence information.

The intelligence community reported regularly on Iraq's safe harbor and financial support for Palestinian rejectionist groups, the Abu Nidal Organization, and others. The February 2002 NIE fully supported the claim that Iraq had, and would continue, to support terrorist groups.

(U) **Conclusion 11**: Statements that Iraq provided safe haven for Abu Musab al-Zargawi and other al-Qa'ida-related terrorist members were substantiated by the intelligence assessments.

Intelligence assessments noted Zargawi's presence in Iraq and his ability to travel and operate within the country. . . .

(U) **Conclusion 12**: Statements and implications by the President and Secretary of State suggesting that Iraq and al-Qa'ida had a partnership, or that Iraq had provided al-Qa'ida with weapons training, were not substantiated by the intelligence.

Intelligence assessments, including multiple CIA reports and the November 2002 NIE, dismissed the claim that Iraq and al-Qa'ida were cooperating partners. . . .

(U) **Conclusion 15**: Statements by the President and the Vice President indicating that Saddam Hussein was prepared to give weapons of mass destruction to terrorist groups for attacks against the United States were contradicted by available intelligence information. . . . The October 2002 National Intelligence Estimate assessed that Saddam Hussein did not have nuclear weapons, and was unwilling to conduct terrorist attacks the US using conventional, chemical or biological weapons at that time, in part because he feared that doing so would give the US a stronger case for war with Iraq. This judgment was echoed by both earlier and later intelligence community assessments. All of these assessments noted that gauging Saddam's intentions was quite difficult, and most suggested that he would be more likely to initiate hostilities if he felt that a US invasion was imminent. . . .

[Additional views of Senators Rockefeller, Feinstein, Feingold, Hagel, and Snowe are omitted.]

Minority Views of Vice Chairman Bond and Senators Chambliss, Hatch, and Burr

This majority-only written report by the Senate Intelligence Committee is a great disappointment to us and an unfortunate commentary on the political nature of intelligence oversight in the Congress today. . . . We have rarely seen such a poorly handled congressional investigation . . . .

. . . As the Committee's Phase I report showed, it was the intelligence that was faulty. In the cases in which the majority concluded that statements were not substantiated by intelligence or did not convey fully the intelligence community's analysis, it is clear that either the words of the policymakers in question or the body of intelligence available at the time were distorted in order to make these false charges. . . .

In the nuclear area, for example, the majority report's first conclusion notes that policymakers' statements about Iraq's nuclear activities were substantiated by intelligence, but the majority concludes that some statements did not convey disagreements that existed within the intelligence community. Many Democrats in Congress also discussed Iraq's nuclear efforts during the Iraq war debate and in other venues and similarly did not describe disagreements within the intelligence community. . . .

[Additional minority views of Senators Warner, Chambliss, Bond, Hatch, and Burr are omitted.]

* * *

15

Covert Action

D. EXECUTIVE BRANCH REFORMS

Page 397. Replace Executive Order No. 12,333 with the following amended executive order.

Executive Order No. 12,333
United States Intelligence Activities

(as amended by Executive Orders 13,284 (2003),
13,355 (2004), and 13,470 (2008))
___ Fed. Reg. ___ (July 30, 2008)
http://www.whitehouse.gov/infocus/nationalsecurity/amended12333.pdf

Timely, insightful, and accurate information about the activities, capabilities, plans, and intentions of foreign powers, organizations, and persons and their agents, is essential to the national security of the United States. All reasonable and lawful means must be used to ensure that the United States will receive the best intelligence possible. For that purpose, by virtue of the authority vested in me by the Constitution and the laws of the United States of America, including the National Security Act of 1947, as amended, and as President of the United States of America, in order to provide for the effective conduct of United States intelligence activities and the protection of constitutional rights, it is hereby ordered as follows:

PART 1. *Goals, Directions, Duties, and Responsibilities with Respect to United States Intelligence Efforts*

1.1 *Goals*. The United States intelligence effort shall provide the President, the National Security Council, and the Homeland Security

Council with the necessary information on which to base decisions concerning the development and conduct of foreign, defense, and economic policies, and the protection of United States national interests from foreign security threats. All departments and agencies shall cooperate fully to fulfill this goal.

(a) All means, consistent with applicable Federal law and this order, and with full consideration of the rights of United States persons, shall be used to obtain reliable intelligence information to protect the United States and its interests. . . .

(g) All departments and agencies have a responsibility to prepare and to provide intelligence in a manner that allows the full and free exchange of information, consistent with applicable law and presidential guidance.

1.2 *The National Security Council.*

(a) *Purpose.* The National Security Council (NSC) shall act as the highest ranking executive branch entity that provides support to the President for review of, guidance for, and direction to the conduct of all foreign intelligence, counterintelligence, and covert action, and attendant policies and programs.

(b) *Covert Action and Other Sensitive Intelligence Operations.* The NSC shall consider and submit to the President a policy recommendation, including all dissents, on each proposed covert action and conduct a periodic review of ongoing covert action activities, including an evaluation of the effectiveness and consistency with current national policy of such activities and consistency with applicable legal requirements. The NSC shall perform such other functions related to covert action as the President may direct, but shall not undertake the conduct of covert actions. The NSC shall also review proposals for other sensitive intelligence operations.

1.3 *Director of National Intelligence.* Subject to the authority, direction, and control of the President, the Director of National Intelligence (Director) shall serve as the head of the Intelligence Community, act as the principal adviser to the President, to the NSC, and to the Homeland Security Council for intelligence matters related to national security, and shall oversee and direct the implementation of the National Intelligence Program and execution of the National Intelligence Program budget. The Director will lead a unified, coordinated, and effective intelligence effort. In addition, the Director shall, in carrying out the duties and responsibilities under this section, take into account the views of the heads of departments containing an element of the Intelligence Community and of the Director of the Central Intelligence Agency.

(a) Except as otherwise directed by the President or prohibited by law, the Director shall have access to all information and intelligence described in section 1.5(a) of this order. For the purpose of access to and sharing of information and intelligence, the Director: . . .

(2) Shall develop guidelines for how information or intelligence is provided to or accessed by the Intelligence Community in accordance with section 1.5(a) of this order, and for how the information or intelligence may be used and shared by the Intelligence Community. All guidelines developed in accordance with this section shall be approved by the Attorney General and, where applicable, shall be consistent with guidelines issued pursuant to section 1016 of the Intelligence Reform and Terrorism Protection Act of 2004 (Public Law 108-458) (IRTPA).

(b) In addition to fulfilling the obligations and responsibilities prescribed by the Act, the Director:

(1) Shall establish objectives, priorities, and guidance for the Intelligence Community to ensure timely and effective collection, processing, analysis, and dissemination of intelligence, of whatever nature and from whatever source derived; . . .

(3) Shall oversee and provide advice to the President and the NSC with respect to all ongoing and proposed covert action programs;

(4) In regard to the establishment and conduct of intelligence arrangements and agreements with foreign governments and international organizations:

(A) May enter into intelligence and counterintelligence arrangements and agreements with foreign governments and international organizations;

(B) Shall formulate policies concerning intelligence and counterintelligence arrangements and agreements with foreign governments and international organizations; and

(C) Shall align and synchronize intelligence and counterintelligence foreign relationships among the elements of the Intelligence Community to further United States national security, policy, and intelligence objectives; . . .

(6) Shall establish common security and access standards for managing and handling intelligence systems, information,

and products, with special emphasis on facilitating:

(A) The fullest and most prompt access to and dissemination of information and intelligence practicable, assigning the highest priority to detecting, preventing, preempting, and disrupting terrorist threats and activities against the United States, its interests, and allies; and

(B) The establishment of standards for an interoperable information sharing enterprise that facilitates the sharing of intelligence information among elements of the Intelligence Community;

(7) Shall ensure that appropriate departments and agencies have access to intelligence and receive the support needed to perform independent analysis;

(8) Shall protect, and ensure that programs are developed to protect, intelligence sources, methods, and activities from unauthorized disclosure;

(9) Shall, after consultation with the heads of affected departments and agencies, establish guidelines for Intelligence Community elements for:

(A) Classification and declassification of all intelligence and intelligence-related information classified under the authority of the Director or the authority of the head of a department or Intelligence Community element; . . .

(14) Shall have ultimate responsibility for production and dissemination of intelligence produced by the Intelligence Community and authority to levy analytic tasks on intelligence production organizations within the Intelligence Community, in consultation with the heads of the Intelligence Community elements concerned; . . .

(16) Shall ensure the timely exploitation and dissemination of data gathered by national intelligence collection means, and ensure that the resulting intelligence is disseminated immediately to appropriate government elements, including military commands;

(17) Shall determine requirements and priorities for, and manage and direct the tasking, collection, analysis, production, and dissemination of, national intelligence by elements of the Intelligence Community, including approving requirements for collection and analysis and resolving conflicts in collection requirements and in the tasking of national collection assets of Intelligence Community elements (except when otherwise

directed by the President or when the Secretary of Defense exercises collection tasking authority under plans and arrangements approved by the Secretary of Defense and the Director); . . .

(20) Shall ensure, through appropriate policies and procedures, the deconfliction, coordination, and integration of all intelligence activities conducted by an Intelligence Community element or funded by the National Intelligence Program. In accordance with these policies and procedures:

(A) The Director of the Federal Bureau of Investigation shall coordinate the clandestine collection of foreign intelligence collected through human sources or through human-enabled means and counterintelligence activities inside the United States;

(B) The Director of the Central Intelligence Agency shall coordinate the clandestine collection of foreign intelligence collected through human sources or through human-enabled means and counterintelligence activities outside the United States;

(C) All policies and procedures for the coordination of counterintelligence activities and the clandestine collection of foreign intelligence inside the United States shall be subject to the approval of the Attorney General; and

(D) All policies and procedures developed under this section shall be coordinated with the heads of affected departments and Intelligence Community elements; . . .

(c) The Director's exercise of authorities in the Act and this order shall not abrogate the statutory or other responsibilities of the heads of departments of the United States Government or the Director of the Central Intelligence Agency. Directives issued and actions taken by the Director in the exercise of the Director's authorities and responsibilities to integrate, coordinate, and make the Intelligence Community more effective in providing intelligence related to national security shall be implemented by the elements of the Intelligence Community, provided that any department head whose department contains an element of the Intelligence Community and who believes that a directive or action of the Director violates the requirements of section 1018 of the IRTPA or this subsection shall bring the issue to the attention of the Director, the NSC, or the President for resolution in a manner that respects and does not abrogate the statutory responsibilities of the heads of the departments.

(d) Appointments to certain positions.

(1) The relevant department or bureau head shall provide recommendations and obtain the concurrence of the Director for the selection of: the Director of the National Security Agency, the Director of the National Reconnaissance Office, the Director of the National Geospatial-Intelligence Agency, the Under Secretary of Homeland Security for Intelligence and Analysis, the Assistant Secretary of State for Intelligence and Research, the Director of the Office of Intelligence and Counterintelligence of the Department of Energy, the Assistant Secretary for Intelligence and Analysis of the Department of the Treasury, and the Executive Assistant Director for the National Security Branch of the Federal Bureau of Investigation. If the Director does not concur in the recommendation, the department head may not fill the vacancy or make the recommendation to the President, as the case may be. If the department head and the Director do not reach an agreement on the selection or recommendation, the Director and the department head concerned may advise the President directly of the Director's intention to withhold concurrence. . . .

(e) Removal from certain positions.

(1) Except for the Director of the Central Intelligence Agency, whose removal the Director may recommend to the President, the Director and the relevant department head shall consult on the removal, or recommendation to the President for removal, as the case may be, of: the Director of the National Security Agency, the Director of the National Geospatial-Intelligence Agency, the Director of the Defense Intelligence Agency, the Under Secretary of Homeland Security for Intelligence and Analysis, the Assistant Secretary of State for Intelligence and Research, and the Assistant Secretary for Intelligence and Analysis of the Department of the Treasury. If the Director and the department head do not agree on removal, or recommendation for removal, either may make a recommendation to the President for the removal of the individual. . . .

1.4. *The Intelligence Community.* Consistent with applicable Federal law and with the other provisions of this order, and under the leadership of the Director, as specified in such law and this order, the Intelligence Community shall:

(a) Collect and provide information needed by the President

and, in the performance of executive functions, the Vice President, the NSC, the Homeland Security Council, the Chairman of the Joint Chiefs of Staff, senior military commanders, and other executive branch officials and, as appropriate, the Congress of the United States;

(b) In accordance with priorities set by the President, collect information concerning, and conduct activities to protect against, international terrorism, proliferation of weapons of mass destruction, intelligence activities directed against the United States, international criminal drug activities, and other hostile activities directed against the United States by foreign powers, organizations, persons, and their agents;

(c) Analyze, produce, and disseminate intelligence; . . .

(f) Protect the security of intelligence related activities, information, installations, property, and employees by appropriate means, including such investigations of applicants, employees, contractors, and other persons with similar associations with the Intelligence Community elements as are necessary; . . .

(i) Perform such other functions and duties related to intelligence activities as the President may direct.

1.5. *Duties and Responsibilities of the Heads of Executive Branch Departments and Agencies.* The heads of all departments and agencies shall:

(a) Provide the Director access to all information and intelligence relevant to the national security or that otherwise is required for the performance of the Director's duties, to include administrative and other appropriate management information, except such information excluded by law, by the President, or by the Attorney General acting under this order at the direction of the President;

(b) Provide all programmatic and budgetary information necessary to support the Director in developing the National Intelligence Program;

(c) Coordinate development and implementation of intelligence systems and architectures and, as appropriate, operational systems and architectures of their departments, agencies, and other elements with the Director to respond to national intelligence requirements and all applicable information sharing and security guidelines, information privacy, and other legal requirements; . . .

(f) Ensure that all elements within the department or agency comply with the provisions of Part 2 of this order, regardless of

Intelligence Community affiliation, when performing foreign intelligence and counterintelligence functions; . . .

(h) Inform the Attorney General, either directly or through the Federal Bureau of Investigation, and the Director of clandestine collection of foreign intelligence and counterintelligence activities inside the United States not coordinated with the Federal Bureau of Investigation;

(i) Pursuant to arrangements developed by the head of the department or agency and the Director of the Central Intelligence Agency and approved by the Director, inform the Director and the Director of the Central Intelligence Agency, either directly or through his designee serving outside the United States, as appropriate, of clandestine collection of foreign intelligence collected through human sources or through human-enabled means outside the United States that has not been coordinated with the Central Intelligence Agency; . . .

1.6. *Heads of Elements of the Intelligence Community.* The heads of elements of the Intelligence Community shall:

(a) Provide the Director access to all information and intelligence relevant to the national security or that otherwise is required for the performance of the Director's duties, to include administrative and other appropriate management information, except such information excluded by law, by the President, or by the Attorney General acting under this order at the direction of the President;

(b) Report to the Attorney General possible violations of Federal criminal laws by employees and of specified Federal criminal laws by any other person as provided in procedures agreed upon by the Attorney General and the head of the department, agency, or establishment concerned, in a manner consistent with the protection of intelligence sources and methods, as specified in those procedures;

(c) Report to the Intelligence Oversight Board, consistent with Executive Order 13462 of February 29, 2008, and provide copies of all such reports to the Director, concerning any intelligence activities of their elements that they have reason to believe may be unlawful or contrary to executive order or presidential directive;

(d) Protect intelligence and intelligence sources, methods, and activities from unauthorized disclosure in accordance with guidance from the Director;

(e) Facilitate, as appropriate, the sharing of information or intelligence, as directed by law or the President, to State, local, tribal, and private sector entities;

(f) Disseminate information or intelligence to foreign governments and international organizations under intelligence or counterintelligence arrangements or agreements established in accordance with section 1.3(b)(4) of this order; . . .

(h) Ensure that the inspectors general, general counsels, and agency officials responsible for privacy or civil liberties protection for their respective organizations have access to any information or intelligence necessary to perform their official duties.

1.7. *Intelligence Community Elements.* Each element of the Intelligence Community shall have the duties and responsibilities specified below, in addition to those specified by law or elsewhere in this order. Intelligence Community elements within executive departments shall serve the information and intelligence needs of their respective heads of departments and also shall operate as part of an integrated Intelligence Community, as provided in law or this order.

(a) The Central Intelligence Agency. The Director of the Central Intelligence Agency shall:

(1) Collect (including through clandestine means), analyze, produce, and disseminate foreign intelligence and counterintelligence;

(2) Conduct counterintelligence activities without assuming or performing any internal security functions within the United States;

(3) Conduct administrative and technical support activities within and outside the United States as necessary for cover and proprietary arrangements;

(4) Conduct covert action activities approved by the President. No agency except the Central Intelligence Agency (or the Armed Forces of the United States in time of war declared by the Congress or during any period covered by a report from the President to the Congress consistent with the War Powers Resolution, Public Law 93-148) may conduct any covert action activity unless the President determines that another agency is more likely to achieve a particular objective;

(5) Conduct foreign intelligence liaison relationships with intelligence or security services of foreign governments or international organizations consistent with section 1.3(b)(4) of this order;

(6) Under the direction and guidance of the Director, and in accordance with section 1.3(b)(4) of this order, coordinate the implementation of intelligence and counterintelligence relationships between elements of the Intelligence Community and the intelligence or security services of foreign governments or international organizations; and

(7) Perform such other functions and duties related to intelligence as the Director may direct. . . .

(c) The National Security Agency. The Director of the National Security Agency shall:

(1) Collect (including through clandestine means), process, analyze, produce, and disseminate signals intelligence information and data for foreign intelligence and counterintelligence purposes to support national and departmental missions;

(2) Establish and operate an effective unified organization for signals intelligence activities, except for the delegation of operational control over certain operations that are conducted through other elements of the Intelligence Community. No other department or agency may engage in signals intelligence activities except pursuant to a delegation by the Secretary of Defense, after coordination with the Director;

(3) Control signals intelligence collection and processing activities, including assignment of resources to an appropriate agent for such periods and tasks as required for the direct support of military commanders;

(4) Conduct administrative and technical support activities within and outside the United States as necessary for cover arrangements;

(5) Provide signals intelligence support for national and departmental requirements and for the conduct of military operations; . . .

(g) Intelligence Elements of the Federal Bureau of Investigation. Under the supervision of the Attorney General and pursuant to such regulations as the Attorney General may establish, the intelligence elements of the Federal Bureau of Investigation shall:

(1) Collect (including through clandestine means), analyze, produce, and disseminate foreign intelligence and counterintelligence to support national and departmental missions, in accordance with procedural guidelines approved by the Attorney General, after consultation with the Director;

(2) Conduct counterintelligence activities; and

(3) Conduct foreign intelligence and counterintelligence liaison relationships with intelligence, security, and law enforcement services of foreign governments or international organizations in accordance with sections 1.3(b)(4) and 1.7(a)(6) of this order. . . .

(j) The Office of the Director of National Intelligence. The Director shall collect (overtly or through publicly available sources), analyze, produce, and disseminate information, intelligence, and counterintelligence to support the missions of the Office of the Director of National Intelligence, including the National Counter-terrorism Center, and to support other national missions. . . .

1.10. *The Department of Defense.* The Secretary of Defense shall:

(a) Collect (including through clandestine means), analyze, produce, and disseminate information and intelligence and be responsive to collection tasking and advisory tasking by the Director;

(b) Collect (including through clandestine means), analyze, produce, and disseminate defense and defense related intelligence and counterintelligence, as required for execution of the Secretary's responsibilities;

(c) Conduct programs and missions necessary to fulfill national, departmental, and tactical intelligence requirements;

(d) Conduct counterintelligence activities in support of Department of Defense components and coordinate counterintelligence activities in accordance with section 1.3(b)(20) and (21) of this order;

(e) Act, in coordination with the Director, as the executive agent of the United States Government for signals intelligence activities; . . .

PART 2. ***Conduct of Intelligence Activities*** . . .

2.2. *Purpose*. . . . Set forth below are certain general principles that, in addition to and consistent with applicable laws, are intended to achieve the proper balance between the acquisition of essential information and protection of individual interests. Nothing in this Order shall be construed to apply to or interfere with any authorized civil or criminal law enforcement responsibility of any department or agency.

2.3. *Collection of Information*. Elements of the Intelligence Community are authorized to collect, retain or disseminate information concerning United States persons only in accordance with procedures established by the head of the Intelligence Community element concerned . . . and approved by the Attorney General . . . after consultation with the Director. Those procedures shall permit collection, retention, and dissemination of the following types of information: . . .

(b) Information constituting foreign intelligence or counterintelligence, including such information concerning corporations or other commercial organizations. Collection within the United States of foreign intelligence not otherwise obtainable shall be undertaken by the Federal Bureau of Investigation (FBI) or, when significant foreign intelligence is sought, by other authorized elements of the Intelligence Community, provided that no foreign intelligence collection by such elements may be undertaken for the purpose of acquiring information concerning the domestic activities of United States persons; . . .

(e) Information needed to protect foreign intelligence or counterintelligence sources, methods, and activities from unauthorized disclosure. Collection within the United States shall be undertaken by the FBI except that other elements of the Intelligence Community may also collect such information concerning present or former employees, present or former intelligence element contractors or their present or former employees, or applicants for such employment or contracting; . . .

2.4. *Collection Techniques*. Elements of the Intelligence Community shall use the least intrusive collection techniques feasible within the United States or directed against United States persons abroad. Elements of the Intelligence Community are not authorized to use such techniques as electronic surveillance, unconsented physical searches, mail surveillance, physical surveillance, or monitoring devices unless they are in accordance with procedures established by the head of the Intelligence Community element concerned or the head of a department containing such element and approved by the Attorney General, after consultation with the Director. Such procedures shall protect constitutional and other legal rights and limit use of such information to lawful governmental purposes. These procedures shall not authorize:

(a) The Central Intelligence Agency (CIA) to engage in electronic surveillance within the United States except for the purpose of training, testing, or conducting countermeasures to hostile electronic surveillance;

(b) Unconsented physical searches in the United States by elements of the Intelligence Community other than the FBI, except for:

(1) Searches by counterintelligence elements of the military services directed against military personnel within the United States or abroad for intelligence purposes, when authorized by a military commander empowered to approve physical searches for law enforcement purposes, based upon a finding of probable cause to believe that such persons are acting as agents of foreign powers; and

(2) Searches by CIA of personal property of non-United States persons lawfully in its possession;

(c) Physical surveillance of a United States person in the United States by elements of the Intelligence Community other than the FBI, except for:

(1) Physical surveillance of present or former employees, present or former intelligence element contractors or their present or former employees, or applicants for any such employment or contracting; and

(2) Physical surveillance of a military person employed by a non-intelligence element of a military service; and

(d) Physical surveillance of a United States person abroad to collect foreign intelligence, except to obtain significant information that cannot reasonably be acquired by other means.

2.5. *Attorney General Approval.* The Attorney General hereby is delegated the power to approve the use for intelligence purposes, within the United States or against a United States person abroad, of any technique for which a warrant would be required if undertaken for law enforcement purposes, provided that such techniques shall not be undertaken unless the Attorney General has determined in each case that there is probable cause to believe that the technique is directed against a foreign power or an agent of a foreign power. The authority delegated pursuant to this paragraph, including the authority to approve the use of electronic surveillance as defined in the Foreign Intelligence Surveillance Act of 1978, as amended, shall be exercised in accordance with that Act.

2.6. *Assistance to Law Enforcement and Other Civil Authorities.* Elements of the Intelligence Community are authorized to: . . .

(b) Unless otherwise precluded by law or this Order, participate in law enforcement activities to investigate or prevent clandestine intelligence activities by foreign powers, or international terrorist or narcotics activities; . . .

2.7. *Contracting.* Elements of the Intelligence Community are authorized to enter into contracts or arrangements for the provision of goods or services with private companies or institutions in the United States and need not reveal the sponsorship of such contracts or arrangements for authorized intelligence purposes. Contracts or arrangements with academic institutions may be undertaken only with the consent of appropriate officials of the institution.

2.8. *Consistency with Other Laws.* Nothing in this Order shall be construed to authorize any activity in violation of the Constitution or statutes of the United States.

2.9. *Undisclosed Participation in Organizations Within the United States.* No one acting on behalf of elements of the Intelligence Community may join or otherwise participate in any organization in the United States on behalf of any element within the Intelligence Community without disclosing such person's intelligence affiliation to appropriate officials of the organization, except in accordance with procedures established by the head of the Intelligence Community element concerned or the head of a department containing such element and approved by the Attorney General, after consultation with the Director. Such participation shall be authorized only if it is essential to achieving lawful purposes as determined by the Intelligence Community element head or designee. No such participation may be undertaken for the purpose of influencing the activity of the organization or its members except in cases where:

(a) The participation is undertaken on behalf of the FBI in the course of a lawful investigation; or

(b) The organization concerned is composed primarily of individuals who are not United States persons and is reasonably believed to be acting on behalf of a foreign power. . . .

2.11. *Prohibition on Assassination.* No person employed by or acting on behalf of the United States Government shall engage in, or conspire to engage in, assassination.

2.12. *Indirect Participation.* No element of the Intelligence Community shall participate in or request any person to undertake activities forbidden by this Order.

2.13. *Limitation on Covert Action.* No covert action may be conducted which is intended to influence United States political processes, public opinion, policies, or media.

PART 3. *General Provisions*

3.1. *Congressional Oversight.* The duties and responsibilities of the Director and the heads of other departments, agencies, elements, and entities engaged in intelligence activities to cooperate with the Congress in the conduct of its responsibilities for oversight of intelligence activities shall be implemented in accordance with applicable law, including title V of the [National Security Act of 1947, as amended]. The requirements of applicable law, including title V of the [National Security Act of 1947, as amended], shall apply to all covert action activities as defined in this Order. . . .

3.5. *Definitions.* For the purposes of this Order, the following terms shall have these meanings:

(a) *Counterintelligence* means information gathered and activities conducted to identify, deceive, exploit, disrupt, or protect against espionage, other intelligence activities, sabotage, or assassinations conducted for or on behalf of foreign powers, organizations, or persons, or their agents, or international terrorist organizations or activities.

(b) *Covert action* means an activity or activities of the United States Government to influence political, economic, or military conditions abroad, where it is intended that the role of the United States Government will not be apparent or acknowledged publicly, but does not include:

(1) Activities the primary purpose of which is to acquire intelligence, traditional counterintelligence activities, traditional activities to improve or maintain the operational security of United States Government programs, or administrative activities;

(2) Traditional diplomatic or military activities or routine support to such activities;

(3) Traditional law enforcement activities conducted by United States Government law enforcement agencies or routine support to such activities; or

(4) Activities to provide routine support to the overt activities (other than activities described in paragraph (1), (2), or (3)) of other United States Government agencies abroad.

(c) *Electronic surveillance* means acquisition of a nonpublic communication by electronic means without the consent of a person who is a party to an electronic communication or, in the case of a nonelectronic communication, without the consent of a person who is visibly present at the place of communication, but not including the use of radio direction-finding equipment solely to determine the location of a transmitter. . . .

(e) *Foreign intelligence* means information relating to the capabilities, intentions, or activities of foreign governments or elements thereof, foreign organizations, foreign persons, or international terrorists.

(f) *Intelligence* includes foreign intelligence and counterintelligence.

(g) *Intelligence activities* means all activities that elements of the Intelligence Community are authorized to conduct pursuant to this order.

(h) *Intelligence Community* and agencies within the Intelligence Community refers to:

(1) The Office of the Director of National Intelligence;

(2) The Central Intelligence Agency;

(3) The National Security Agency;

(4) The Defense Intelligence Agency;

(5) The National Geospatial-Intelligence Agency;

(6) The National Reconnaissance Office;

(7) The other offices within the Department of Defense for the collection of specialized national foreign intelligence through reconnaissance programs;

(8) The intelligence and counterintelligence elements of the Army, the Navy, the Air Force, and the Marine Corps;

(9) The intelligence elements of the Federal Bureau of Investigation;

(10) The Office of National Security Intelligence of the Drug Enforcement Administration;

(11) The Office of Intelligence and Counterintelligence of the Department of Energy;

(12) The Bureau of Intelligence and Research of the Department of State;

(13) The Office of Intelligence and Analysis of the Department of the Treasury;

(14) The Office of Intelligence and Analysis of the Department of Homeland Security;

(15) The intelligence and counterintelligence elements of the Coast Guard; and

(16) Such other elements of any department or agency as may be designated by the President, or designated jointly by the Director and the head of the department or agency concerned, as an element of the Intelligence Community.

(i) *National Intelligence and Intelligence Related to National Security* means all intelligence, regardless of the source from which derived and including information gathered within or outside the United States, that pertains, as determined consistent with any guidance issued by the President, or that is determined for the purpose of access to information by the Director in accordance with section 1.3(a)(1) of this order, to pertain to more than one United States Government agency; and that involves threats to the United States, its people, property, or interests; the development, proliferation, or use of weapons of mass destruction; or any other matter bearing on United States national or homeland security.

(j) *The National Intelligence Program* means all programs, projects, and activities of the Intelligence Community, as well as any other programs of the Intelligence Community designated jointly by the Director and the head of a United States department or agency or by the President. Such term does not include programs, projects, or activities of the military departments to acquire intelligence solely for the planning and conduct of tactical military operations by United States Armed Forces. . . .

NOTES AND QUESTIONS

Page 400. Replace the introductory paragraph to Notes and Questions with the following material.

The July 30, 2008, amendment to Executive Order No. 12,333 made many significant revisions to the original Reagan order that require changes to the cross-references in some of the following notes and questions, as well as some changes to the answers. Nevertheless, questions concerning the evolution of the order and the control over the intelligence community that it asserts remain valid and relevant and have therefore been retained. References to the "Reagan order" should simply be read as references to amended Executive Order 12,333, except where the supplemental material refers to the "original Reagan order."

Preamble language typically sets forth the presumed authority for the prescriptions that follow. Precisely what constitutional or statutory authority empowered the President to promulgate this executive order?

Page 402. Add "DNI" to the entities listed in Note 2.

Page 402. In Note 3, replace "§3.4(h)" with "§3.5(b)," and replace the second paragraph of the Note with the following material.

The Ford and Carter executive orders, unlike the original Reagan order, formally included the Justice Department in the covert action decision-making process. What role, if any, is assigned the Attorney General in covert action approval by the amended order? What other provisions does it make for lawyers to participate in the intelligence activities it addresses? Does their involvement really matter if the President is free to ignore their advice?

Page 403. Delete Note 1.

Page 403. Replace the text of Note 4 with the following material.

Section 1.7(a)(3) of the amended order provides that the CIA may "conduct administrative and technical support activities within and outside the United States as necessary for cover and proprietary arrangements." What kinds of activities does this provision contemplate?

Page 403. Replace the text of Note 5 with the following material.

The original Reagan order listed seven entities in the "intelligence community." The amended order now lists fifteen. §3.5(h). Some have simply been renamed or subdivided in the re-organization of the community. Others are new, however, or have been assigned expanded roles that merit their identification as parts of the community. Is the list broad enough to cover all entities conducting intelligence activities? Do you think that the apparent expansion of the intelligence community is permanent, or merely a transient by-product of the war on terrorism? Is the apparent expansion likely to improve the community's performance? Or enhance the likelihood that its activities will comply with U.S. law or American principles?

Page 404. Replace the text of Note 6 with the following material.

Look closely at §3.5(b). Does it provide a clear and workable definition of covert action? How would you synthesize the criteria the entire amended order sets out for the approval of covert action? Does any problematic covert activity escape the definition or the criteria?

E. THE REFORMS TESTED: A CASE STUDY OF THE IRAN CONTRA AFFAIR

2. Presidents' Rules: Executive Orders and Decision Directives

Page 410. Replace the text of Note 1 with the following material.

The original Reagan order stated that only the CIA could conduct "special" (i.e., covert) activities unless the President determined that "another agency is more likely to achieve a particular objective." Could the NSC legitimately have carried out the arms sales and Contra supply missions without such a presidential determination? Do you see any practical difference in the language of §1.7(a)(4) of the order as amended in 2008? What is the effect of §1.2(b) of the amended order.

* * *

16

Other Legal Problems in the Intelligence Field

A. DOMESTIC COLLECTION

3. The NSA

Page 444. Replace the excerpt of Executive Order No. 12,333 with §1.7(c) of the amended order, reproduced *supra* p. 18.

* * *

19

Congressional Authority for National Security Surveillance

C. FISA, LAW ENFORCEMENT, AND "THE WALL"

Page 546. Add this case at the end of Note 6.

Mayfield v. United States

United States District Court, Oregon, 2007
504 F. Supp. 2d 1023

AIKEN, J. Plaintiffs' Amended Complaint requests declaratory relief that the Foreign Intelligence Surveillance Act ("FISA"), as amended by the Patriot Act, is unconstitutional. . . .

In brief, the facts as alleged by plaintiffs are as follows: On March 11, 2004, in Madrid, Spain, terrorists' bombs exploded on commuter trains, murdering 191 persons, and injuring another 1600 persons, including three United States citizens. Shortly after the bombings, the Spanish National Police ("SNP") recovered fingerprints from a plastic bag containing explosive detonators. The bag was found in a Renault van located near the bombing site. . . .

[Brandon Mayfield, a U.S. citizen born in Oregon and a practicing Oregon lawyer, was arrested and detained for two weeks after the FBI mistakenly matched his fingerprints to the terrorist attack in Spain. The FBI used FISA to search Mayfield's house and law office, copy computer files and photos, tape his telephone conversations, and place surveillance bugs in his office. In a settlement announced in

November 2006, the government agreed to pay $2 million to Mayfield and his family, but the agreement allowed him to proceed with a challenge to the constitutionality of the Patriot Act amendment to the "purpose" requirement of FISA.]

Here, the government chose to go to the FISC, despite the following evidence: Mayfield did not have a current passport; he had not been out of the country since completing his military duty as a U.S. Army lieutenant in Germany during the early 1990s; the fingerprint identification had been determined to be "negative" by the SNP; the SNP believed the bombings were conducted by persons from northern Africa; and there was no evidence linking Mayfield with Spain or North Africa. The government nevertheless made the requisite showing to the FISC that Mayfield was an "agent of a foreign power." That representation, which by law the FISC could not ignore unless clearly erroneous, provided the government with sufficient justification to compel the FISC to authorize covert searches and electronic surveillance in support of a criminal investigation. . . .

[The court found that Mayfield had standing to challenge the constitutionality of FISA and that the lawsuit was ripe for hearing.]

At issue here are two fundamental concerns: the safety of our nation and the constitutional rights of citizens. With the passage of the Patriot Act, these concerns are now placed in conflict. The court recognizes that a difficult balance must be struck in a manner that preserves the peace and security of our nation while at the same time preserving the constitutional rights and civil liberties of all Americans.

Prior to passage of the Patriot Act, the government would have been required to follow the traditional process and demonstrate probable cause to a "detached and neutral magistrate" that Mayfield had committed a crime. Therefore, prior to issuing a search warrant, the Fourth Amendment required that law enforcement have reasonable grounds to believe that the law was being violated. FISA does not contain this criminal standard of probable cause. Instead, FISA contains a "foreign intelligence standard" of probable cause which requires a showing that the target may be an agent of a foreign government and the place or facility to be searched is being used in furtherance of espionage or terrorist activities.

Significantly, a seemingly minor change in wording has a dramatic and significant impact on the application of FISA. A warrant under FISA now issues if "a significant purpose" of the surveillance is foreign intelligence. Now, for the first time in our Nation's history, the government can conduct surveillance to gather evidence for use in a criminal case without a traditional warrant, as long as it presents a non-reviewable assertion that it also has a significant interest in the targeted person for foreign intelligence purposes.

Since the adoption of the Bill of Rights in 1791, the government has been prohibited from gathering evidence for use in a prosecution against an American citizen in a courtroom unless the government could prove the existence of probable cause that a crime has been committed. The hard won legislative compromise previously embodied in FISA reduced the probable cause requirement only for national security intelligence gathering. The Patriot Act effectively eliminates that compromise by allowing the Executive Branch to bypass the Fourth Amendment in gathering evidence for a criminal prosecution.

In 1967, the Supreme Court held that a New York statute authorizing electronic surveillance violated the Fourth Amendment because: (1) "it did not requir[e] the belief that any particular offense has been or is being committed; nor that the 'property' sought, the conversations, be particularly described;" (2) it failed to limit the duration of the surveillance to impose sufficiently stringent requirements on renewals of the authorization; and (3) the statute "has no requirement for notice as do conventional warrants, nor does it overcome this defect by requiring some showing of special facts." Berger v. New York, 388 U.S. 41, 58-60 (1967).

The Court specifically rejected the state's argument that Fourth Amendment requirements should be relaxed because the surveillance statute was essential in its fight against organized crime. The Court held:

> [W]e cannot forgive the requirements of the Fourth Amendment in the name of law enforcement. This is no formality that we require today but a fundamental rule that has long been recognized as basic to the privacy of every home in America. While the requirements of the Fourth Amendment are not inflexible, or obtusely unyielding to the legitimate needs of law enforcement, it is not asking too much that officers be required to comply with the basic command of the Fourth Amendment before the innermost secrets of one's home or office are invaded. Few threats to liberty exist which are greater than that posed by the use of eavesdropping devices.

Id. at 62-63 (internal quotation and citation omitted). . . .

The government does not refute plaintiffs' historical recitation of law leading up to the enactment of FISA. Similarly, the parties agree that when surveying the case law prior to In re Sealed Case, 310 F.3d 717 (Foreign Int. Surv. Ct. Rev. 2003), every Article III court that had considered the issue directly concluded that to justify non-probable cause searches and electronic surveillance, the government's purpose, or at least its primary purpose, must have been the collection of foreign intelligence. Specifically, as originally drafted and implemented over its 24-year history, FISA applications were properly granted only when "the purpose" of the surveillance was foreign intelligence gathering. . . .

In this case, the court declines to adopt the analysis and conclusion reached by the FISCR in *In re Sealed Case.* Notably, the FISCR's two fundamental premises underlying its ruling are contradictory. FISCR determined both that FISA never contained a purpose requirement, and that in altering the purpose requirement, Congress did not undermine the validity of searches conducted pursuant to FISA. Regarding FISCR's second premise, FISCR found that the primary purpose test "generates dangerous confusion and creates perverse organizational incentives arising from the purported need to distinguish between intelligence gathering and criminal investigation." *Id.* at 743. However, a provision of the Patriot Act, unchallenged by plaintiffs here, eliminates the DOJ "wall" and with it the "dangerous confusion" and "perverse organizational incentives" referred to and relied on by the FISCR. Moreover, to the extent the "primary purpose" test imposes any restraint on the sharing of FISA surveillance with criminal investigators, investigators are, of course, free to seek orders authorizing surveillance under Title III, and traditional search warrants that satisfy Fourth Amendment requirements. Finally, Title III includes predicate offenses for which surveillance is justified for virtually all terrorism and espionage-related offenses. 18 U.S.C. §2516(1). As such, Title III provides a satisfactory alternative when criminal investigators cannot have access to FISA surveillance.

The FISCR also attempts, without merit, to distinguish the Supreme Court's "special needs" cases. *In re Sealed Case,* 310 F.3d at 745-46 n.33. "Special needs" cases are those where the Supreme Court has found it appropriate to carve out an exception to the Fourth Amendment's requirement of probable cause based upon an individualized suspicion of wrongdoing. In these cases, the Court found that special needs, beyond the normal need of law enforcement, might justify an otherwise unconstitutional search. Skinner v. Railway Labor Executives' Assn., 489 U.S. 602, 619 (1989). Prior to the Patriot Act, FISA may have had as its "general programmatic purpose . . . to protect the nation against terrorism and espionage threats directed by foreign powers." *In re Sealed Case,* 310 F.3d at 746. After the Patriot Act, however, FISA surveillance, including the surveillance at bar, may have as its "programmatic purpose" the generation of evidence for law enforcement purposes – which is forbidden without criminal probable cause and a warrant.

Finally and perhaps most significantly, *In re Sealed Case* ignores congressional concern with the appropriate balance between intelligence gathering and criminal law enforcement. It is notable that our Founding Fathers anticipated this very conflict as evidenced by the discussion in the Federalist Papers. Their concern regarding unrestrained government resulted in the separation of powers, checks and balances, and ultimately, the Bill of Rights. Where these important objectives merge, it is critical that we, as a democratic Nation, pay close attention to traditional Fourth Amendment principles. The Fourth Amendment has served this Nation well for 220 years, through many other perils. Title III, like the Supreme Court's pronouncements in *Katz* and *Berger,* recognizes that wiretaps are searches requiring fidelity to the Fourth Amendment.

Moreover, the constitutionally required interplay between Executive action, Judicial decision, and Congressional enactment, has been eliminated by the FISA amendments. Prior to the amendments, the three branches of government operated with thoughtful and deliberate checks and balances – a principle upon which our Nation was founded. These constitutional checks and balances effectively curtail overzealous executive, legislative, or judicial activity regardless of the catalyst for overzealousness. The Constitution contains bedrock principles that the framers believed essential. Those principles should not be easily altered by the expediencies of the moment.

Despite this, the FISCR holds that the Constitution need not control the conduct of criminal surveillance in the United States. In place of the Fourth Amendment, the people are expected to defer to the Executive Branch and its representation that it will authorize such surveillance only when appropriate. The defendant here is asking this court to, in essence, amend the Bill of Rights, by giving it an interpretation that would deprive it of any real meaning. This court declines to do so.

For over 200 years, this Nation has adhered to the rule of law – with unparalleled success. A shift to a Nation based on extra-constitutional authority is prohibited, as well as ill-advised. In this regard, the Supreme Court has cautioned:

> The price of lawful public dissent must not be a dread of subjection to an unchecked surveillance power. Nor must the fear of unauthorized official eavesdropping deter vigorous citizen dissent and discussion of Government action in private conversation. For private dissent, no less than open public discourse, is essential to our free society.

Keith, 407 U.S. at 314.

Therefore, I conclude that 50 U.S.C. §§1804 and 1823, as amended by the Patriot Act, are unconstitutional because they violate the Fourth Amendment of the United States Constitution. Plaintiffs' Amended Complaint for declaratory relief is granted. . . .

D. FISA TRENDS

Page 556. Add the following materials after Note 9.

American Civil Liberties Union v. National Security Agency

United States Court of Appeals, Sixth Circuit, 2007
493 F.3d 644, *cert. denied*, 128 S. Ct. 1334 (2008)

ALICE M. BATCHELDER, Circuit Judge. The United States National Security Agency ("NSA") appeals from the decision of the District Court for the Eastern District of Michigan that granted summary judgment against the NSA and imposed a permanent injunction. [American Civil Liberties Union v. National Security Agency, 438 F. Supp. 2d 754 (E.D. Mich. 2006).] The plaintiffs are a collection of associations and individuals led by the American Civil Liberties Union, and they cross-appeal. Because we cannot find that any of the plaintiffs have standing for any of their claims, we must vacate the district court's order and remand for dismissal of the entire action.

I.

Sometime after the September 11, 2001, terrorist attacks, President Bush authorized the NSA to begin a counter-terrorism operation that has come to be known as the Terrorist Surveillance Program ("TSP"). Although the specifics remain undisclosed, it has been publicly acknowledged that the TSP includes the interception (i.e., wiretapping), without warrants, of telephone and email communications where one party to the communication is located outside the United States and the NSA has "a reasonable basis to conclude that one party to the communication is a member of al Qaeda, affiliated with al Qaeda, or a member of an organization affiliated with al Qaeda, or working in support of al Qaeda." *See* Press Briefing by Att'y Gen. Alberto Gonzales and Gen. Michael Hayden, Principal Deputy Dir. for Nat'l Intelligence

(Dec. 19, 2005).

The plaintiffs in this action include journalists, academics, and lawyers who regularly communicate with individuals located overseas, who the plaintiffs believe are the types of people the NSA suspects of being al Qaeda terrorists, affiliates, or supporters, and are therefore likely to be monitored under the TSP. From this suspicion, and the limited factual foundation in this case, the plaintiffs allege that they have a "well founded belief" that their communications are being tapped. According to the plaintiffs, the NSA's operation of the TSP – and the possibility of warrantless surveillance – subjects them to conditions that constitute an irreparable harm. . . .

II. . . .

The "particular plaintiffs" to this action are a diverse group of associations and individuals, and it would require a rigorous undertaking to assure that each has standing to litigate. However, for purposes of the asserted declaratory judgment – though not necessarily for the requested injunction – it is only necessary that one plaintiff [have] standing. The injunction in this case is predicated on the declaratory judgment (i.e., a determination that the NSA's conduct is unlawful), so it follows that if the plaintiffs lack standing to litigate their declaratory judgment claim, they must also lack standing to pursue an injunction. The question is whether *any* plaintiff has standing to litigate the declaratory judgment claim.

As for the "particular claims," the plaintiffs have asserted six separate claims or causes of action – three constitutional (First Amendment, Fourth Amendment, and Separation of Powers) and three statutory (APA, Title III, and FISA) – and the plaintiffs must establish that at least one plaintiff has standing for each. Because a cause of action is intertwined with an injury, the injuries being alleged must be described as precisely and unambiguously as possible. A particularized analysis is therefore necessary.

The conduct giving rise to the alleged injuries is undisputed: the NSA (1) eavesdrops, (2) without warrants, (3) on international telephone and email communications in which at least one of the parties is reasonably suspected of al Qaeda ties. The plaintiffs' objection to this conduct is also undisputed, and they demand that the NSA discontinue it. The plaintiffs do not contend – nor could they – that the mere practice of wiretapping (i.e., eavesdropping) is, by itself, unconstitutional, illegal, or even improper. Rather, the plaintiffs object to the NSA's eavesdropping without warrants, specifically FISA warrants with their associated limitations and minimization requirements. *See* 50 U.S.C. §§1804-06. According to the plaintiffs, it is the absence of these warrants that renders the NSA's conduct illegal and unconstitutional. But the plaintiffs do not . . . produce any evidence that any of their own communications have ever been intercepted by the NSA, under the TSP, or without warrants. Instead, they assert a mere belief, which they contend is reasonable and which they label a "well founded belief," that: their overseas contacts are the types of people targeted by the NSA; the plaintiffs are consequently subjected to the NSA's eavesdropping; the eavesdropping leads the NSA to discover (and possibly disclose) private or privileged information; and the mere possibility of such discovery (or disclosure) has injured them in three particular ways.

Notably, the plaintiffs do *not* allege as injury that they personally, either as individuals or associations, anticipate or fear any form of direct reprisal by the government (e.g., the NSA, the Justice Department, the Department of Homeland Security, etc.), such as criminal prosecution, deportation, administrative inquiry, civil litigation, or even public exposure. The injuries that these plaintiffs allege are not so direct; they are more amorphous and necessitate a pointed description.

The plaintiffs' primary alleged injury – the first of three – is their inability to communicate with their overseas contacts by telephone or email due to their self-governing ethical obligations. Under this claim, the *immediate* injury results directly from the plaintiffs' own actions and decisions, based on (1) their subjective belief that the NSA might be intercepting their communications, and (2) the ethical requirements governing such circumstances, as dictated by their respective professional organizations or affiliations. Relying on the district court's three facts, the plaintiffs allege their "well founded belief" that the NSA is intercepting their communications with overseas contacts, to the perceived detriment of those overseas contacts. The plaintiffs explain that they have an ethical duty to keep their communications confidential, which, under the circumstances, requires that they refrain from communicating with the overseas contacts by telephone or email, lest they violate that duty. The possibility that private communications may be revealed burdens the plaintiffs' pursuit of their chosen professions or organizational objectives – i.e., in order to comply with their ethical duties, the plaintiffs must refrain from communicating by telephone or email, and are instead required either to travel overseas to meet with these contacts in person or else refrain from communicating with them altogether. The injury manifests itself in both a quantifiable way (as the added time and expense of traveling overseas) and a non-quantifiable way (as the incomplete or substandard performance of their professional responsibilities and obligations). . . .

The second alleged injury . . . is the "chilling effect" on the overseas contacts' willingness to communicate with the plaintiffs by telephone or email. Under this claim, the *immediate* injury results directly from the actions of the overseas contacts who, the plaintiffs contend, fear that the NSA's discovery of otherwise private or privileged information (being communicated by telephone or email) will lead to some direct reprisal by the United States government, their own governments, or others. This fear causes the overseas contacts to refuse to communicate with the plaintiffs by telephone or email, and this refusal to communicate burdens the plaintiffs in the performance of their jobs or other lawful objectives, because, in order to pursue their chosen professions or organizational objectives, the plaintiffs must travel overseas to meet with these contacts in person. This injury manifests itself as both an added expense and an added burden.

The plaintiffs' third alleged injury is the NSA's violation of their legitimate expectation of privacy in their overseas telephone and email communications. Under this claim, the *immediate* injury comes directly from the actions of the NSA. The plaintiffs assert that the Fourth Amendment, Title III, and FISA limit the occasions and circumstances in which, and the manner by which, the government can lawfully intercept overseas electronic communications, giving rise to a legitimate expectation that their overseas communications will be intercepted only in accordance with these limits. The plaintiffs conclude that, because the NSA has conducted foreign electronic surveillance without obtaining FISA warrants (and presumably, without strict adherence to FISA's minimization requirements), the NSA has breached their legitimate expectation of privacy, thereby causing them injury. . . .

This third kind of injury, unlike the other two, is direct and personal; under this theory, the NSA has directly invaded the plaintiffs' interest and proof of such invasion is all that is necessary to establish standing. If, for instance, a plaintiff could demonstrate that her privacy had actually been breached (i.e., that her communications had actually been wiretapped), then she would have standing to assert a Fourth Amendment cause of action for breach of privacy. In the present case, the plaintiffs concede that there is no single plaintiff who can show that he or she has actually been wiretapped. . . . This injury is not concrete or imminent under these circumstances, and this opinion focuses on the plaintiffs' two other alleged injuries.

One other issue demands attention, namely, that the plaintiffs' failure to subject themselves to actual harm does not, by itself, prevent a finding that they have standing – specifically, it does not deprive them of the right to seek declaratory judgment. *See* 28 U.S.C. §2201(a) (empowering courts to "declare the rights and other legal relations of any interested party seeking such declaration, whether or not further relief is or could be sought"). Implicit in each of the plaintiffs' alleged injuries is the underlying *possibility* – which the plaintiffs label a "well founded belief" and seek to treat as a probability or even a certainty – that the NSA is presently intercepting, or will eventually intercept, communications to or from one or more of these particular plaintiffs, and that such interception would be detrimental to the plaintiffs' clients, sources, or overseas contacts. This is the premise upon which the plaintiffs' entire theory is built. But even though the plaintiffs' beliefs – based on their superior knowledge of their contacts' activities – may be reasonable, the alternative possibility remains that the NSA might *not* be intercepting, and might *never* actually intercept, any communication by any of the plaintiffs named in this lawsuit.

A plaintiff's refusal to engage in potentially harmful activities is the typical substance of a declaratory judgment action and does not, by itself, preclude a finding that the plaintiff has standing. *See* MedImmune, Inc. v. Genentech, Inc., 549 U.S. [118], 127 S. Ct. 764, 772-73 (2007). But it is important to distinguish the two harms that surround a declaratory judgment action. The anticipated harm that *causes* one to refrain from the activities may satisfy the "injury-in-fact" element of standing if it is sufficiently imminent and concrete. For reasons that will be made clear in the analysis, the other harm – the harm that *results* from refraining from the potentially harmful activities – is another matter. In the present case, the plaintiffs anticipate that the NSA's interception of telephone and email communications might be detrimental to their overseas contacts, and this perceived harm *causes* the plaintiffs to refrain from that communication (i.e., potentially harmful activity). Because there is no evidence that any plaintiff's communications have ever been intercepted . . . there is no proof that interception would be detrimental to the plaintiffs' contacts, and the anticipated harm is neither imminent nor concrete – it is hypothetical, conjectural, or speculative. Therefore, this harm cannot satisfy the "injury in fact" requirement of standing. Because the plaintiffs cannot avoid this shortcoming, they do not propose this harm – the harm that *causes* their refusal to communicate – as an "injury" that warrants redress. Instead, they propose the injuries that *result* from their refusal to communicate and those injuries do appear imminent and concrete.

Thus, in crafting their declaratory judgment action, the plaintiffs have attempted (unsuccessfully) to navigate the obstacles to stating a justiciable claim. By refraining from communications (i.e., the potentially harmful conduct), the plaintiffs have negated any possibility that the NSA will ever actually intercept their communications and thereby avoided the anticipated harm – this is typical of declaratory judgment and perfectly permissible. *See MedImmune,* 127 S. Ct. at 772-73. But, by proposing only injuries that *result* from this refusal to engage in communications (e.g., the inability to conduct their professions without added burden and expense), they attempt to supplant an insufficient, speculative injury with an injury that appears sufficiently imminent and concrete, but is only incidental to the alleged wrong (i.e., the NSA's conduct) – this is atypical and, as will be discussed, impermissible.

Therefore, the injury that would support a declaratory judgment action (i.e., the anticipated interception of communications resulting in harm to the contacts) is too speculative, and the injury that is imminent and concrete (i.e., the burden on professional performance) does not support a declaratory judgment action. This general proposition – the doctrine of standing – is explained more fully in the sections of the analysis regarding each individual cause of action.

III.

By claiming six causes of action, the plaintiffs have actually engaged in a thinly veiled, though perfectly acceptable, ruse. To call a spade a spade, the plaintiffs have only one claim, namely, breach of privacy, based on a purported violation of the Fourth Amendment or FISA – i.e., the plaintiffs do not want the NSA listening to their phone calls or reading their emails. That is really all there is to it. On a straightforward reading, this claim does not implicate the First Amendment. The problem with asserting only a breach-of-privacy claim is that, because the plaintiffs cannot show that they have been or will be subjected to surveillance personally, they clearly cannot establish standing under the Fourth Amendment or FISA. The plaintiffs concede as much. In an attempt to avoid this problem, the plaintiffs have recast their injuries as a matter of free speech and association, characterized their claim as a violation of the First Amendment, and engaged the First Amendment's relaxed rules on standing. . . .

IV. . . .

A. Constitutional Claims . . .

1. First Amendment

The plaintiffs allege that the NSA has, by conducting the warrantless wiretaps, violated the free speech and free association clauses of the First Amendment. The district court assumed that the plaintiffs had engaged in certain "protected expression," apparently referring to the telephone and email communications. Although the plaintiffs' painstaking efforts to keep these communications confidential belies the contention that this case involves *expression,* I nonetheless assume this is a viable First Amendment cause of action. Standing to litigate this claim requires a showing of three elements: (1) injury in fact, (2) causation, and (3) redressability.

Injury in Fact . . .

. . . [T]o allege a sufficient injury under the First Amendment, a plaintiff must establish that he or she is regulated, constrained, or compelled directly by the government's actions, instead of by his or her own subjective chill. . . . "'Chilling effect' is cited as the *reason* why the governmental imposition is invalid [under the First Amendment] rather than as the *harm* which entitles the plaintiffs to challenge it." [United Presb. Church v. Reagan, 738 F.2d 1375, 1378 (D.C. Cir. 1984)]. In an attempt to establish harm, the *Reagan* plaintiffs claimed that they were "especially likely to be targets of the unlawful [surveillance] authorized by the order," but the court explained:

> Even if it were conceded that . . . the plaintiffs [were] at greater risk than the public at large, that would still fall far short of the "genuine threat" required to support this theory of standing, as opposed to mere "speculative" harm. It must be borne in mind that this order does not *direct* intelligence-gathering activities against all persons who could conceivably come within its scope, but merely *authorizes* them.

Id. at 1380 (citations omitted). The *Reagan* court therefore held that the plaintiffs failed to satisfy the injury-in-fact requirement because they did not allege that "any direct governmental constraint" was "threatened or even contemplated against them." *Id.* The present case is no different.

The plaintiffs here contend that the NSA has inflicted First

Amendment injury in two ways, both of which prevent them from performing their jobs or pursuing other lawful objectives. The first injury, which went unaddressed by the district court, involves the plaintiffs' own unwillingness to communicate with their overseas contacts by telephone or email. The plaintiffs fear that the NSA may intercept their communications, and therefore, their ethical obligations require them to forgo the communications in order to avoid interception. The injurious consequence of the NSA's conduct, the plaintiffs contend, is that they must either suffer diminished performance in their jobs for lack of communication, or else bear the cost of traveling overseas to meet with these contacts in person.

Even accepting this as a good faith assertion and assuming the factual statements are true, the plaintiffs' first injury still involves two purely speculative fears: (1) that the NSA will actually intercept the plaintiffs' particular communications, and (2) that armed with the fruit of those interceptions, the NSA will take action detrimental to the contacts. If, on the other hand, the plaintiffs could be assured that the NSA would not intercept their communications, or, if interception occurs, that no harm would befall the overseas contacts, then the NSA could continue the TSP wiretapping without harm to the plaintiffs. It is not the mere existence of the TSP, but the possibility that the plaintiffs' overseas contacts will be subjected to it, that ultimately results in the alleged harm. Even assuming these fears are imminent rather than speculative, this is still a tenuous basis for proving a *concrete* and *actual* injury. That is, even if it were certain that the NSA would intercept these particular plaintiffs' overseas communications, if the overseas contacts were nonetheless willing to communicate with the plaintiffs by telephone or email in spite of the impending interception, then it is doubtful that the plaintiffs (journalists, academics, lawyers, or organizations), who have themselves alleged no personal fear of our government (or basis for fear of our government), would still be unwilling or unable to communicate. The plaintiffs' unwillingness comes not from any anticipated harm to themselves, but from their apprehension for and duty to their overseas contacts.

Moreover, even if their allegations are true, the plaintiffs still allege only a subjective apprehension and a personal (self-imposed) unwillingness to communicate . . . . Indeed, the district court stated that, to date, no one has been exposed or prosecuted based on information collected under the TSP. *ACLU v. NSA,* 438 F. Supp. 2d at 771. . . .

The plaintiffs' second injury is the unwillingness of their overseas contacts, clients, witnesses, and sources to communicate by telephone or email, due to their fear that the NSA will intercept the communications. The district court, in its standing analysis, framed the issue this way:

> The Plaintiffs in this case are not claiming simply that the [NSA]'s surveillance has "chilled" them from making international calls to sources and clients. *Rather, they claim that Defendants' surveillance has chilled their sources, clients, and potential witnesses from communicating with them.* The alleged effect on Plaintiffs is a concrete, actual inability to communicate with witnesses, sources, clients and others without great expense which has significantly crippled Plaintiffs, at a minimum, in their ability to report the news and competently and effectively represent their clients.

ACLU v. NSA, 438 F. Supp. 2d at 769 (emphasis added). Under this view, the plaintiffs claim that their contacts have been chilled, which prevents them from communicating with these contacts.

In Presbyterian Church v. United States, 870 F.2d 518, 520 (9th Cir. 1989), the Ninth Circuit considered a claim by plaintiff churches that "INS agents entered the churches wearing 'body bugs' and surreptitiously recorded church services" in violation of the First and Fourth Amendments. The district court had dismissed the claims for lack of standing, based on the plaintiffs' failure to show injury in fact, opining that the protections of the First Amendment extend not to corporations but to individuals, because "churches don't go to heaven." *Id.* at 521. On appeal, the Ninth Circuit reversed, finding that the plaintiff churches had pled a sufficient injury:

> When congregants are chilled from participating in worship activities [and] refuse to attend church services because they fear the government is spying on them and taping their every utterance, all as alleged in the complaint, we think a church suffers *organizational injury* because its ability to carry out its ministries has been impaired.

Id. at 522 (emphasis added). The Ninth Circuit then distinguished *Laird* [v. Tatum, 408 U.S. 1 (1972)]:

> Although *Laird* establishes that a litigant's allegation that it has suffered a subjective "chill" does not necessarily confer Article III standing, *Laird* does not control this case. The churches in this case are not claiming simply that the INS surveillance has "chilled" them from holding worship services. Rather, they claim that the INS surveillance has chilled individual congregants from attending worship services, and that this effect on the congregants has in turn interfered with the churches' ability to carry out

> their ministries. The alleged effect on the churches is not a mere subjective chill on their worship activities; it is a concrete, demonstrable decrease in attendance at those worship activities. The injury to the churches is "distinct and palpable." *Laird* has no application here.

Id. (citations omitted).

In one sense, the Ninth Circuit's decision could be read as concluding that the churches suffered injury based on the actions of third parties (i.e., individual parishioners) – a reading that supports the plaintiffs' arguments in favor of standing. In another sense, however, the Ninth Circuit's decision may be confined to the unique idea of "organizational injury"; a church is, after all, an organization comprising a congregation of parishioners, and these congregants are properly viewed as intrinsic to the church organization, rather than as separate third parties. This reading of *Presbyterian Church* would weaken its application to the present context because the overseas third-party clients, contacts, and sources in this case are not affiliated with the plaintiffs in the same intrinsic manner as are parishioners with a church. None of the plaintiffs have alleged any "organizational injury" in the present context.

Having acknowledged these alternative interpretations of *Presbyterian Church,* it is unnecessary to resolve that issue definitively on this record. Injury in fact is but one of the criteria necessary to establish standing, and ultimately, it is not determinative of this case. Either of the other two criteria – causation or redressability – might ultimately defeat the plaintiffs' claim of standing, even if the plaintiffs' alleged injury is deemed adequate to state an injury in fact.

Causation . . .

In the present case, the "putatively illegal action" is the NSA's interception of overseas communications without warrants (specifically FISA warrants), and the "threatened or actual injury" is the added cost of in-person communication with the overseas contacts (or correspondingly, the diminished performance resulting from the inability to communicate). Therefore, to show causation, the plaintiffs must show that, but for the lack of warrants (or FISA compliance), they would not incur this added cost. There are two causal pathways based on the two types of alleged injury. In the first: (1) the NSA's warrantless wiretapping, (2) creates in the plaintiffs a "well founded belief" that their overseas telephone and email communications are being intercepted, which (3) requires the plaintiffs to refrain from these communications (i.e., chills communication), and (4) compels the plaintiffs to travel overseas to meet personally with these contacts in order to satisfy their professional responsibilities, thereby (5) causing the plaintiffs to incur additional costs. In the second: (1) the NSA's warrantless wiretapping (2) causes the "well founded belief," which (3) compels the overseas contacts to refuse to communicate by telephone or email (i.e., chills communication), thereby (4) requiring in-person communication, with its (5) associated additional costs. The district court attempted to articulate this relationship: "All of the Plaintiffs contend that the TSP has caused clients, witnesses and sources to discontinue their communications with plaintiffs out of fear that their communications will be intercepted." *ACLU v. NSA,* 438 F. Supp. 2d at 767 (footnote omitted). From this, the district court theorized: "Plaintiffs would be able to continue using the telephone and email in the execution of their professional responsibilities if the Defendants were not undisputedly and admittedly conducting warrantless wiretaps of conversations." *Id.* at 769. In considering these causal pathways, I question the second step (whether the "well founded belief" is actually founded on the warrantless wiretapping) and refute the third step (whether the unwillingness to communicate is actually caused by the warrantless character of the wiretaps).

The underpinning of the second step is questionable. The plaintiffs allege that they have a "well founded belief" that their overseas contacts are likely targets of the NSA and that their conversations are being intercepted. The plaintiffs have no evidence, however, that the NSA has actually intercepted (or will actually intercept) any of their conversations. No matter what the plaintiffs and others might find "reasonable," the evidence establishes only a *possibility* – not a probability or certainty – that these calls might be intercepted, that the information might be disclosed or disseminated, or that this might lead to some harm to the overseas contacts. While this lack of evidence is not, by itself, enough to *disprove* causation, the absence of this evidence makes the plaintiffs' showing of causation less certain and the likelihood of causation more speculative.

The third step is unsupportable. In this step, the plaintiffs allege, and the district court found, that it is *the absence of a warrant* (and all that goes with it) that has chilled the plaintiffs and their overseas contacts from communicating by telephone or email. This allegation does not stand up under scrutiny, however, and it is not clear whether the chill can fairly be traced to the absence of a warrant, or if the chill would still exist without regard to the presence or absence of a warrant. The insufficiency of this step leads to a breakdown in the causal pathway.

A wiretap is always "secret" – that is its very purpose – and because of this secrecy, neither the plaintiffs nor their overseas contacts would know, with or without a warrant, whether their communications were being tapped. Therefore, the NSA's secret possession of a warrant would have no more effect on the subjective willingness or unwillingness of these parties to "freely engage in conversations and correspond via email," *see ACLU v. NSA,* 438 F. Supp. 2d at 770, than would the secret absence of that warrant. The plaintiffs have neither asserted nor proven any basis upon which to justifiably conclude that the mere absence of a warrant – rather than some other reason, such as the prosecution of the War on Terror, in general, or the NSA's targeting of communications involving suspected al Qaeda terrorists, affiliates, and supporters, in particular – is the cause of the plaintiffs' (and their overseas contacts') reluctance to communicate by telephone or email.

The plaintiffs have argued that if the NSA were to conduct its surveillance in compliance with FISA, they would no longer feel compelled to cease their international telephone and email communications. But again, even if the NSA had (secretly) obtained FISA warrants for each of the overseas contacts, who the plaintiffs themselves assert are likely to be monitored, the plaintiffs would still not have known their communications were being intercepted, still faced the same fear of harm to their contacts, still incurred the same self-imposed (or contact-imposed) burden on communications and, therefore, still suffered the same alleged injury. The plaintiffs' theory relies on their contention that their ethical obligations require them to cease telephone or email communications any time they believe the private or privileged information in those communications might be discovered or disclosed to the detriment of their clients, sources, or contacts. Assuming that this contention is true, it must also be true that this ethical obligation would arise whenever, and continue so long as, the plaintiffs believe their contacts to be the types of people likely to be monitored by the NSA.

The imposition of FISA requirements into this scenario would not change the likelihood that these overseas contacts are the types of people who the plaintiffs believe would be monitored. Nor would it change the plaintiffs' "well founded belief" that the NSA is intercepting their communications with these individuals, the plaintiffs' ethical obligations, or the overseas contacts' subjective fears. Even under the plaintiffs' depiction, it would merely assure the plaintiffs and their contacts that – while their international telephone and email communications with al Qaeda affiliates are still just as likely to be intercepted – the NSA will obtain FISA Court orders, which will presumably limit the duration and content of the acquisition and the use and dissemination of the acquired information. The plaintiffs, however, have not asserted, explained, or proven how a change in the duration or content of the NSA's interceptions – purely hypothetical changes that are unknown and unknowable based on the established record and the State Secrets Doctrine – would alleviate their fears. Specifically, the plaintiffs have not proffered any types or topics of communication, from which they are currently refraining, but about which – upon the imposition of FISA's limitations and protections – they would thereafter "freely engage in conversations and correspond[ence] via email." *See ACLU v. NSA,* 438 F. Supp. 2d at 770.

Some plaintiffs (especially those who are lawyers) assert that the imposition of FISA minimization – to limit the use and dissemination of the information acquired – would relieve their fears sufficiently to satisfy their ethical obligations because it would ensure that those communications would remain confidential and privileged in the event of a subsequent criminal prosecution, removal proceeding, military tribunal, etc. Therefore, they argue, imposition of FISA requirements would alter the type and content of their communications. This theory, however, is predicated on the assumption that their current fears and apprehensions are justified – and there is no support for this assumption. First, there is no evidence in the current record from which to presume that the information collected by the NSA via warrantless wiretapping will be used or disclosed for any purpose other than national security. Next, there is no evidence in the record from which to presume that the NSA is not complying with, or even exceeding, FISA's restrictions on the acquisition, retention, use, or disclosure of this information (i.e., FISA's minimization techniques). Finally, there is no basis to presume that traditional *post-hoc* remedies, such as the Exclusionary Rule or FISA's civil suit provision, 50 U.S.C. §1810, would not adequately deter the use or dissemination of this information. Consequently, this disconnect in the plaintiffs' theory is unavoidable, and the plaintiffs' injury is not fairly traceable to the mere absence of FISA compliance. . . .

The plaintiffs have not shown a sufficient causal connection between the complained-of conduct (i.e., the absence of a warrant or FISA protection) and the alleged harm (i.e., the inability to communicate). This inadequacy is further exemplified in the analysis of redressability.

Redressability . . .

In the present case, the plaintiffs requested a declaratory judgment and an injunction. They theorize that their injury (i.e., deficient professional performance or the additional cost of in-person communication) will be redressed by a declaration that the NSA's practice of warrantless wiretapping is unlawful, because it naturally follows that the unlawful conduct will be prohibited. The declaratory judgment thus forms the basis for an injunction prohibiting interception of communications without FISA compliance. The district court agreed, declaring the NSA's conduct illegal and imposing an injunction, on the belief that its injunction would redress the plaintiffs' injury by assuring them "that they could freely engage in conversations and correspond via email without concern, at least without notice, that such communications were being monitored." *ACLU v. NSA,* 438 F. Supp. 2d at 770-71. This theory of redressability rests on the premise that the NSA's compliance with FISA's warrant requirements will entice the plaintiffs and their contacts to "freely engage in conversations and correspond via email without concern." The likelihood of this outcome, however, "can, at best, be termed only speculative," *see Linda R.S.* [v. Richard D., 410 U.S. 614 (1973),] at 618; it is just as likely (if not more likely) that, even with the imposition of a warrant requirement, the plaintiffs' current situation will not change – their fears will not be abated. . . .

For the foregoing reasons, the plaintiffs in the present action have no standing to pursue their First Amendment claim. Even if they could demonstrate injury, they cannot establish causation, and their alleged injury is not redressable by the remedy they seek.

2. Fourth Amendment

The plaintiffs allege that the NSA has, by conducting the warrantless wiretaps, violated the "plaintiffs' privacy rights guaranteed by the Fourth Amendment." The district court – asserting a heretofore unprecedented, *absolute* rule that the Fourth Amendment "requires prior warrants for *any* reasonable search," *ACLU v. NSA,* 438 F. Supp. 2d at 775 – agreed and granted the plaintiffs' motion for summary judgment on this theory, *id.* at 782.

However, the Supreme Court has made clear that Fourth Amendment rights are "personal rights" which, unlike First Amendment rights, may not be asserted vicariously. *See* Rakas v. Illinois, 439 U.S. 128, 133-34 (1978). . . .

3. Separation of Powers . . .

To prove causation, the plaintiffs must connect the alleged separation-of-powers violation ("the putatively illegal action") to the burden on the performance of their professional obligations (the alleged injury). Six steps separate the putatively illegal conduct from the alleged injury: (1) the President allegedly exceeded his allotted authority by authorizing the NSA to conduct warrantless wiretapping as part of its enhanced national security (i.e., counterterrorism) operations and the worldwide War on Terror, causing (2) the NSA to institute its practice of warrantless wiretapping under the TSP, causing (3) the plaintiffs' "well founded belief" that the NSA is intercepting their telephone and email communications, causing (4) either the plaintiffs themselves or the overseas contacts to refrain from these communications, causing (5) the plaintiffs either to underperform in their professional capacities or to travel to meet personally with these contacts, causing (6) the additional burden on performance of the plaintiffs' professional duties.

This record simply does not permit the kind of particularized analysis that is required to determine causation. Ignoring for a moment the first two steps in the analysis, it is clear that the third and fourth are problematic. The plaintiffs have presented no evidence to support their alleged "well founded belief" that their conversations are being intercepted. The evidence establishes only a *possibility* – not a probability or certainty – that these communications might be intercepted, disclosed, or disseminated. . . .

B. Statutory Claims . . .

When considering statutory claims, "the inquiry as to standing must begin with a determination of whether the statute in question authorizes review at the behest of the plaintiff." *Sierra Club* [v. Morton, 405 U.S. 727 (1972),] at 732. The plaintiffs asserted three statutory bases – the APA, Title III, and FISA – and none of these three statutes, individually or collectively, provides an express or implied cause of action that "authorizes review" of the plaintiffs claims. *See id.* Therefore, the plaintiffs cannot establish standing to litigate their statutory claims, and further explanation is unnecessary. . . .

V.

The district court dismissed the data mining aspect of the plaintiffs' claim, finding that the plaintiffs could not establish a *prima facie* case without resorting to privileged information. *ACLU v. NSA,* 438 F. Supp. 2d at 765. The plaintiffs press this issue as a cross-appeal.

A thorough review of the complaint, the district court opinion, and the arguments presented on appeal, makes it clear that the plaintiffs allege no separate injury in connection with the alleged data-mining aspect of the TSP. Therefore, this standing analysis applies equally, and the plaintiffs' cross-appeal must be dismissed for lack of jurisdiction.

VI.

We hold that the plaintiffs do not have standing to assert their claims in federal court. Accordingly, we VACATE the order of the district court and REMAND this case to the district court with instructions to DISMISS for lack of jurisdiction.

JULIA SMITH GIBBONS, Circuit Judge, concurring. [omitted]

RONALD LEE GILMAN, Circuit Judge, dissenting. [omitted]

Page 556. Add the following materials after Note 9.

After a FISC judge decided in May 2007 not to continue approval of what had been the TSP under FISC supervision, the Bush administration urged Congress to pass statutory authorization for its program. In August 2007, Congress enacted the Protect America Act, Pub. L. No. 110-55, 121 Stat. 552, which permitted the DNI and the Attorney General to authorize collection of foreign intelligence concerning persons reasonably believed to be outside the United States, without obtaining an order from the FISC, even if one party to the communication was a U.S. citizen inside the United States. The Protect

America Act expired by its own terms in February 2008, leading to the enactment on July 10, 2008, of the FISA amendments excerpted below.

FISA Amendments Act of 2008

Pub. L. No. 110-261, 122 Stat. 2436

[Section 101 of the 2008 Act struck Title VII of FISA as it existed (containing the expired Protect America Act), and added the following new Title VII:]

TITLE VII – ADDITIONAL PROCEDURES REGARDING CERTAIN PERSONS OUTSIDE THE UNITED STATES. . . .

§702. Procedures for Targeting Certain Persons Outside the United States Other than United States Persons.

(a) Authorization – Notwithstanding any other provision of law, upon the issuance of an order in accordance with subsection (i)(3) or a determination under subsection (c)(2), the Attorney General and the Director of National Intelligence may authorize jointly, for a period of up to 1 year from the effective date of the authorization, the targeting of persons reasonably believed to be located outside the United States to acquire foreign intelligence information.

(b) Limitations – An acquisition authorized under subsection (a) –

(1) may not intentionally target any person known at the time of acquisition to be located in the United States;

(2) may not intentionally target a person reasonably believed to be located outside the United States if the purpose of such acquisition is to target a particular, known person reasonably believed to be in the United States;

(3) may not intentionally target a United States person reasonably believed to be located outside the United States;

(4) may not intentionally acquire any communication as to which the sender and all intended recipients are known at the time of the acquisition to be located in the United States; and

(5) shall be conducted in a manner consistent with the fourth amendment to the Constitution of the United States.

(c) Conduct of Acquisition –

(1) In General – An acquisition authorized under subsection (a) shall be conducted only in accordance with –

(A) the targeting and minimization procedures adopted in

accordance with subsections (d) and (e); and

(B) upon submission of a certification in accordance with subsection (g), such certification.

(2) Determination – A determination under this paragraph and for purposes of subsection (a) is a determination by the Attorney General and the Director of National Intelligence that exigent circumstances exist because, without immediate implementation of an authorization under subsection (a), intelligence important to the national security of the United States may be lost or not timely acquired and time does not permit the issuance of an order pursuant to subsection (i)(3) prior to the implementation of such authorization. . . .

(4) Construction – Nothing in title I shall be construed to require an application for a court order under such title for an acquisition that is targeted in accordance with this section at a person reasonably believed to be located outside the United States.

(d) Targeting Procedures –

(1) Requirement to Adopt – The Attorney General, in consultation with the Director of National Intelligence, shall adopt targeting procedures that are reasonably designed to –

(A) ensure that any acquisition authorized under subsection (a) is limited to targeting persons reasonably believed to be located outside the United States; and

(B) prevent the intentional acquisition of any communication as to which the sender and all intended recipients are known at the time of the acquisition to be located in the United States.

(2) Judicial Review – The procedures adopted in accordance with paragraph (1) shall be subject to judicial review pursuant to subsection (i).

(e) Minimization Procedures –

(1) Requirement to Adopt – The Attorney General, in consultation with the Director of National Intelligence, shall adopt minimization procedures that meet the definition of minimization procedures under section 101(h) or 301(4) [*see* casebook p. 528, Note 8], as appropriate, for acquisitions authorized under subsection (a).

(2) Judicial Review – The minimization procedures adopted in accordance with paragraph (1) shall be subject to judicial review pursuant to subsection (i).

(f) Guidelines for Compliance with Limitations –

(1) Requirement to Adopt – The Attorney General, in consultation with the Director of National Intelligence, shall adopt

guidelines to ensure –

(A) compliance with the limitations in subsection (b); and

(B) that an application for a court order is filed as required by this Act.

(2) Submission of Guidelines – The Attorney General shall provide the guidelines adopted in accordance with paragraph (1) to –

(A) the congressional intelligence committees;

(B) the Committees on the Judiciary of the Senate and the House of Representatives; and

(C) the Foreign Intelligence Surveillance Court.

(g) Certification –

(1) In General –

(A) Requirement – Subject to subparagraph (B), prior to the implementation of an authorization under subsection (a), the Attorney General and the Director of National Intelligence shall provide to the Foreign Intelligence Surveillance Court a written certification and any supporting affidavit, under oath and under seal, in accordance with this subsection.

(B) Exception – If the Attorney General and the Director of National Intelligence make a determination under subsection (c)(2) and time does not permit the submission of a certification under this subsection prior to the implementation of an authorization under subsection (a), the Attorney General and the Director of National Intelligence shall submit to the Court a certification for such authorization as soon as practicable but in no event later than 7 days after such determination is made.

(2) Requirements – A certification made under this subsection shall –

(A) attest that –

(i) there are procedures in place that have been approved, have been submitted for approval, or will be submitted with the certification for approval by the Foreign Intelligence Surveillance Court that are reasonably designed to –

(I) ensure that an acquisition authorized under subsection (a) is limited to targeting persons reasonably believed to be located outside the United States; and

(II) prevent the intentional acquisition of any communication as to which the sender and all intended recipients are known at the time of the acquisition to be located in the United States;

(ii) the minimization procedures to be used with respect to such acquisition –

(I) meet the definition of minimization procedures under section 101(h) or 301(4), as appropriate; and

(II) have been approved, have been submitted for approval, or will be submitted with the certification for approval by the Foreign Intelligence Surveillance Court;

(iii) guidelines have been adopted in accordance with subsection (f) to ensure compliance with the limitations in subsection (b) and to ensure that an application for a court order is filed as required by this Act;

(iv) the procedures and guidelines referred to in clauses (i), (ii), and (iii) are consistent with the requirements of the fourth amendment to the Constitution of the United States;

(v) a significant purpose of the acquisition is to obtain foreign intelligence information;

(vi) the acquisition involves obtaining foreign intelligence information from or with the assistance of an electronic communication service provider; and

(vii) the acquisition complies with the limitations in subsection (b);

(B) include the procedures adopted in accordance with subsections (d) and (e);

(C) be supported, as appropriate, by the affidavit of any appropriate official in the area of national security who is –

(i) appointed by the President, by and with the advice and consent of the Senate; or

(ii) the head of an element of the intelligence community;

(D) include –

(i) an effective date for the authorization that is at least 30 days after the submission of the written certification to the court; or

(ii) if the acquisition has begun or the effective date is less than 30 days after the submission of the written certification to the court, the date the acquisition began or the effective date for the acquisition; and

(E) if the Attorney General and the Director of National Intelligence make a determination under subsection (c)(2), include a statement that such determination has been made. . . .

(6) Review – A certification submitted in accordance with this

subsection shall be subject to judicial review pursuant to subsection (i).

(h) Directives and Judicial Review of Directives –

(1) Authority – With respect to an acquisition authorized under subsection (a), the Attorney General and the Director of National Intelligence may direct, in writing, an electronic communication service provider to –

(A) immediately provide the Government with all information, facilities, or assistance necessary to accomplish the acquisition in a manner that will protect the secrecy of the acquisition and produce a minimum of interference with the services that such electronic communication service provider is providing to the target of the acquisition; . . .

(3) Release from Liability – No cause of action shall lie in any court against any electronic communication service provider for providing any information, facilities, or assistance in accordance with a directive issued pursuant to paragraph (1).

(4) Challenging of Directives –

(A) Authority to Challenge – An electronic communication service provider receiving a directive issued pursuant to paragraph (1) may file a petition to modify or set aside such directive with the Foreign Intelligence Surveillance Court, which shall have jurisdiction to review such petition. . . .

(5) Enforcement of Directives –

(A) Order to Compel – If an electronic communication service provider fails to comply with a directive issued pursuant to paragraph (1), the Attorney General may file a petition for an order to compel the electronic communication service provider to comply with the directive with the Foreign Intelligence Surveillance Court, which shall have jurisdiction to review such petition. . . .

(6) Appeal –

(A) Appeal to the Court of Review – The Government or an electronic communication service provider receiving a directive issued pursuant to paragraph (1) may file a petition with the Foreign Intelligence Surveillance Court of Review for review of a decision issued pursuant to paragraph (4) or (5). . . .

(B) Certiorari to the Supreme Court – The Government or an electronic communication service provider receiving a directive issued pursuant to paragraph (1) may file a petition for a writ of certiorari for review of a decision of the Court of Review issued under subparagraph (A). . . .

(i) Judicial Review of Certifications and Procedures –

(1) In General –

(A) Review by the Foreign Intelligence Surveillance Court – The Foreign Intelligence Surveillance Court shall have jurisdiction to review a certification submitted in accordance with subsection (g) and the targeting and minimization procedures adopted in accordance with subsections (d) and (e), and amendments to such certification or such procedures. . . .

(2) Review – The Court shall review the following:

(A) Certification – A certification submitted in accordance with subsection (g) to determine whether the certification contains all the required elements.

(B) Targeting Procedures – The targeting procedures adopted in accordance with subsection (d) to assess whether the procedures are reasonably designed to –

(i) ensure that an acquisition authorized under subsection (a) is limited to targeting persons reasonably believed to be located outside the United States; and

(ii) prevent the intentional acquisition of any communication as to which the sender and all intended recipients are known at the time of the acquisition to be located in the United States.

(C) Minimization Procedures – The minimization procedures adopted in accordance with subsection (e) to assess whether such procedures meet the definition of minimization procedures under section 101(h) or section 301(4), as appropriate.

(3) Orders –

(A) Approval – If the Court finds that a certification submitted in accordance with subsection (g) contains all the required elements and that the targeting and minimization procedures adopted in accordance with subsections (d) and (e) are consistent with the requirements of those subsections and with the fourth amendment to the Constitution of the United States, the Court shall enter an order approving the certification and the use, or continued use in the case of an acquisition authorized pursuant to a determination under subsection (c)(2), of the procedures for the acquisition.

(B) Correction of Deficiencies – If the Court finds that a certification submitted in accordance with subsection (g) does not contain all the required elements, or that the procedures adopted in accordance with subsections (d) and (e) are not consistent with the requirements of those subsections or the fourth amendment to the Constitution of the United States, the Court shall issue an order directing the Government to, at the Government's election and to the extent required by the Court's order –

(i) correct any deficiency identified by the Court's order not later than 30 days after the date on which the Court issues the order; or

(ii) cease, or not begin, the implementation of the authorization for which such certification was submitted. . . .

(4) Appeal –

(A) Appeal to the Court of Review – The Government may file a petition with the Foreign Intelligence Surveillance Court of Review for review of an order under this subsection. . . .

(D) Certiorari to the Supreme Court – The Government may file a petition for a writ of certiorari for review of a decision of the Court of Review issued under subparagraph (A). . . .

(l) Assessments and Reviews –

(1) Semiannual Assessment – Not less frequently than once every 6 months, the Attorney General and Director of National Intelligence shall assess compliance with the targeting and minimization procedures adopted in accordance with subsections (d) and (e) and the guidelines adopted in accordance with subsection (f) and shall submit each assessment to –

(A) the Foreign Intelligence Surveillance Court; and

(B) consistent with the Rules of the House of Representatives, [and] the . . . Rules of the Senate . . . –

(i) the congressional intelligence committees; and

(ii) the Committees on the Judiciary of the House of Representatives and the Senate.

(2) Agency Assessment – The Inspector General of the Department of Justice and the Inspector General of each element of the intelligence community authorized to acquire foreign intelligence information under subsection (a), with respect to the department or element of such Inspector General –

(A) are authorized to review compliance with the targeting and minimization procedures adopted in accordance with subsections (d) and (e) and the guidelines adopted in accordance with subsection (f); . . . [and]

(D) shall provide each such review to –

(i) the Attorney General;

(ii) the Director of National Intelligence; and

(iii) consistent with the Rules of the House of Representatives, [and] the . . . Rules of the Senate. . . –

(I) the congressional intelligence committees; and

(II) the Committees on the Judiciary of the House of Representatives and the Senate.

(3) Annual Review –

(A) Requirement to Conduct – The head of each element of the intelligence community conducting an acquisition authorized under subsection (a) shall conduct an annual review to determine whether there is reason to believe that foreign intelligence information has been or will be obtained from the acquisition. The annual review shall provide, with respect to acquisitions authorized under subsection (a) –

(i) an accounting of the number of disseminated intelligence reports containing a reference to a United States-person identity; . . .

(iii) the number of targets that were later determined to be located in the United States and, to the extent possible, whether communications of such targets were reviewed; and

(iv) a description of any procedures developed by the head of such element of the intelligence community and approved by the Director of National Intelligence to assess, in a manner consistent with national security, operational requirements and the privacy interests of United States persons . . . .

(C) Provision of Review – The head of each element of the intelligence community that conducts an annual review under subparagraph (A) shall provide such review to –

(i) the Foreign Intelligence Surveillance Court;

(ii) the Attorney General;

(iii) the Director of National Intelligence; and

(iv) consistent with the Rules of the House of Representatives, [and] the . . . Rules of the Senate . . . –

(I) the congressional intelligence committees; and

(II) the Committees on the Judiciary of the House of Representatives and the Senate.

§703. Certain Acquisitions Inside the United States Targeting United States Persons Outside the United States.

(a) Jurisdiction of the Foreign Intelligence Surveillance Court –

(1) in General – The Foreign Intelligence Surveillance Court shall have jurisdiction to review an application and to enter an order approving the targeting of a United States person reasonably believed to be located outside the United States to acquire foreign intelligence information, if the acquisition constitutes electronic surveillance or the acquisition of stored electronic communications or stored electronic data that requires an order under this Act, and such acquisition is conducted within the United States.

(2) Limitation – If a United States person targeted under this subsection is reasonably believed to be located in the United States during the effective period of an order issued pursuant to subsection (c), an acquisition targeting such United States person under this section shall cease unless the targeted United States person is again reasonably believed to be located outside the United States while an order issued pursuant to subsection (c) is in effect. Nothing in this section shall be construed to limit the authority of the Government to seek an order or authorization under, or otherwise engage in any activity that is authorized under, any other title of this Act.

(b) Application –

(1) In General – Each application for an order under this section shall be made by a Federal officer in writing upon oath or affirmation to a judge having jurisdiction under subsection (a)(1). Each application shall require the approval of the Attorney General based upon the Attorney General's finding that it satisfies the criteria and requirements of such application, as set forth in this section, and shall include –

(A) the identity of the Federal officer making the application;

(B) the identity, if known, or a description of the United States person who is the target of the acquisition;

(C) a statement of the facts and circumstances relied upon to justify the applicant's belief that the United States person who is the target of the acquisition is –

(i) a person reasonably believed to be located outside the United States; and

(ii) a foreign power, an agent of a foreign power, or an officer or employee of a foreign power;

(D) a statement of proposed minimization procedures that meet the definition of minimization procedures under section 101(h) or 301(4), as appropriate;

(E) a description of the nature of the information sought and the type of communications or activities to be subjected to acquisition;

(F) a certification made by the Attorney General or an official specified in section 104(a)(6) that –

(i) the certifying official deems the information sought to be foreign intelligence information;

(ii) a significant purpose of the acquisition is to obtain foreign intelligence information;

(iii) such information cannot reasonably be obtained by normal investigative techniques;

(iv) designates the type of foreign intelligence information being sought according to the categories described in section 101(e) [*see* casebook p. 514]; . . .

(G) a summary statement of the means by which the acquisition will be conducted and whether physical entry is required to effect the acquisition;

(H) the identity of any electronic communication service provider necessary to effect the acquisition, provided that the application is not required to identify the specific facilities, places, premises, or property at which the acquisition authorized under this section will be directed or conducted; . . . [and]

(J) a statement of the period of time for which the acquisition is required to be maintained, provided that such period of time shall not exceed 90 days per application. . . .

(c) Order –

(1) Findings – Upon an application made pursuant to subsection (b), the Foreign Intelligence Surveillance Court shall enter an ex parte order as requested or as modified by the Court approving the acquisition if the Court finds that – . . .

(B) on the basis of the facts submitted by the applicant, for the United States person who is the target of the acquisition, there is probable cause to believe that the target is –

(i) a person reasonably believed to be located outside the United States; and

(ii) a foreign power, an agent of a foreign power, or an officer or employee of a foreign power; . . .

(D) the application that has been filed contains all statements and certifications required by subsection (b) and the certification or certifications are not clearly erroneous on the basis of the statement made under subsection (b)(1)(F)(v) and any other information furnished under subsection (b)(3).

(2) Probable Cause – In determining whether or not probable cause exists for purposes of paragraph (1)(B), a judge having jurisdiction under subsection (a)(1) may consider past activities of the target and facts and circumstances relating to current or future activities of the target. No United States person may be considered a foreign power, agent of a foreign power, or officer or employee of a foreign power solely upon the basis of activities protected by the first amendment to the Constitution of the United States.

(3) Review –

(A) Limitation on Review – Review by a judge having jurisdiction under subsection (a)(1) shall be limited to that required to make the findings described in paragraph (1). . . .

(6) Duration – An order approved under this subsection shall be effective for a period not to exceed 90 days and such order may be renewed for additional 90-day periods upon submission of renewal applications meeting the requirements of subsection (b). . . .

(d) Emergency Authorization – [This provision substantially repeats the authority set out in FISA §105, 50 U.S.C. §1805 (*see* casebook p. 528, Note 9), except that it extends from 48 hours to 7 days the time for the Attorney General to apply for a judicial order after authorizing acquisition in an emergency.]

(e) Release From Liability – No cause of action shall lie in any court against any electronic communication service provider for providing any information, facilities, or assistance in accordance with an order or request for emergency assistance issued pursuant to subsection (c) or (d), respectively.

(f) Appeal –

(1) Appeal to the Foreign Intelligence Surveillance Court of Review – The Government may file a petition with the Foreign Intelligence Surveillance Court of Review for review of an order issued pursuant to subsection (c). . . .

(2) Certiorari to the Supreme Court – The Government may file a petition for a writ of certiorari for review of a decision of the Court of Review issued under paragraph (1). . . .

(g) Construction – Except as provided in this section, nothing in this Act shall be construed to require an application for a court order for an acquisition that is targeted in accordance with this section at a United

States person reasonably believed to be located outside the United States.

§704. Other Acquisitions Targeting United States Persons Outside the United States.

(a) Jurisdiction and Scope –

(1) Jurisdiction – The Foreign Intelligence Surveillance Court shall have jurisdiction to enter an order pursuant to subsection (c).

(2) Scope – No element of the intelligence community may intentionally target, for the purpose of acquiring foreign intelligence information, a United States person reasonably believed to be located outside the United States under circumstances in which the targeted United States person has a reasonable expectation of privacy and a warrant would be required if the acquisition were conducted inside the United States for law enforcement purposes, unless a judge of the Foreign Intelligence Surveillance Court has entered an order with respect to such targeted United States person or the Attorney General has authorized an emergency acquisition pursuant to subsection (c) or (d), respectively, or any other provision of this Act. . . .

(b) Application – Each application for an order under this section shall be made by a Federal officer in writing upon oath or affirmation to a judge having jurisdiction under subsection (a)(1). Each application shall require the approval of the Attorney General based upon the Attorney General's finding that it satisfies the criteria and requirements of such application as set forth in this section and shall include – . . .

(3) a statement of the facts and circumstances relied upon to justify the applicant's belief that the United States person who is the target of the acquisition is –

(A) a person reasonably believed to be located outside the United States; and

(B) a foreign power, an agent of a foreign power, or an officer or employee of a foreign power; . . .

(5) a certification made by the Attorney General, an official specified in section 104(a)(6), or the head of an element of the intelligence community that –

(A) the certifying official deems the information sought to be foreign intelligence information; and

(B) a significant purpose of the acquisition is to obtain foreign intelligence information; . . . [and]

(7) a statement of the period of time for which the acquisition is required to be maintained, provided that such period of time shall not

exceed 90 days per application.

[§704(c)-(e) generally repeats the requirements of §703(c)-(f).] . . .

§705. Joint Applications and Concurrent Authorizations.

(a) Joint Applications and Orders – If an acquisition targeting a United States person under section 703 or 704 is proposed to be conducted both inside and outside the United States, a judge having jurisdiction under section 703(a)(1) or 704(a)(1) may issue simultaneously, upon the request of the Government in a joint application complying with the requirements of sections 703(b) and 704(b), orders under sections 703(c) and 704(c), as appropriate.

(b) Concurrent Authorization – If an order authorizing electronic surveillance or physical search has been obtained under section 105 or 304, the Attorney General may authorize, for the effective period of that order, without an order under section 703 or 704, the targeting of that United States person for the purpose of acquiring foreign intelligence information while such person is reasonably believed to be located outside the United States. . . .

§707. Congressional Oversight.

(a) Semiannual Report – Not less frequently than once every 6 months, the Attorney General shall fully inform, in a manner consistent with national security, the congressional intelligence committees and the Committees on the Judiciary of the Senate and the House of Representatives, consistent with the Rules of the House of Representatives, [and] the . . . Rules of the Senate . . . concerning the implementation of this title. . . .

[Section 102(a) of the 2008 Act amended Title I of FISA by adding at the end the following new section:]

STATEMENT OF EXCLUSIVE MEANS BY WHICH ELECTRONIC SURVEILLANCE AND INTERCEPTION OF CERTAIN COMMUNICATIONS MAY BE CONDUCTED

§112. (a) Except as provided in subsection (b), the procedures of chapters 119, 121, and 206 of title 18, United States Code, and this Act shall be the exclusive means by which electronic surveillance and the interception of domestic wire, oral, or electronic communications may be conducted.

(b) Only an express statutory authorization for electronic surveillance or the interception of domestic wire, oral, or electronic communications, other than as an amendment to this Act or chapters 119, 121, or 206 of title 18, United States Code, shall constitute an additional exclusive means for the purpose of subsection (a).

[Section 102(b) of the 2008 Act provided conforming amendments to FISA §109(a), 50 U.S.C. §1809(a), which criminalizes violations of FISA. *See* casebook pp. 550-551 and p. 552, Note 2.]

[Section 102(c) of the 2008 Act amended FISA §105, 50 U.S.C. §1805, extending from 48 hours to 7 days the time to apply for a judicial order if the Attorney General authorizes electronic surveillance in an emergency. *See* casebook p. 528, Note 9.] . . .

[Sections 107 and 108 of the 2008 Act provided conforming amendments to FISA's physical search provisions and to its provisions for emergency pen registers and trap and trace devices.] . . .

[Section 110(a)(1) of the 2008 Act amended FISA §101(a), 50 U.S.C. §1801(a), by adding the following new definition of a "foreign power" (*see* casebook p. 522, Note 4):]

> (7) an entity not substantially composed of United States persons that is engaged in the international proliferation of weapons of mass destruction.

[Section 110(a)(2) of the 2008 Act amended FISA §101(b)(1), 50 U.S.C. §1801(b)(1), by adding the following new definitions of "agent of a foreign power" (*see* casebook p. 522, Note 4), to include "any person other than a United States person, who":]

> (D) engages in the international proliferation of weapons of mass destruction, or activities in preparation therefor; or
>
> (E) engages in the international proliferation of weapons of mass destruction, or activities in preparation therefor for or on behalf of a foreign power; or

[Section 110(a)(3) of the 2008 Act amended FISA §101(e)(1)(B), 50 U.S.C. §1801(e)(1)(B), which offers one definition of "foreign intelligence information," by striking "sabotage or international terrorism" and inserting "sabotage, international terrorism, or the international proliferation of weapons of mass destruction."] . . .

[Section 201 of the 2008 Act amended FISA as it existed by adding the following new title:]

TITLE VIII – PROTECTION OF PERSONS ASSISTING THE GOVERNMENT

§801. Definitions.

In this title:

(1) Assistance – The term "assistance" means the provision of, or the provision of access to, information (including communication contents, communications records, or other information relating to a customer or communication), facilities, or another form of assistance. . . .

§802. Procedures for Implementing Statutory Defenses.

(a) Requirement for Certification – Notwithstanding any other provision of law, a civil action may not lie or be maintained in a Federal or State court against any person for providing assistance to an element of the intelligence community, and shall be promptly dismissed, if the Attorney General certifies to the district court of the United States in which such action is pending that –

(1) any assistance by that person was provided pursuant to an order of the court established under section 103(a) directing such assistance;

(2) any assistance by that person was provided pursuant to a certification in writing under section 2511(2)(a)(ii)(B) or 2709(b) of title 18, United States Code;

(3) any assistance by that person was provided pursuant to a directive under section 102(a)(4), 105B(e), as added by section 2 of the Protect America Act of 2007 (Public Law 110-55), or 702(h) directing such assistance;

(4) in the case of a covered civil action, the assistance alleged to have been provided by the electronic communication service provider was –

(A) in connection with an intelligence activity involving communications that was –

(i) authorized by the President during the period beginning on September 11, 2001, and ending on January 17, 2007; and

(ii) designed to detect or prevent a terrorist attack, or activities in preparation for a terrorist attack, against the United States; and

(B) the subject of a written request or directive, or a series of written requests or directives, from the Attorney General or the head of an element of the intelligence community (or the deputy of such person) to the electronic communication service provider indicating that the activity was –

(i) authorized by the President; and

(ii) determined to be lawful; or

(5) the person did not provide the alleged assistance.

(b) Judicial Review –

(1) Review of Certifications – A certification under subsection (a) shall be given effect unless the court finds that such certification is not supported by substantial evidence provided to the court pursuant to this section. . . .

[Section 301 of the 2008 Act requires that the Inspectors General of agencies that participated in the TSP complete a comprehensive review of the program and provide a preliminary report to congressional committees within 60 days after enactment and a final report within 1 year of enactment.] . . .

* * *

20

Third-Party Records and Data Mining

A. FINDING THE DOTS – THIRD-PARTY RECORDS

1. Expectations of Privacy Regarding Transactional Data

Page 559. Insert the following case after Note 2.

Warshak v. United States

United States Court of Appeals, 6th Circuit, 2007
490 F.3d 455
vacated on ripeness grounds, 2008 WL 2698177
(6th Cir. July 11, 2008) (en banc)

BOYCE F. MARTIN, JR., Circuit Judge. The government appeals the district court's entry of a preliminary injunction, prohibiting it from seizing "the contents of any personal e-mail account maintained by an Internet Service Provider in the name of any resident of the Southern District of Ohio without providing the relevant account holder or subscriber prior notice and an opportunity to be heard on any complaint, motion, or other pleading seeking issuance of such an order." For the reasons discussed below, we largely affirm the district court's decision, requiring only that the preliminary injunction be slightly modified on remand.

I. . . .

[During a criminal investigation of Steven Warshak for mail and wire fraud, money laundering, and related federal offenses, the government obtained an order from a United States Magistrate Judge directing an internet service provider ("ISP") to turn over to government agents information pertaining to Warshak's e-mail account, including (1) customer account information, such as application information, "account identifiers," "[b]illing information to include bank account numbers," contact information, and "[any] other information pertaining to the customer, including set up, synchronization, etc."; (2) "[t]he contents of wire or electronic communications (not in electronic storage unless greater than 181 days old) that were placed or stored in directories or files owned or controlled" by the ISP; and (3) "[a]ll Log files and backup tapes." At a later date, Warshak was informed of the order and sought an injunction prohibiting future searches. The district court issued a preliminary injunction.]

The gist of this remedy appears to be that when a hearing is required and the e-mail account holder is given an opportunity in court to resist the disclosure of information, any resulting order is more like a subpoena than a search warrant. Therefore the standard necessary to obtain an order under the [Stored Communications Act (SCA), 18 U.S.C. §§2701-2712] – that the government introduce "specific and articulable facts showing that there are reasonable grounds to believe that the contents" of the e-mail to be seized "are relevant and material to an ongoing criminal investigation" [18 U.S.C. §2705(d)] – is permissible as the functional equivalent of a subpoena given the subject's ability to contest the order in court. Because this standard is lower than the probable cause standard necessary to obtain a search warrant, it is sufficient to justify a warrantless search only in instances where notice is provided to the account holder.

The government appeals from the district court's ruling. . . .

III. . . .

B. Likelihood of Success on the Merits: Probable Cause versus Reasonableness and Fourth Amendment Implications of SCA Orders

1. Probable Cause versus Reasonableness

With respect to the merits of the preliminary injunction, the government argues that court orders issued under section 2703 are not searches but rather compelled disclosures, akin to subpoenas. As a result, according to the government, the more stringent showing of probable cause, a prerequisite to the issuance of a warrant under the Fourth Amendment, is inapplicable, and an order under section 2703 need only be supported by a showing of "reasonable relevance."

The government is correct that "whereas the Fourth Amendment mandates a showing of probable cause for the issuance of search warrants, subpoenas are analyzed only under the Fourth Amendment's general reasonableness standard." Doe v. United States, 253 F.3d 256, 263-64 (6th Cir. 2001). As this Court has explained, "[o]ne primary reason for this distinction is that, unlike 'the immediacy and intrusiveness of a search and seizure conducted pursuant to a warrant[,]' the reasonableness of an administrative subpoena's command can be contested in federal court before being enforced." *Id.* at 264 (quoting In Re Subpoena Duces Tecum, 228 F.3d 341, 347-49 (4th Cir. 2000)); *see also* Donovan v. Lone Steer, 464 U.S. 408, 415 (1984). The government is also correct that this principle extends to subpoenas to third-parties – that is, entities other than the subject of the investigation, like NuVox and Yahoo in this case. *See* United States v. Phibbs, 999 F.2d 1053, 1077 (6th Cir. 1993).

Phibbs makes explicit, however, a necessary Fourth Amendment caveat to the rule regarding third-party subpoenas: the party challenging the subpoena has "standing to dispute [its] issuance on Fourth Amendment grounds" if he can "demonstrate that he had a legitimate expectation of privacy attaching to the records obtained." *Id.*; *see also* United States v. Miller, 425 U.S. 435, 444 (1976) ("Since **no Fourth Amendment interests of the depositor are implicated here,** this case is governed by the general rule that the issuance of a subpoena to a third party to obtain the records of that party does not violate the rights of a defendant." (emphasis added)). This language reflects the rule that where the party challenging the disclosure has voluntarily disclosed his records to a third party, he maintains no expectation of privacy in the disclosure vis-a-vis that individual, and assumes the risk of that person disclosing (or being compelled to disclose) the shared information to the authorities. *See, e.g.,* United States v. Jacobsen, 466 U.S. 109, 117 (1984) ("[W]hen an individual reveals private information to another, he assumes the risk that his confidant will reveal that information to the authorities, and if that occurs the Fourth Amendment does not prohibit governmental use of that information.").

Combining this disclosure to a third party with the government's ability to subpoena the third party alleviates any need for the third-party subpoena to meet the probable cause requirement, if the challenger has not maintained an expectation of privacy with respect to the individual being compelled to make the disclosure. For example, in *Phibbs,* the documents in question were credit card and phone records that were "readily accessible to employees during the normal course of business." 999 F.2d at 1078. A similar rationale was employed by the Supreme Court in *Miller.* 425 U.S. at 442 ("The checks are not confidential communications but negotiable instruments to be used in commercial transactions. All of the documents obtained, including financial statements and deposit slips, contain only information voluntarily conveyed to the banks and exposed to their employees in the ordinary course of business."). *See also* SEC v. Jerry T. O'Brien, Inc., 467 U.S. 735, 743 (1984) ("When a person communicates information to a third party even on the understanding that the communication is confidential, he cannot object if the third party conveys that information or records thereof to law enforcement authorities."). The government's compelled disclosure argument, while relevant, therefore begs the critical question of whether an e-mail user maintains a reasonable expectation of privacy in his e-mails vis-a-vis the party who is subject to compelled disclosure – in this instance, the ISPs. If he does not, as in *Phibbs* or *Miller,* then the government must meet only the reasonableness standard applicable to compelled disclosures to obtain the material. If, on the other hand, the e-mail user does maintain a reasonable expectation of privacy in the content of the e-mails with respect to the ISP, then the Fourth Amendment's probable cause standard controls the e-mail seizure.

2. *Reasonable expectation of privacy in e-mail content*

Two amici curiae convincingly analogize the privacy interest that e-mail users hold in the content of their e-mails to the privacy interest in the content of telephone calls, recognized by the Supreme Court in its line of cases involving government eavesdropping on telephone conversations. *See* Smith v. Maryland, 442 U.S. 735 (1979); Katz v. United States, 389 U.S. 347 (1967); Berger v. New York, 388 U.S. 41 (1967). In *Berger* and *Katz,* telephone surveillance that intercepted the content of a conversation was held to constitute a search, because the caller "is surely entitled to assume that the words he utters into the mouthpiece will not be broadcast to the world," and therefore cannot be said to have forfeited his privacy right in the conversation. *Katz,* 389 U.S. at 352. This is so even though "[t]he telephone conversation itself must be electronically transmitted by telephone company equipment, and may be recorded or overheard by the use of other company equipment." *Smith,* 442 U.S. at 746 (Stewart, J., dissenting). On the other hand, in

Smith, the Court ruled that the use of [a] pen register, installed at the phone company's facility to record the numbers dialed by the telephone user, did not amount to a search. This distinction was due to the fact that "a pen register differs significantly from the listening device employed in *Katz,* for pen registers do not acquire the *contents* of communications." 442 U.S. at 741 (emphasis in original).

The distinction between *Katz* and *Miller* makes clear that the reasonable expectation of privacy inquiry in the context of shared communications must necessarily focus on two narrower questions than the general fact that the communication was shared with another. First, we must specifically identify the party with whom the communication is shared, as well as the parties from whom disclosure is shielded. Clearly, under *Katz,* the mere fact that a communication is shared with another person does not entirely erode all expectations of privacy, because otherwise eavesdropping would never amount to a search. It is true, however, that by sharing communications with someone else, the speaker or writer assumes the risk that it could be revealed to the government by that person, or obtained through a subpoena directed to that person. *See Miller,* 425 U.S. at 443 ("[T]he Fourth Amendment does not prohibit the obtaining of information revealed to a third party and conveyed by him to Government authorities."). The same does not necessarily apply, however, to an intermediary that merely has the ability to access the information sought by the government. Otherwise phone conversations would never be protected, merely because the telephone company can access them; letters would never be protected, by virtue of the Postal Service's ability to access them; the contents of shared safe deposit boxes or storage lockers would never be protected, by virtue of the bank or storage company's ability to access them.

The second necessary inquiry pertains to the precise information actually conveyed to the party through whom disclosure is sought or obtained. This distinction provides the obvious crux for the different results in *Katz* and *Smith,* because although the conduct of the telephone user in *Smith* "may have been calculated to keep the *contents* of his conversation private, his conduct was not and could not have been calculated to preserve the privacy of the number he dialed." 442 U.S. at 743. Like the depositor in *Miller,* the caller in *Smith* "assumed the risk" of the phone company disclosing the records that he conveyed to it. *Id.* Yet this assumption of the risk is limited to the specific information conveyed to the service provider, which in the telephone context excludes the content of the conversation. It is apparent, therefore, that although the government can compel disclosure of a shared communication from the party with whom it was shared, it can only compel disclosure of the specific information to which the subject of its compulsion has been granted access. It cannot, on the other hand, bootstrap an intermediary's limited access to one part of the communication (e.g., the phone number) to allow it access to another part (the content of the conversation).

This focus on the specific information shared with the subject of compelled disclosure applies with equal force in the e-mail context. Compelled disclosure of subscriber information and related records through the ISP might not undermine the e-mail subscriber's Fourth Amendment interest under *Smith,* because like the information obtained through the pen register in *Smith* and like the bank records in *Miller,* subscriber information and related records are records of the service provider as well, and may likely be accessed by ISP employees in the normal course of their employment. Consequently, the user does not maintain the same expectation of privacy in them vis-a-vis the service provider, and a third party subpoena to the service provider to access information that is shared with it likely creates no Fourth Amendment problems. The combined precedents of *Katz* and *Smith,* however, recognize a heightened protection for the **content** of the communications. Like telephone conversations, simply because the phone company or the ISP **could** access the content of e-mails and phone calls, the privacy expectation in the content of either is not diminished, because there is a societal expectation that the ISP or the phone company will not do so as a matter of course.

Similarly, under both *Miller* and *Katz,* if the government in this case had received the content of Warshak's e-mails by subpoenaing the person with whom Warshak was e-mailing, a Fourth Amendment challenge brought by Warshak would fail, because he would not have maintained a reasonable expectation of privacy vis-a-vis his e-mailing partners. *See Phibbs,* 999 F.2d at 1077. But this rationale is inapplicable where the party subpoenaed is not expected to access the content of the documents, much like the phone company in *Katz*. Thus, as Warshak argues, the government could not get around the privacy interest attached to a private letter by simply subpoenaing the postal service with no showing of probable cause, because unlike in *Phibbs,* postal workers would not be expected to read the letter in the normal course of business. *See* Ex Parte Jackson, 96 U.S. 727, 733 (1878) ("No law of Congress can place in the hands of officials connected with the postal service any authority to invade the secrecy of letters and such sealed packages in the mail; and all regulations adopted as to mail matter of this kind must be in subordination to the great principle embodied in the fourth amendment of the Constitution."). Similarly, a bank customer maintains an expectation of privacy in a safe deposit box to which the bank lacks access (as opposed to bank records, like checks or account statements), and the government could not compel disclosure of the contents of the safe deposit box only by subpoenaing the bank.

This analysis is consistent with other decisions that have addressed an individual's expectation of privacy in particular electronic communications. In Guest v. Leis, 255 F.3d 325, 333 (6th Cir. 2001), we concluded that users of electronic bulletin boards lacked an expectation of privacy in material posted on the bulletin board, as such materials were "intended for publication or public posting." Of course the public disclosure of material to an untold number of readers distinguishes bulletin board postings from e-mails, which typically have a limited, select number of recipients. *See also Jackson,* 96 U.S. at 733 ("[A] distinction is to be made between different kinds of mail matter, – between what is intended to be kept free from inspection, such as letters, and sealed packages subject to letter postage; and what is open to inspection, such as newspapers, magazines, pamphlets, and other printed matter, purposely left in a condition to be examined."). Although we stated that an e-mail sender would "lose a legitimate expectation of privacy in an e-mail that had already reached its recipient," analogizing such an e-mailer to "a letter-writer," this diminished privacy is only relevant with respect to the recipient, as the sender has assumed the risk of disclosure by or through the recipient. *Id.* at 333 (citing United States v. King, 55 F.3d 1193, 1196 (6th Cir. 1995)). *Guest* did not hold that the mere use of an intermediary such as an ISP to send and receive e-mails amounted to a waiver of a legitimate expectation of privacy.

Other courts have addressed analogous situations where electronic communications were obtained based on the sender's use of a computer network. In *United States v. Simons,* the Fourth Circuit held that a government employee lacked a reasonable expectation of privacy in electronic files on his office computer, in light of the employer's policy that explicitly notified the employee of its intention to "audit, inspect, and monitor" his computer files. 206 F.3d 392, 398 (4th Cir. 2000). In light of this explicit policy, the employee's belief that his files were private was not objectively reasonable. *Id.* On the other hand, in *United States v. Heckenkamp*, the Ninth Circuit held that a university student did have a reasonable expectation of privacy in his computer files even though he "attached [his computer] to the university network," because the "university policies do not eliminate Heckenkamp's expectation of privacy in his computer." 482 F.3d 1142, 1147 (9th Cir. 2007). Although the university did "establish limited instances in which university administrators may access his computer in order to protect the university's systems," this exception fell far short of a blanket monitoring or auditing policy, and the Ninth Circuit deemed it insufficient to waive the user's expectation of privacy.

Heckenkamp and *Simons* provide useful bookends for the question before us, regarding when the use of some intermediary provider of computer and e-mail services – be it a commercial ISP, a university, an employer, or another type of entity – amounts to a waiver of the user's reasonable expectation of privacy in the content of the e-mails with respect to that intermediary. In instances where a user agreement explicitly provides that e-mails and other files will be monitored or audited, as in *Simons,* the user's knowledge of this fact may well extinguish his reasonable expectation of privacy. Without such a statement, however, the service provider's control over the files and ability to access them under certain limited circumstances will not be enough to overcome an expectation of privacy, as in *Heckenkamp.*

Turning to the instant case, we have little difficulty agreeing with the district court that individuals maintain a reasonable expectation of privacy in e-mails that are stored with, or sent or received through, a commercial ISP. The content of e-mail is something that the user "seeks to preserve as private," and therefore "may be constitutionally protected." *Katz,* 389 U.S. at 351. It goes without saying that like the telephone earlier in our history, e-mail is an ever-increasing mode of private communication, and protecting shared communications through this medium is as important to Fourth Amendment principles today as protecting telephone conversations has been in the past. *See Katz,* 389 U.S. at 352 ("To read the Constitution more narrowly is to ignore the vital role that the public telephone has come to play in private communication.").

The government asserts that ISPs have the contractual right to access users' e-mails. The district court's ruling was based on its willingness to credit Warshak's contrary factual argument that "employees of commercial ISPs [do not] open and read – [nor do] their subscribers reasonably expect them to open and read – individual subscriber e-mails as a matter of course." This factual determination tracks the language from *Miller* and *Phibbs* that suggests a privacy interest in records held by a third party is only undermined where the documents are accessed by the third party or its employees "in the ordinary course of business." *Miller,* 425 U.S. at 442. Moreover, as explained in the Ninth Circuit's decision in *Heckenkamp,* mere accessibility is not enough to waive an expectation of privacy. *See Heckenkamp,* 482 F.3d at 1147 (holding that university policies establishing "limited instances in which university administrators may access [the user's] computer in order to protect the university's systems" was insufficient to eliminate an expectation of privacy); *see also Katz,* 389 U.S. at 351 ("[W]hat [a pay phone user] seeks to preserve as private, **even in an area accessible to the public,** may be constitutionally protected." (emphasis added)). Where a user agreement calls for regular auditing, inspection, or monitoring of e-mails, the expectation may well be different, as the potential for an administrator to read the content of e-mails in the account should be apparent to the user. *See Simons,* 206 F.3d at 398. Where there is such an arrangement, compelled disclosure by means of an SCA order at the ISP would be akin to the third party subpoena directed at a bank, as in *Miller* and *Jerry T. O'Brien.* In contrast, the terms of service in question here, which the government has cited to in both the district court and this Court, clearly provide for access only in limited circumstances, rather than wholesale inspection, auditing, or monitoring of e-mails.[7] Because the ISP's right to access e-mails under these user agreements is reserved for extraordinary circumstances, much like the university policy in *Heckenkamp,* it is similarly insufficient to undermine a user's expectation of privacy. For now, the government has made no showing that e-mail content is regularly accessed by ISPs, or that users are aware of such access of content.

The government also insists that ISPs regularly screen users' e-mails for viruses, spam, and child pornography. Even assuming that this is true, however, such a process does not waive an expectation of privacy in the content of e-mails sent through the ISP, for the same reasons that the terms of service are insufficient to waive privacy expectations. The government states that ISPs "are developing technology that will enable them to scan user images" for child pornography and viruses. The

---

7. *See* Gov't Br. at 34 (citing Yahoo terms of service which allow access where "reasonably necessary to: (a) comply with legal process; (b) enforce the [Terms of Service]; (c) respond to claims that any Content violates the rights of third parties; (d) respond to your requests for customer service; or (e) protect the rights, property or personal safety of Yahoo!, its users and the public."). As amicus Electronic Frontier Foundation points out, each instance involves outside prompting for an ISP to review content, and does not occur in the normal course of business. This type of accessibility by the service provider was rejected as diminishing the expectation of privacy in *Katz,* as well as in *Heckenkamp.*

government's statement that this process involves "technology," rather than manual, human review, suggests that it involves a computer searching for particular terms, types of images, or similar indicia of wrongdoing that would not disclose the content of the e-mail to any person at the ISP or elsewhere, aside from the recipient. But the reasonable expectation of privacy of an e-mail user goes to the **content** of the e-mail message. The fact that a computer scans millions of e-mails for signs of pornography or a virus does not invade an individual's content-based privacy interest in the e-mails and has little bearing on his expectation of privacy in the content. In fact, these screening processes are analogous to the post office screening packages for evidence of drugs or explosives, which does not expose the content of written documents enclosed in the packages. The fact that such screening occurs as a general matter does not diminish the well-established reasonable expectation of privacy that users of the mail maintain in the packages they send.

It is also worth noting that other portions of the SCA itself strongly support an e-mail user's reasonable expectation of privacy in the content of his e-mails. Section 2701 prohibits unauthorized users from accessing e-mails. Section 2702 generally prohibits an ISP from disclosing e-mail content without the permission of the user. Further, section 2703 makes it easier for the government to get an order requiring the disclosure of records and subscriber information, in which the user does not maintain a privacy interest vis-a-vis the ISP, than to obtain an order requiring the disclosure of content. The statute also requires a warrant to search the content of e-mails that have been stored for 180 days or less. 18 U.S.C. [2]703(a). Thus, even though the contested exception in section 2703(b) creates tension with the Fourth Amendment's requirements for a warrant, independent provisions support the proposition that a user maintains a reasonable expectation of privacy in the content of his e-mails.

The government's compelled disclosure argument is initially on point, but fails to address adequately the caveat relating to a party's maintenance of a reasonable expectation of privacy in documents in the custody of a third party. A warrant based on probable cause would not have been necessary had the government subpoenaed Warshak or given him prior notice of its intent to seek an SCA order, because the need for this higher showing would be offset by his ability to obtain judicial review before producing any e-mails. *See Phibbs,* 999 F.2d at 1077 ("The subpoena has to be 'sufficiently limited in scope, relevant in purpose, and specific in directive so that compliance [would] not be unreasonable.' If it is a subpoena duces tecum, the government does not have to secure a judicial warrant before service is effectuated. Nonetheless, 'the subpoenaed party [must be able to] obtain judicial review of the reasonableness of the demand prior to suffering penalties for refusing to comply.'") (citing See v. City of Seattle, 387 U.S. 541, 544 (1967)). The same rationale would apply if the government subpoenaed a third party that had access to the content of the e-mails, and against whom Warshak had no claim of privacy, such as the recipient of one of his e-mails. By the same token, an SCA order that provided notice to the ISP alone, and not to the user, would be appropriate in the limited instances where the user had waived his expectation of privacy with respect to the ISP, such as where the government can show that auditing, monitoring, or inspection are expressly provided for in the terms of service, or where the user has e-mailed content directly to the ISP. Where the third party is not expected to access the e-mails in the normal course of business, however, the party maintains a reasonable expectation of privacy, and subpoenaing the entity with mere custody over the documents is insufficient to trump the Fourth Amendment warrant requirement.

The district court enjoined the United States "from seizing, pursuant to court order under 18 U.S.C. §2703(d), the contents of any personal e-mail account maintained by an Internet Service Provider in the name of any resident of the Southern District of Ohio without providing the relevant account holder or subscriber prior notice and an opportunity to be heard. . . ." Our discussion above necessitates one modification to this injunction, which counsel for Warshak agreed at oral argument would be appropriate. If the government can show, based on specific facts, that an e-mail account holder has waived his expectation of privacy vis-a-vis the ISP, compelled disclosure of e-mails through notice to the ISP alone would be appropriate. This is a narrow modification, however, as a right to access e-mails in an account only in certain limited circumstances would not be sufficient. Rather, the government must show that the ISP or other intermediary clearly established and utilized the right to inspect, monitor, or audit the content of e-mails, or otherwise had content revealed to it. In such cases the SCA order will operate as the functional equivalent of a third party subpoena, allowing disclosure through a party that has total access to the documents in question. On remand, therefore, the preliminary injunction shall allow seizures of e-mail in three situations: (1) if the government obtains a search warrant under the Fourth Amendment, based on probable cause and in with the particularity requirement; (2) if the government provides notice to the account holder in seeking an SCA order, according him the same judicial review he would be allowed were he to be subpoenaed; or (3) if the government can show specific, articulable facts, demonstrating that an ISP or other entity has complete access to the e-mails in question and that it actually relies on and utilizes this access in the normal course of business, sufficient to establish that the user has waived his expectation of privacy with respect to that entity, in which case compelled disclosure may occur if that entity is afforded notice and an opportunity to be heard. . . .

IV.

The district court correctly determined that e-mail users maintain a reasonable expectation of privacy in the content of their e-mails, and we agree that the injunctive relief it crafted was largely appropriate, although we find necessary one modification. On remand, the preliminary injunction should be modified to prohibit the United States from seizing the contents of a personal e-mail account maintained by an ISP in the name of any resident of the Southern District of Ohio, pursuant to a court order issued under 18 U.S.C. §2703(d), without either (1) providing the relevant account holder or subscriber prior notice and an opportunity to be heard, or (2) making a fact-specific showing that the account holder maintained no expectation of privacy with respect to the ISP, in which case only the ISP need be provided prior notice and an opportunity to be heard.

2. Techniques and Authorities for Collection of Transactional Data

Page 581. Insert the following case after Note 7.

Doe v. Gonzales (*Doe IV*)

United States District Court, Southern District of New York, 2007
500 F. Supp. 2d 379

[After the first decision in this case, *Doe I*, reported at casebook pp. 562, Congress passed the USA Patriot Improvement and Reauthorization Act of 2005, Pub. L. No. 109-177, 120 Stat. 192 (2006). The Act is summarized at casebook pp. 579-580, Notes 3-5. The Court of Appeals then remanded the case for reconsideration in light of the new act. *See* casebook p. 575. This decision followed.]

MARRERO, District Judge. . . .

II. *BACKGROUND*

C. *THE REVISED NONDISCLOSURE PROVISION*

As indicated above, while the Government's appeals were pending before the Second Circuit, Congress enacted the Reauthorization Act. The Government contends that the revised §2709(c) and the newly enacted §3511 directly address[] the concerns raised by this Court in its *Doe I* decision and rectif[y] any constitutional deficiencies. Instead of a categorical, blanket prohibition on disclosure with respect to the issuance of any NSL, §2709(c) now calls for a case-by-case determination of the need for a nondisclosure order to accompany an NSL. Specifically, the statute provides that a recipient of an NSL is barred from disclosing that the FBI "has sought or obtained access to information or records" under the NSL statute if the Director of the FBI, or his designee, "certifies" that disclosure "may result" in "a danger to the national security of the United States, interference with a criminal, counterterrorism, or counterintelligence investigation, interference with diplomatic relations, or danger to the life or physical safety of any person" (here collectively referred to as the "Enumerated Harms"). 18 U.S.C. §2709(c)(1).

The newly enacted §3511 provides an opportunity for judicial review of NSLs. Section 3511(a) explicitly allows the recipient of an NSL to petition a United States district court "for an order modifying or setting aside the request," which the court "may" grant "if compliance would be unreasonable, oppressive, or otherwise unlawful." 18 U.S.C. §3511(a). Additionally, under §3511(b), an NSL recipient may seek an order modifying or setting aside a nondisclosure requirement.

If a petition to modify or set aside the nondisclosure requirement is filed within one year of the NSL request, the reviewing court may grant such relief only if it finds that "there is no reason to believe" disclosure "may result" in one or more of the Enumerated Harms. 18 U.S.C. §3511(b)(2). Moreover, if one of several authorized senior FBI officials "certifies that disclosure may endanger the national security of the United States or interfere with diplomatic relations, such certification shall be treated as conclusive unless the court finds that the certification was made in bad faith." *Id.*

If the petition to modify or set aside the nondisclosure requirement is filed one year or more after the NSL request was issued, the FBI must either terminate the nondisclosure requirement or re-certify that disclosure may result in one of the Enumerated Harms, in which case the court could grant the petition only in accordance with the standards described above. *See* 18 U.S.C. §3511(b)(3). Additionally, if the court denies the petition, the NSL recipient is precluded from filing another petition for one year.

As §3511 now explicitly permits challenges to NSLs, Plaintiffs do not renew their Fourth Amendment challenge. However, Plaintiffs contend that the amendments do not cure the statute's First Amendment deficiencies, and that it remains an unconstitutional prior restraint and a content-based restriction on speech because it (1) fails to provide constitutionally mandated procedural safeguards, (2) invests the FBI with unbridled discretion to suppress speech, (3) forecloses reviewing courts from applying a constitutionally mandated standard of review, and (4) authorizes the issuance of nondisclosure orders that are not narrowly tailored.

As the Second Circuit vacated this Court's prior decision in light of the Reauthorization Act, the Court must now consider whether the nondisclosure provision, with the judicial review now contemplated, still runs afoul of the First Amendment. For the reasons set forth below, the Court finds that it does.

D. *THE FBI'S USE OF NSLs* . . .

As part of the Reauthorization Act, Congress directed the Department of Justice, Office of the Inspector General ("OIG"), to review the "effectiveness and use, including any improper or illegal use, o[f] national security letters issued by the Department of Justice." *See* Pub. L. No. 109-177, §119. In March, 2007, the OIG issued its first public report pursuant to this statute, entitled "A Review of the Federal Bureau of Investigation's Use of National Security Letters" (the "OIG Report"). The OIG Report addresses the FBI's use of NSLs for calendar years 2003 through 2005.

The OIG Report confirms that the Patriot Act transformed NSLs into a much more frequently employed investigatory tool. Specifically, it states that "the FBI issued approximately 8,500 NSL requests in CY 2000, the year prior to passage of the Patriot Act. After the Patriot Act, according to FBI data, the number of NSL requests increased to approximately 39,000 in 2003, approximately 56,000 in 2004, and approximately 47,000 in 2005." While the number of NSL requests issued under each separate NSL provision is not publicly available, the report does indicate that "the overwhelming majority of the NSL requests sought telephone toll billing records information, subscriber information (telephone or e-mail), or electronic communication transactional records" under §2709. In considering these statistics, it is important to distinguish between "NSLs" and "NSL requests" – a single NSL may contain multiple requests for information. The OIG Report specifies that "the 39,000 NSL requests in 2003 were contained in approximately 12,000 letters, and the 47,000 requests in 2005 were contained in approximately 19,000 letters.

According to the OIG Report, there are three main reasons for the dramatic increase in the number of NSL requests issued starting in 2003. First, the Patriot Act eliminated the requirement that an NSL be issued only if "there are specific and articulable facts giving reason to believe that the person or entity to whom the information sought pertains is a foreign power or an agent of a foreign power." 18 U.S.C. §2709(b) (2000). Instead, the information must currently satisfy only the lower standard of being "relevant to an authorized investigation to protect against international terrorism or clandestine intelligence activities." 18 U.S.C. §2709(b). Second, whereas previously an NSL had to be approved by a senior FBI official at FBI headquarters, NSLs can now be authorized by Special Agents in Charge at FBI field offices. As a result, approval is no longer a lengthy process, and generally takes only two to five days. Third, in 2003, the Attorney General issued revised guidelines governing the use of NSLs in FBI national security investigations (the "NSI Guidelines"). The revised NSI Guidelines permit NSLs to be issued during preliminary investigations; under the prior NSI Guidelines, they could be issued only during full investigations. The OIG Report concludes that "[t]aken together, these three expansions of the FBI's [NSL] authorities resulted in significantly greater use" of NSLs.

FBI officials describe NSLs as "indispensable investigative tools that serve as building blocks in many counterterrorism and counterintelligence investigations." In particular, the most important use of §2709 NSLs, as described by FBI officials, is "to support FISA applications for electronic surveillance, physical searches, or pen register/trap and trace orders." NSLs are also important in that they assist the FBI in collecting information sufficient to eliminate concerns about investigative subjects and close national security investigations with a greater degree of confidence. Moreover, often the target of an NSL is not necessarily the main target of an investigation, and an NSL thus serves as a key tool in allowing the FBI to follow leads. As the OIG Report notes, "[f]or example, if the response to an NSL for toll billing records on the subject's telephone number identifies a telephone number that the subject contacted frequently during a time period relevant to the investigation, the FBI may issue another NSL requesting subscriber information for that telephone number.

While the OIG Report provides helpful background on how NSLs are actually used by the FBI, Plaintiffs emphasize that the report also details significant misuse of NSLs by the FBI, which Plaintiffs claim supports their argument that the statute, in its current form, is too susceptible to abuse to survive First Amendment scrutiny. Specifically, the OIG Report found that in addition to significantly under-reporting the number of NSL requests issued, the FBI: (1) under-reported violations arising from the use of NSLs; (2) sought information not permitted by the statute; (3) issued NSLs without proper authorization; (4) issued over 700 "exigent letters" requesting the type of information covered by §2709 without following the process for obtaining an NSL; and (5) repeatedly failed to properly adhere to the FBI's own internal documentation requirements for the approval of an NSL. In summary, while noting the significant challenges and major structural changes the FBI was facing during the period covered and the lack of any misuse rising to the level of criminal misconduct, the OIG Report nonetheless concluded that "the FBI used NSLs in violation of applicable NSL statutes, Attorney General Guidelines, and internal FBI policies." . . .

III. *DISCUSSION*

. . . In light of the seriousness of the potential intrusion into the individual's personal affairs and the significant possibility of a chilling effect on speech and association – particularly of expression that is critical of the government or its policies – a compelling need exists to ensure that the use of NSLs is subject to the safeguards of public accountability, checks and balances, and separation of powers that our Constitution prescribes.

Accordingly, the issue now before the Court is not whether, or under what circumstances, the government should possess the authority to issue NSLs. Rather, the more fundamental question is the extent of the authority that the First Amendment allows the government to exercise in keeping its use of NSLs secret, insofar as such secrecy inhibits freedom of speech.

The Court's review of First Amendment jurisprudence yields two primary conclusions. First, the government's use of nondisclosure orders must be narrowly-tailored on a case-by-case basis. That is, a nondisclosure order may not be broader in either scope or duration than the degree of secrecy required to serve the government's interest in protecting national security. Second, the nondisclosure orders must be subject to meaningful judicial review. To conform to prevailing constitutional norms as read by this Court, taking into account the unique latitude and added flexibility national security needs demand under ordinary circumstances, as well as the practicalities of surveillance work before a target is adequately identified, in issuing an NSL the government must either affirmatively terminate the nondisclosure requirement or bear the burden of justifying to a court why continued secrecy is necessary within a reasonable period of time after the FBI issues an NSL containing a nondisclosure order.

Additionally, and in many ways most troubling, this Court finds that the standard of review the Reauthorization Act directs that the courts must apply when a nondisclosure order is challenged, offends the fundamental constitutional principles of checks and balances and separation of powers. Independent of the First Amendment deficiencies identified by the Court, the deferential standard of review imposed on reviewing courts by §3511(b) fails not only because it creates too great a danger that constitutionally protected speech will be suppressed, but more fundamentally because it reflects an attempt by Congress and the executive to infringe upon the judiciary's designated role under the Constitution. To conform with §3511(b) as drafted, a court reviewing a nondisclosure order must apply not the standard of review the judge determines is mandated by constitutional law, but an overly deferential standard imposed by Congress. It is axiomatic that in our system of government it is the province of the courts to say what the law is. When Congress attempts to curtail or supersede this role, it jeopardizes the delicate balance of powers among the three branches of government and endangers the very foundations of our constitutional system. Thus, for this reason as well, §3511(b) fails. . . .

D. *PROCEDURAL SAFEGUARDS*

Plaintiffs contend that the NSL nondisclosure provision, §2709(c), constitutes a "paradigmatic licensing scheme," in that "the FBI is invested with the discretion to determine, on a case-by-case basis, whether a gag order should be issued with respect to any given NSL." Plaintiffs argue that §2709(c) is therefore unconstitutional because it fails to provide the requisite procedural safeguards set forth by the Supreme Court in *Freedman* [v. Maryland, 380 U.S. 51 (1965)].

[The court first held that the government must bear "the burden of going to court to suppress the speech and . . . the burden of proof once in court." Although the government can obtain a temporary nondisclosure order before getting court approval, it must within a reasonable time either lift the order or "justify to a court the need for a continued period of nondisclosure."] . . .

E. *DISCRETION*

Plaintiffs argue that §2709(c) violates the First Amendment because the standard governing the issuance of nondisclosure orders provides the FBI with unbridled discretion to suppress speech. Plaintiffs assert that a scheme that invests executive officers with such broad discretion to suppress speech is unconstitutional even if it otherwise affords adequate procedural safeguards. . . .

Plaintiffs argue that a standard based on "a danger to national security," among other potential harms, is simply not susceptible to an objective test. They contend that the term "national security" is inherently vague, and they point out that it has been used in the past to "cloak many questionable executive practices." Additionally, Plaintiffs express concern that there is no objective criteri[on] to guide the FBI in determining what level of threat is sufficient to require nondisclosure of the NSL.

Indeed, the Supreme Court has indicated that "[t]he danger to political dissent is acute where the Government attempts to act under so vague a concept as the power to protect 'domestic security.' Given the difficulty in defining the domestic security interest, the danger of abuse in acting to protect that interest becomes apparent." United States v. United States District Court, 407 U.S. 297, 314 (1972); *see also New York Times* [v. United States, 403 U.S. 713 (1971),] at 719 ("The word 'security' is a broad, vague generality whose contours should not be invoked to abrogate the fundamental law embodied in the First Amendment.") (Black, J. and Douglas, J., concurring).

The invitation to abuse of discretion, Plaintiffs contend, is compounded by the breadth of discretion conferred on the FBI; the FBI, without any prior independent review, merely needs to certify that disclosure "may" result in any one of the Enumerated Harms. *Cf. New York Times,* 403 U.S. at 725-26 ("The entire thrust of the Government's claim throughout these cases has been that publication of the material sought to be enjoined 'could,' or 'might,' or 'may' prejudice the national interest in various ways. But the First Amendment tolerates absolutely no prior judicial restraints of the press predicated upon surmise or conjecture that untoward consequences may result.") (Brennan, J., concurring).

Plaintiffs' arguments are not without merit. Without doubt, §2709(c) confers broad discretion to the FBI to accompany NSLs with nondisclosure orders – it may do so upon certification that disclosure of the NSL "may" result in any of the several Enumerated Harms. In particular, the Court agrees that a standard relating to endangering "national security" is susceptible to very broad interpretation. However, the Court is not persuaded that the FBI's discretion under §2709(c) is so unrestrained as to rise to the level of a constitutional infirmity. While the Court recognizes that the standard is broadly phrased, it is also mindful of the limitations of language to capture the fine lines distinguishing the permissible from the proscribed, and the legitimate exercise of government discretion from the infringement on protected rights. As the Second Circuit has observed, "'[p]erfect clarity and precise guidance have never been required even of regulations that restrict expressive activity,' and 'flexible' standards granting 'considerable discretion' to public officials can pass constitutional muster." Field Day, LLC v. County of Suffolk, 463 F.3d 167, 179 (2d Cir. 2006) (*quoting* Ward v. Rock Against Racism, 491 U.S. [781 (1989),] at 794).

That the rubric of "national security" has been abused on occasion does not imply that the Court should presume the language of "national security" in §2709(c) necessarily affords unfettered discretion to the FBI likely to result in abuse. Despite past abuses, it remains "well-settled doctrine that courts grant substantial deference to the political branches in national security matters." *Doe I,* 334 F. Supp. 2d 523; *see also* Zadvydas v. Davis, 533 U.S. 678, 696 (2001) (courts may afford "heightened deference to the judgments of the political branches with respect to matters of national security").

The context of counterterrorism investigations requires that the FBI have a degree of discretion in using NSLs to gather information about the targets of investigations and others who may be involved peripherally. Deference by courts to executive determinations of threats to "national security" exists in part because evaluating such threats is not a precise science, and some flexibility is necessary in making such determinations in the first instance. Thus, the Court is convinced that requiring further tailoring of the discretionary standard of §2709(c) would be unlikely to offer significant benefits to First Amendment concerns and could lead to "regulations that are so tightly worded that the flexibility needed for administration is lacking." [MacDonald v. Safir, 206 F.3d 183 (2d Cir. 2000),] at 191.

As the Court stated in *Doe I,* "[t]he high stakes here pressing the scales . . . compel the Court to strike the most sensitive judicial balance, calibrating by delicate increments toward a result that adequately protects national security without unduly sacrificing individual freedoms." 334 F. Supp. 2d at 478. In striking this balance, the Court finds that the FBI's discretion in certifying a need for nondisclosure of an NSL is broad but not inappropriately so under the circumstances. As detailed elsewhere in this opinion, the best protection against abuse of the FBI's discretion in certifying nondisclosure is to ensure that such discretion is checked by meaningful and reasonably expeditious judicial review.

F. *PRESCRIBING THE STANDARD OF JUDICIAL REVIEW*

As the Court has already made clear, judicial review of the Reauthorization Act's nondisclosure requirement is subject to strict scrutiny. Section 3511(b) allows a reviewing court to modify or set aside the nondisclosure requirement of an NSL issued under §2709 only "if it finds that there is no reason to believe that disclosure" will lead to one of the Enumerated Harms. 18 U.S.C. §3511(b)(2). Moreover, if an authorized Justice Department or FBI official certifies that disclosure may "endanger the national security of the United States or interfere with diplomatic relations, such certification shall be treated as conclusive unless the court finds that the certification was made in bad faith." *Id.* The Court agrees with Plaintiffs that this standard is plainly at odds with First Amendment jurisprudence which requires that courts strictly construe content-based restrictions and prior restraints to ensure they are narrowly tailored to advance a compelling government interest. A court reviewing a statute implicating the First Amendment must review that statute in accordance with First Amendment doctrine. *See Blount* [v. Rizzi, 400 U.S. 410 (1971),] at 420 (provision which required a district court to "grant the relief sought by the Postmaster General upon a showing merely of 'probable cause'" did not "satisfy the demands of the First Amendment," which required more meaningful judicial review).

1. *Congress Cannot Legislate a Standard of Review at Odds with First Amendment Jurisprudence . . .*

b. *Application of the Principles [of] Separation of Powers*

Against this backdrop of history and constitutional premises, §3511(b) is invalid because it does not reflect full account of these controlling principles and the long-standing national experience from which their force derives. That provision amounts to a significant congressional incursion, one with profound implications, into exclusive jurisdictional ground the Constitution reserves for the judiciary's role in our government. Of greatest concern, the law encroaches onto what is perhaps the most consequential authority the courts possess: the sole power to judge how to take the proper measure of the validity of a statute as aligned against the precepts of the Constitution itself, and to that end decide what constitutional rule of law must apply to guide that crucial test. Thus, this aspect of the Reauthorization Act, however legitimate and compelling the national interests it otherwise embodies, fails a test of recognition, insofar as it breaches the proper constitutional limits drawn for our government by the concepts of separation and balance of power. In this respect, the statute overlooks a potential risk, weighty in its far-reaching implications. All could be lost of the judiciary's most vital function, and hence of the individual freedoms of Americans, if the courts were to cede fundamental decisional power to Congress, and were Congress in turn empowered to override the courts in laying down the law that governs constitutional review of legislation or of an action of the executive.

Moving from the general to the particulars, the Court finds that the standard of review prescribed in §3511(b) is sharply at odds with the standard of review the Supreme Court has explicitly held is required to assess the conformance of a statute with the strictures of the First Amendment. Congress cannot legislate a constitutional standard of review that contradicts or supercedes what the courts have determined to be the standard applicable under the First Amendment for that purpose. *See* Dickerson v. United States, 530 U.S. 428, 437 (2000) ("Congress may not legislatively supersede our decisions interpreting and applying the Constitution."); *Marbury* [v. Madison, 5 U.S. (1 Cranch) 137 (1803),] at 177 ("It is a proposition too plain to be contested, that the constitution controls any legislative act repugnant to it; or, that the legislature may [not] alter the constitution by an ordinary act.").

The Government argues that the standard set forth in §3511 is merely a codification of the deferential standard of review applied by courts to executive determinations to prohibit disclosure of information in the interest of national security. The Government points out that in *Doe I* this Court specifically acknowledged that deference. But even while acknowledging that the Government should be accorded a due measure of deference when it asserts that secrecy is necessary for national security, the Court in *Doe I* nonetheless applied strict scrutiny to the nondisclosure provision of §2709.

The Court begins with the observation that a distinguishing factor between the review standard codified in §3511(b) and cases of national security deference cited by the Government – and this Court in *Doe I* – generally involve the courts *voluntarily* crediting an invocation of national security and *voluntarily* deferring to the executive in a particular instance. Thus, in those cases, judicial deference and restraint was self-imposed, in the courts' own recognition of their lack of expertise in assessing highly sensitive matters under the particular circumstances of the case before them. Here, §3511(b) *mandates* when and how deference should be accorded. Congress has in effect prescribed to the judiciary the standard of review a court must apply in assessing the validity of a government restriction on First Amendment rights in every case and every circumstance arising under the statute, thereby transforming judicial deference into subservience to executive judgments.

It is well settled by many years of judicial interpretation of the First Amendment that a statute which constitutes a prior restraint on speech or a content-based restriction on speech must be strictly construed, meaning that it must be narrowly tailored to advance a compelling government interest. That is what the judiciary has said the constitutional law is on this vital principle. Congress, even as an accommodation to the executive branch on matters of national security, cannot say that that constitutional standard is something else. That is precisely what §3511 attempts to do insofar as it decrees the standard of review and level of deference the judiciary must accord to the executive in adjudicating a challenged restriction on protected speech. . . .

What these cases make clear is that when the judiciary has established a "constitutional rule," such as requiring that any prior restraint or content-based restriction on speech be narrowly tailored to support a compelling government interest, the courts must respect and apply such previously established rules in reviewing a challenge to a government curtailment of constitutionally protected expression, even if Congress and the executive branch urge otherwise.

c. *Prospective Concerns*

Having found that in adopting the Reauthorization Act's standard of review provision Congress impermissibly crossed over its jurisdictional bounds under the letter of the Constitution, the Court deems it appropriate at this point to identify the specific dangers to our form of government that it finds deeply problematic in respect of the statute under the spirit of the Constitution as well, and that potentially lurk in the shadows of the law if the encroachment were allowed to stand. For §3511 raises grave concerns not just for what it is, but for what it could become if not effectively checked. Under these circumstances, a court should present the clearest and most instructive articulation of the pertinent law, offering guidance not only as to what is wrong with the particular statute under judicial consideration in the light of constitutional imperatives but also of potential pitfalls, as viewed from all relevant perspectives. As drafted, §3511(b) could serve as a precedential step toward the development of a much larger and more fearsome vehicle for legislative or executive intrusion into the business of the courts. Conceivably, what might commence as an innocent legislative step over a blurry line in the dark, could later stretch into a means of farther and more detrimental invasion of the courts' prerogatives – the legislative equivalent of breaking and entering, with an ominous free pass to the hijacking of constitutional values.

The pernicious consequences which that prospect could trigger cannot be overstated, or lightly discounted. If Congress were able not only to enact the substance of legislation, but also to prescribe the precise corresponding rule telling the courts what level of scrutiny to apply in properly gauging the constitutionality of the statute's application in practice, the barriers against government abuse that the principles of separation and balance of powers were designed to erect could be severely compromised, and may eventually collapse, with consequential diminution of the judiciary's function, and hence potential dire effects to individual freedoms. In that event, the courts' exercise of judicial review could effectively be reduced to that of a mere mouthpiece of the legislature. And with the courts so enervated, Congress would possess what would amount to a self-regulated means, by way of a back door when it so elected, to decide that the Constitution means whatever Congress says it means. Any piece of legislation could then be equipped, as a standard feature, with its own brand of judicial review of Congress's choosing, which could be styled to make the validation of the law foolproof.

Once embarked on such a course, how far the legislative limits may be pushed before they go too far and the harms become intolerable is uncertain. More certain is that few of the possible outcomes are likely to end happily. What would deter the legislative branch, dispensing with niceties and formalities altogether, from eventually superseding the standards of review the courts have devised for application in deciding First Amendment disputes – the concept of strict scrutiny, for example, –

and formulating its own rules to govern such judicial oversight?

These concerns may be readily dismissed as protesting too much, as conjuring a remote, unduly alarmist parade of horrors. But those who are inclined, for the risk of the moment, to give chance a chance by wagering against the improbable, should consult history for its guidance as to what the roll of the dice may hold in predictable situations. The past is long, and so is the future we want to protect. But too often memory is short. The pages of this nation's jurisprudence cry out with compelling instances illustrating that, called upon to adjudicate claims of extraordinary assertions of executive or legislative or even state power, such as by the high degree of deference to the executive that the Government here contends §3511(b) demands of the courts, when the judiciary lowers its guard on the Constitution, it opens the door to far-reaching invasions of liberty. *See, e.g.,* Korematsu v. United States, 323 U.S. 214 (1944); Plessy v. Ferguson, 163 U.S. 537 (1896). These examples, however few in number, loom large in proportions of the tragic ill-effects felt in the wake of the courts' yielding fundamental ground to other branches of government on the constitutional role the judiciary must play in protecting the fundamental freedoms of the American people. Viewed from the standpoint of the many citizens who lost essential human rights as a result of such expansive exercises of governmental power unchecked by judicial rulings appropriate to the occasion, the only thing left of the judiciary's function for those Americans in that experience was a symbolic act: to sing a requiem and lower the flag on the Bill of Rights.

To cite the teaching of one case, in 1944 the Supreme Court, amidst public passions wartime aroused, and under the mantle of national security and military expediency, endorsed the president's exercise of unilateral authority to relocate all Americans of Japanese descent (but not those of other nations also at war with the United States) to internment camps for the duration of the hostilities. *See Korematsu,* 323 U.S. at 216-18. Later, that ruling was much regretted not only for what it represented as a retreat from the judiciary's constitutional function in safeguarding American liberties and democratic principles, but for the potentially deleterious precedent it set of the courts' bowing unjustifiably to extraordinary actions of the other branches of the government. *See* Korematsu v. United States, 584 F. Supp. 1406, 1420 (N.D. Cal. 1984) ("As historical precedent [*Korematsu*] stands as a constant caution that in times of war or declared military necessity our institutions must be vigilant in protecting constitutional guarantees. It stands as a caution that in times of distress the shield of military necessity and national security must not be used to protect governmental actions from close scrutiny and accountability.").

Indeed, just eight years after *Korematsu,* the president, invoking the same theory of inherent power, national defense, and military exigency that prevailed in *Korematsu,* sought to nationalize the nation's steel mills in order to avert a strike by steelworkers. *See* Youngstown Sheet & Tube Co. v. Sawyer, 343 U.S. 579, 582-83 (1952). But, by contrast, on that occasion the Supreme Court was not deferential to a comparably extraordinary claim of unbounded executive power that would have trampled upon the principle of separation of powers. While *Youngstown Sheet* concerned executive encroachment on Congress's authority under the Constitution, the separation of powers principle the Supreme Court reaffirmed applies with equal force in this context as well[:] "The Founders of this Nation entrusted [the power to say what the law is under the Constitution to the courts] alone in both good times and bad times. It would do no good to recall the historical events, the fears of power and the hopes for freedom that lay behind their choice." *Id.* at 589.

As *Doe I* noted, the Court recognized the "heavy weight" of September 11, 2001, "a murderous attack of international terrorism, unparalleled in its magnitude, and unprecedented in America's national security," that looms over this proceeding. *See* 334 F. Supp. 2d at 477-78. Its effect is still felt and acknowledged by this Court, which sits just a few blocks from where the World Trade Center towers fell. The Court is also mindful of the executive's need to meet new threats to national security with new and ever more effective means of detecting and stopping those perils. Indeed, since September 11, 2001 the executive has sought additional ways of securing the nation, which is its prerogative, including efforts at expanding its surveillance powers. However, new methods of protecting and combating threats that result in asserted expansions of executive power underscore the courts' concerns of the dangers in suffering any infringement on their essential role under the Constitution. The Constitution was designed so that the dangers of any given moment would never suffice as justification for discarding fundamental individual liberties or circumscribing the judiciary's unique role under our governmental system in protecting those liberties and upholding the rule of law. It is the judiciary's independent function to uphold the Constitution even if to do so may mean curtailing Congress's efforts to confer greater freedom on the executive to investigate national security threats.

2. *The Review Prescribed by §3511(b) Does Not Comport with First Amendment Jurisprudence*

The Government attempts to minimize or dismiss the separation of powers concern raised by §3511(b) by insisting that the provision is not at odds with strict scrutiny. The cases cited by the Government do not support its assertion that the standard of review mandated by §3511(b) is simply a codification of case law on the substantial deference courts afford the executive in matters of national security in which the information sought to be suppressed is of the government's own creation. . . .

While the Court acknowledges that it is entirely appropriate for the judiciary, in the proper exercise of judicial power, to defer to executive determinations that a specific disclosure of sensitive information may result in a specific harm to national security interests, that is not the end of the analysis, but merely the beginning. Because the First Amendment is implicated, a reviewing court must still satisfy itself that the harm asserted by the government justifies the curtailment of the specific individual liberties implicated. Although the Executive's tasks "include the protection of national security and the maintenance of the secrecy of sensitive information, the judiciary's tasks include the protection of individual rights." *Id.* at 1149. The standard of review required by §3511(b) impermissibly ties the judiciary's hands by requiring a reviewing court to effectively end its analysis as long [as] the court finds a reason – any reason – to believe disclosure "may" lead to one of the Enumerated Harms. . . .

In an analogous context, the Fourth Circuit noted, in rejecting the government's argument that national security interests preclude the application of strict scrutiny with respect to the First Amendment right of access to judicial documents, that it was "troubled by the notion that the judiciary should abdicate its decisionmaking responsibility to the executive branch whenever national security concerns are present. . . . A blind acceptance by the courts of the government's insistence on the need for secrecy . . . would impermissibly compromise the independence of the judiciary and open the door to possible abuse." In re Washington Post Co., 807 F.2d 383, 391-92 (4th Cir. 1986). This Court is similarly troubled by the suggestion that even though First Amendment rights are implicated, its ability to review a government restriction on speech is limited to situations where there is "no reason to believe" that disclosure may result in one of the Enumerated Harms. Such a review deprives the judiciary of its ability to properly balance the government's compelling national security interests against the First Amendment rights of persons affected by the nondisclosure requirement.

More problematic still, while the "no reason to believe" standard impermissibly constrains the Court's First Amendment review, the requirement that the Court credit the government's invocation of national security as *conclusive* absent evidence of bad faith eviscerates any meaningful judicial review, as it clearly equates to an uncritical acceptance of the government's insistence of the need for secrecy. In requiring the Court to accept the government's certification as conclusive, §3511(b) effectively allows the government to determine the constitutionality of its own actions, leaving only the difficult to prove and narrow issue of the existence of "bad faith" to the judiciary. As the Supreme Court has previously noted in the Fourth Amendment context, "those charged with . . . investigative and prosecutorial duty *should not be the sole judges of when to utilize constitutionally sensitive means in pursuing their tasks*. . . . [U]nreviewed executive discretion may yield too readily to pressures to obtain incriminating evidence and overlook potential invasions of privacy and protected speech." *United States District Court,* 407 U.S. at 317 (emphasis added). For the reasons discussed, a standard of review which eliminates any meaningful check on executive discretion to suppress protected speech offends both the First Amendment and the basic constitutional principle of separation of powers.

G. *NARROW TAILORING*

Section 2709(c) prohibits an NSL recipient from "disclos[ing] to any person . . . that the [FBI] has sought or obtained access to information or records under this section." This nondisclosure provision contains no time limit. Plaintiffs argue that §2709(c) violates the First Amendment by allowing the issuance of nondisclosure orders that are not narrowly tailored – either in scope or duration – to a compelling government interest.

The Court addressed this issue at length in *Doe I* with respect to the prior version of §2709(c). It stated that although nondisclosure may be justified under certain circumstances, the government must show "that secrecy is necessary for national security purposes in a *particular situation* involving *particular persons* at a *particular time*." The Court concluded that "the Government cannot cast §2709 – a blunt agent of secrecy applying in perpetuity to all persons affected in every case – as narrowly-tailored." *Id.* at 516.

The revised provision incorporates case-by-case analysis in the determination as to whether nondisclosure of a particular NSL is necessary under the circumstances, but it continues to authorize nondisclosure orders that *permanently* restrict an NSL recipient from engaging in *any* discussion related to its receipt of the NSL. . . .

The potentially broad effect of the nondisclosure order is demonstrated in the present case. Asserting a risk to national security, the Government has invoked the nondisclosure order to attempt to prevent Plaintiffs from publically disclosing through their court filings a wide range of information, such as statements disclosing the mere fact that the FBI issued an NSL to an unspecified internet service provider ("ISP"), the general type of information about its clients that the ISP in question maintains, the kinds of services the ISP provides to its clients, and, most troubling to the Court, statements critical of the way that the government uses NSLs and expressing concern that free expression and association might be chilled.

Additionally, it is worth noting that, in response to Plaintiffs' Motion to Set Aside Request for Records, the FBI has withdrawn its NSL request in this case. Essentially, the FBI has conceded that the information that it would obtain by way of the NSL at issue is no longer relevant to an international terrorism investigation, but it continues to assert that any disclosure otherwise related to the NSL would endanger national security.

With respect to duration, it is hard to conceive of any circumstances that would justify a permanent bar on disclosure. *See Doe v. Gonzales,* 449 F.3d at 422 ("A permanent ban on speech seems highly unlikely to survive the test of strict scrutiny, one where the government must show that the statute is narrowly tailored to meet a compelling government interest.") (*citing* Ashcroft v. ACLU, 542 U.S. at 665-66 and *Kamasinski* [v. Judicial Review Council, 44 F.3d 106 (2d Cir. 1994),] at 109) (Cardamone, J., concurring); *cf.* Capital Cities Media, Inc. v. Toole, 463 U.S. 1303, 1304-06 (1983). Once disclosure no longer poses a threat to national security, there is no basis for further restricting NSL recipients from communicating their knowledge of the government's activities. International terrorism investigations might generally last longer than run-of-the-mill domestic criminal investigations, but they do not last forever. And, even while an investigation continues, the disclosure regarding the issuance of a particular NSL might not necessarily endanger that investigation. . . .

In addition to the permanent duration of the nondisclosure order contained in the NSL, §3511(b)(3) provides: "If the court denies a petition for an order modifying or setting aside a nondisclosure requirement under this paragraph, the recipient shall be precluded for a period of one year from filing another petition to modify or set aside such nondisclosure requirement." Plaintiffs argue, correctly, that this aspect of the statue is not narrowly tailored because it may call for the period of nondisclosure to extend substantially beyond the time that national security necessitates. For example, the statute contains no requirement that the government act affirmatively and promptly to terminate the nondisclosure order when public knowledge of the NSL no longer poses a threat to national security, or indeed, as occurred in *Doe II,* when the information the government seeks to maintain secret is ascertained and disclosed by third parties through legitimate means. . . .

H. *SCOPE OF 18 U.S.C. §§3511(d) AND 3511(e)*

In amending the NSL statute, Congress added two provisions intended to guide reviewing courts with respect to decisions to close hearings, seal documents, or review evidence ex parte and in camera. Upon review, the Court finds each section constitutional, provided that the attendant language as interpreted by the Court preserves the traditional role of the court in carefully examining the extent to which closure, sealing, and limited evidentiary access by the defendant is necessary. . . .

IV. *CONCLUSION*

For the reasons stated above, the Court concludes that §2709(c) is unconstitutional under the First Amendment because it functions as a licensing scheme that does not afford adequate procedural safeguards, and because it is not a sufficiently narrowly tailored restriction on protected speech. Because the Court finds that §2709(c) cannot be severed from the remainder of the statute, the Court finds the entirety of §2709 unconstitutional. Additionally, the Court concludes that §3511(b) is unconstitutional under the First Amendment and the doctrine of separation of powers.

V. *STAY OF JUDGMENT*

As it did in *Doe I,* in light of the implications of its ruling and the importance of the issues involved, the Court will stay enforcement of its judgment pending appeal, or for the Government otherwise to pursue any alternate course of action, for 90 days. The stay is intended to give the

Government the opportunity to move this Court, or the Court of Appeals, for whatever appropriate relief it may seek to maintain the confidentiality of any information implicated by the Court's ruling. . . .

21

Screening for Security

A. CHECKPOINT SEARCHES

Page 590. Substitute the following case for the District Court decision in *MacWade v. Kelly*.

MacWade v. Kelly

United States Court of Appeals, Second Circuit, 2006
460 F.3d 260

[The New York City subway system, with 26 interconnected lines and 468 passenger stations operating 24 hours a day, is the most heavily used subway in the United States. Experts assert that transportation systems like it are attractive targets for terrorist bombings because they carry large numbers of people. An attack could produce huge casualties, as well as causing widespread economic consequences and public fear. Following the March 11, 2004, Madrid commuter train bombings that killed more than 200 persons, another 2004 train bombing in Moscow that killed 40, and the London subway bombings in July 2005, killing 52 persons, the New York City subway system adopted a random "container inspection program" to address the threat of an explosive device being taken into the subway in a carry-on container or backpack.]

STRAUB, Circuit Judge. We consider whether the government may employ random, suspicionless container searches in order to safeguard mass transportation facilities from terrorist attack. The precise issue before us is whether one such search regime, implemented on the New York City subway system, satisfies the special needs exception to the

Fourth Amendment's usual requirement of individualized suspicion. We hold that it does. . . .

BACKGROUND

I. *The Subway System and the Container Inspection Program*

. . . A "checkpoint" consists of a group of uniformed police officers standing at a folding table near the row of turnstiles disgorging onto the train platform. At the table, officers search the bags of a portion of subway riders entering the station.

In order to enhance the Program's deterrent effect, the NYPD selects the checkpoint locations "in a deliberative manner that may appear random, undefined, and unpredictable." In addition to switching checkpoint locations, the NYPD also varies their number, staffing, and scheduling so that the "deployment patterns . . . are constantly shifting." While striving to maintain the veneer of random deployment, the NYPD bases its decisions on a sophisticated host of criteria, such as fluctuations in passenger volume and threat level, overlapping coverage provided by its other counter-terrorism initiatives, and available manpower.

The officers assigned to each checkpoint give notice of the searches and make clear that they are voluntary. Close to their table they display a large poster notifying passengers that "backpacks and other containers [are] subject to inspection." The Metropolitan Transportation Authority, which operates the subway system, makes similar audio announcements in subway stations and on trains. A supervising sergeant at the checkpoint announces through a bullhorn that all persons wishing to enter the station are subject to a container search and those wishing to avoid the search must leave the station. Although declining the search is not by itself a basis for arrest, the police may arrest anyone who refuses to be searched and later attempts to reenter the subway system with the uninspected container.

Officers exercise virtually no discretion in determining whom to search. The supervising sergeant establishes a selection rate, such as every fifth or tenth person, based upon considerations such as the number of officers and the passenger volume at that particular checkpoint. The officers then search individuals in accordance with the established rate only.

Once the officers select a person to search, they limit their search as to scope, method, and duration. As to scope, officers search only those containers large enough to carry an explosive device, which means, for example, that they may not inspect wallets and small purses. Further, once they identify a container of eligible size, they must limit their inspection "to what is minimally necessary to ensure that the . . . item does not contain an explosive device," which they have been trained to recognize in various forms. They may not intentionally look for other contraband, although if officers incidentally discover such contraband, they may arrest the individual carrying it.[1] Officers may not attempt to read any written or printed material. Nor may they request or record a passenger's personal information, such as his name, address, or demographic data.

The preferred inspection method is to ask the passenger to open his bag and manipulate his possessions himself so that the officer may determine, on a purely visual basis, if the bag contains an explosive device. If necessary, the officer may open the container and manipulate its contents himself. Finally, because officers must conduct the inspection for no "longer than necessary to ensure that the individual is not carrying an explosive device," a typical inspection lasts for a matter of seconds. . . .

DISCUSSION . . .

II. *The Special Needs Doctrine*

. . . As the Fourth Amendment's text makes clear, the concept of reasonableness is the "touchstone of the constitutionality of a governmental search." Bd. of Educ. v. Earls, 536 U.S. 822, 828 (2002). "What is reasonable, of course, depends on all of the circumstances surrounding the search or seizure and the nature of the search or seizure itself." Skinner v. Railway Labor Exec. Ass'n, 489 U.S. 602 (1989) (internal quotation marks omitted). As a "general matter," a search is unreasonable unless supported "by a warrant issued upon probable cause. . . ." Nat'l Treasury Employees Union v. Von Raab, 489 U.S. 656, 665 (1989). However, "neither a warrant nor probable cause, nor, indeed, any measure of individualized suspicion, is an indispensable component of reasonableness in every circumstance." *Id.*

---

1. At oral argument counsel for defendants informed us that thus far there have been no arrests for general crimes stemming from the seizure of non-explosive contraband discovered during a search conducted pursuant to the Program.

In light of those "longstanding" principles, *id.,* we upheld a program employing metal detectors and hand searches of carry-on baggage at airports. *See* United States v. Edwards, 498 F.2d 496, 500-501 (2d Cir. 1974). We determined that the "purpose" of the search program was not to serve "as a general means for enforcing the criminal laws" but rather to "prevent airplane hijacking" by "terrorists[.]" *Id.* at 500. We then dispensed with the traditional warrant and probable cause requirements and instead balanced "the need for a search against the offensiveness of the intrusion." *Id.* We concluded that,

> When the risk is the jeopardy to hundreds of human lives and millions of dollars of property inherent in the pirating or blowing up of a large airplane, the danger alone meets the test of reasonableness, so long as the search is conducted in good faith for the purpose of preventing hijacking or like damage and with reasonable scope and the passenger has been given advance notice of his liability to such a search so that he can avoid it by choosing not to travel by air.

Id. Although at the time we lodged our decision within the broad rubric of reasonableness, *id.* at 498 n.5, our reasoning came to be known as the "special needs exception" roughly one decade later. *See* New Jersey v. T.L.O., 469 U.S. 325, 351 (1985) (Blackmun, J., concurring) ("Only in those exceptional circumstances in which special needs, beyond the need for normal law enforcement, make the warrant and probable-cause requirement impracticable, is a court entitled to substitute its balancing of interests for that of the Framers."). . . .

The doctrine's central aspects are as follows. First, as a threshold matter, the search must "serve as [its] immediate purpose an objective distinct from the ordinary evidence gathering associated with crime investigation." Nicholas v. Goord, 430 F.3d 652, 663 (2d Cir. 2005). Second, once the government satisfies that threshold requirement, the court determines whether the search is reasonable by balancing several competing considerations. These balancing factors include (1) the weight and immediacy of the government interest, *Earls,* 536 U.S. at 834; (2) "the nature of the privacy interest allegedly compromised by" the search, *id.* at 830; (3) "the character of the intrusion imposed" by the search, *id.* at 832; and (4) the efficacy of the search in advancing the government interest.

III. *The Program Is Constitutional* . . .

A. The special needs doctrine does not require that the subject of the search possess a diminished privacy interest

Plaintiffs first raise the purely legal contention that, as a threshold matter, the special needs doctrine applies only where the subject of the search possesses a reduced privacy interest. While it is true that in most special needs cases the relevant privacy interest is somewhat "limited," *see Earls,* 536 U.S. at 832 (considering the privacy interest of public schoolchildren), the Supreme Court never has implied – much less actually held – that a reduced privacy expectation is a *sine qua non* of special needs analysis. . . .

Accordingly, to the extent that the principle needs clarification, we expressly hold that the special needs doctrine does not require, as a threshold matter, that the subject of the search possess a reduced privacy interest. Instead, once the government establishes a special need, the nature of the privacy interest is a factor to be weighed in the balance.

B. The container inspection program serves a special need

Plaintiffs next maintain that the District Court erred in concluding that the Program serves the special need of preventing a terrorist attack on the subway. . . .

As a factual matter, we agree with the District Court's conclusion that the Program aims to prevent a terrorist attack on the subway. Defendants implemented the Program in response to a string of bombings on commuter trains and subway systems abroad, which indicates that its purpose is to prevent similar occurrences in New York City. In its particulars, the Program seeks out explosives only: officers are trained to recognize different explosives, they search only those containers capable of carrying explosive devices, and they may not intentionally search for other contraband, read written or printed material, or request personal information. Additionally, the Program's voluntary nature illuminates its purpose: that an individual may refuse the search *provided* he leaves the subway establishes that the Program seeks to prevent a terrorist, laden with concealed explosives, from boarding a subway train in the first place.

As a legal matter, courts traditionally have considered special the government's need to "prevent" and "discover . . . latent or hidden" hazards, *Von Raab,* 489 U.S. at 668, in order to ensure the safety of mass transportation mediums, such as trains, airplanes, and highways. We have no doubt that concealed explosives are a hidden hazard, that the Program's purpose is prophylactic, and that the nation's busiest subway system implicates the public's safety. Accordingly, preventing a terrorist from bombing the subways constitutes a special need that is distinct from ordinary post hoc criminal investigation. Further, the fact that an officer incidentally may discover a different kind of contraband and arrest its possessor does not alter the Program's intended purpose.

Relying on dicta in [City of Indianapolis v. Edmond, 531 U.S. 32 (2000),] in which the Supreme Court struck down a drug interdiction checkpoint, plaintiffs urge the extraordinarily broad legal principle that a terrorist checkpoint serves a special need only in the face of an imminent attack. The *Edmond* Court merely remarked that under such dire circumstances, "[f]or example," a checkpoint regime "would almost certainly" be constitutional. *Edmond,* 531 U.S. at 44. . . . Where, as here, a search program is designed and implemented to seek out concealed explosives in order to safeguard a means of mass transportation from terrorist attack, it serves a special need.

C. On balance, the Program is constitutional

Having concluded that the Program serves a special need, we next balance the factors set forth above to determine whether the search is reasonable and thus constitutional.

(i) The government interest is immediate and substantial

. . . In light of the thwarted plots to bomb New York City's subway system, its continued desirability as a target, and the recent bombings of public transportation systems in Madrid, Moscow, and London, the risk to public safety is substantial and real. . . .

(ii) A subway rider has a full expectation of privacy in his containers

. . . [A] person carrying items in a closed, opaque bag has manifested his subjective expectation of privacy by keeping his belongings from plain view and indicating "that, for whatever reason, [he] prefer[s] to keep [them] close at hand." [Bond v. United States, 529 U.S. 334, 338 (2000).] Further, the Supreme Court has recognized as objectively reasonable a bus rider's expectation that his bag will not be felt "in an exploratory manner" from the outside, *id.* at 338-39, let alone opened and its contents visually inspected or physically manipulated. Accordingly, a subway rider who keeps his bags on his person possesses an undiminished expectation of privacy therein. We therefore weigh this factor in favor of plaintiffs.

(iii) The search is minimally intrusive

Although a subway rider enjoys a full privacy expectation in the contents of his baggage, the kind of search at issue here minimally intrudes upon that interest. Several uncontested facts establish that the Program is narrowly tailored to achieve its purpose: (1) passengers receive notice of the searches and may decline to be searched so long as they leave the subway, (2) police search only those containers capable of concealing explosives, inspect eligible containers only to determine whether they contain explosives, inspect the containers visually unless it is necessary to manipulate their contents, and do not read printed or written material or request personal information, (3) a typical search lasts only a matter of seconds, (4) uniformed personnel conduct the searches out in the open, which reduces the fear and stigma that removal to a hidden area can cause, and (5) police exercise no discretion in selecting whom to search, but rather employ a formula that ensures they do not arbitrarily exercise their authority. Although defendants need not employ "the least intrusive means" to serve the state interest, it appears they have approximated that model. Given the narrow tailoring that the Program achieves, this factor weighs strongly in favor of defendants, as the District Court properly concluded.

(iv) The Program is reasonably effective

In considering the "degree to which the seizure advances the public interest," we must remember not to wrest "from politically accountable officials . . . the decision as to which among reasonable alternative law enforcement techniques should be employed to deal with a serious public danger." Michigan Dep't of State Police v. Sitz, 496 U.S. 444, 453-454 (1990) (internal quotation marks omitted). That decision is best left to those with "a unique understanding of, and responsibility for, limited public resources, including a finite number of police officers." *Id.* 22 at 454. Accordingly, we ought not conduct a "searching examination of effectiveness." *Id.* at 454 (internal quotation marks omitted). Instead, we need only determine whether the Program is "a reasonably effective means of addressing" the government interest in deterring and detecting a terrorist attack on the subway system. *Earls,* 536 U.S. at 837. . . .

. . . [T]he expert testimony established that terrorists seek predictable and vulnerable targets, and the Program generates uncertainty that frustrates that goal, which, in turn, deters an attack. . . .

Plaintiffs further claim that the Program is ineffective because police notify passengers of the searches, and passengers are free to walk away and attempt to reenter the subway at another point or time. Yet we always have viewed notice and the opportunity to decline as beneficial aspects of a suspicionless search regime because those features minimize intrusiveness. *Edwards,* 498 F.2d at 500 (upholding suspicionless airport searches as reasonable "so long as . . . the passenger has been given advance notice of his liability to such a search so that he can avoid it by choosing not to travel by air"). Striking a search program as ineffective on account of its narrow tailoring would create a most perverse result: those programs "more pervasive and more invasive of privacy" more likely would satisfy the Fourth Amendment. *Von Raab,* 489 U.S. at 676-677 n.4 (internal quotation marks omitted).

Importantly, if a would-be bomber declines a search, he must leave the subway or be arrested – an outcome that, for the purpose of preventing subway bombings, we consider reasonably effective, especially since the record establishes that terrorists prize predictability. An unexpected change of plans might well stymie the attack, disrupt the synchronicity of multiple bombings, or at least reduce casualties by forcing the terrorist to detonate in a less populated location. . . .

CONCLUSION

In sum, we hold that the Program is reasonable, and therefore constitutional, because (1) preventing a terrorist attack on the subway is a special need; (2) that need is weighty; (3) the Program is a reasonably effective deterrent; and (4) even though the searches intrude on a full privacy interest, they do so to a minimal degree. We thus Affirm the judgment of the District Court.

C. PROFILING

Page 613. Add the following case after Note 9.

Tabbaa v. Chertoff

United States Court of Appeals, Second Circuit, 2007
509 F.3d 89

STRAUB, Circuit Judge: . . .

BACKGROUND . . .

In December 2004, CBP [the U.S. Bureau of Customs and Border Protection] received intelligence information that raised "specific concerns about certain national and international conferences," including the Reviving the Islamic Spirit Conference ("RIS Conference") that was being held from December 24 through December 26, 2004 at the Skydome in Toronto, Canada. Specifically, CBP had "reason to believe that certain individuals who were associated with terrorist organizations or activities and might pose a danger to the United States, or who were associated with organizations that provide financial support to terrorists, *would be* in attendance at the 2004 RIS conference." CBP also had reason to believe that the 2004 RIS Conference "*would serve* as a possible meeting point for terrorists" to "coordinate operations, and raise funds intended for terrorist activities," as well as "exchange ideas and documents," including "travel or identification documents such as passports or driver's licenses."[2]

Based on this intelligence, in late December 2004, CBP prepared an Intelligence Driven Special Operation ("IDSO"), which directed CBP officials at various ports of entry, including the one in Buffalo, where plaintiffs entered the United States, to undertake special enforcement

---

2. . . . [W]e viewed, ex parte and in camera, the classified intelligence at issue in order to ensure independently that there was a sufficient basis for [the CBP's statement of reasons for its concerns]. (The District Court was given the option of viewing this classified intelligence, but chose not to do so.) These materials confirmed what the record available to both parties already made plain: CBP had reason to believe that known terrorists, or those with terrorist ties, would be attending the RIS Conference.

actions. The IDSO instructed the officials to: (a) identify and examine all persons associated with any of the Islamic conferences at issue who sought entry into the United States, (b) contact CBP's National Targeting Center upon encountering conference participants "in order to determine whether individuals seeking to enter the United States posed a particular threat," and (c) question conference attendees about their activities during their trip and examine their documentation and persons and vehicles for "evidence of terrorist-related activities, such as plans, money, or even weapons." The IDSO also permitted, but did not require, border officials to fingerprint and photograph conference attendees. The purpose of these measures – which were designed to process travelers who are suspected terrorists – was to "confirm each individual's identity and verify that they were not on any watch list of suspected terrorists, or seeking to use the conference as a cover for crossing the U.S. border, or otherwise involved in illegal activity, or carrying any illegal weapons, documents, monetary instruments, or any other prohibited items across the border." Attendance at one of the Islamic conferences at issue was the sole factor that triggered the enhanced processing.

Plaintiffs – Sawsaan Tabbaa, Hassan Shibly, Asmaa Elshinawy, Karema Atassi, and Galeb Rizek – are U.S. citizens who were among an estimated 13,000 individuals from across North America who attended the RIS Conference. The conference, which lasted three days, included religious and cultural activities, musical performances, a series of prominent Islamic speakers, and communal prayer three times a day. Plaintiffs viewed participation in the conference as an act of religious observance and as a way to learn more about their religion. Tabbaa and Atassi viewed their participation as a "hajj," or pilgrimage; Tabbaa considered attendance to be part of her religious obligations.

Following the conference, plaintiffs reached the U.S. border at various times on December 26 and 27, 2004. Plaintiffs had no criminal records, and at no time did CBP have reasonable suspicion that any particular plaintiff had committed a crime or was associated with terrorists. Yet each experienced similar treatment. Plaintiffs were initially asked where they had been in Canada, and after responding that they had attended an Islamic conference at the Skydome, they were ordered to pull their cars into a separate area and enter a nearby building, where they saw several other people who appeared to be Muslims who also had attended the RIS Conference.

Inside this secondary inspection area, plaintiffs were directed to fill out several forms, and then were questioned about, *inter alia,* their past travels, their relationship to other vehicle occupants, what occurred at the

RIS Conference, and why they had attended the conference. Plaintiffs were frisked, fingerprinted, and photographed, and their cars were searched. They were not told why they were being fingerprinted and photographed, or why they had been detained and inspected so thoroughly. Four of the plaintiffs at some point questioned part of the processing, but, after being told that he or she would not be released until all of the screening measures had been completed, eventually complied. Rizek and Shibly assert, and we assume for the purposes of this appeal, that CBP officers forcibly kicked their feet open and almost knocked them on the ground in order to effectuate the pat-downs. We also assume for the purposes of this appeal that, as plaintiffs allege, some physical force – i.e., grabbing of hands – was used to take the fingerprints of Tabbaa, Shibly, and Elshinawy. All told, each plaintiff was detained and searched for between four and six hours, after which he or she was released into the United States.

Within seven days of the searches, the government removed from its databases plaintiffs' fingerprints and photographs. However, the government continues to hold some information about plaintiffs in its Treasury Enforcement Communication System ("TECS"), including each plaintiff's name, date of birth, address, and the details of their 2004 detentions. . . .

DISCUSSION . . .

II. Defendants Did Not Violate the Administrative Procedure Act

Plaintiffs' first substantive claim is brought pursuant to the APA. Plaintiffs argue that CBP did not have statutory authority to detain them in order to screen for possible association with terrorist activity, in violation of section 706 of the APA. *See* 5 U.S.C. §706(2)(c) (providing that a reviewing court shall set aside agency action "found to be . . . in excess of statutory jurisdiction, authority, or limitations. . . ."). Plaintiffs do not contest that CBP, as a general matter, can implement any of the screening procedures to which plaintiffs were subject, including detailed questioning, fingerprinting, and photographing. . . .

The customs statutes and regulations, however, do not so confine CBP's authority to detain and search individuals, especially in the wake of the creation of the Department of Homeland Security. A crucial aspect of the new "primary mission" of CBP is to "prevent terrorist attacks within the United States" and "reduce the vulnerability of the United States to terrorism." 6 U.S.C. §111(b)(1). The undersecretary in charge of CBP has specific statutory responsibility for "[p]reventing the entry of terrorists and the instruments of terrorism into the United States." 6 U.S.C. §202(1). Given these provisions, we cannot conclude that it is beyond the power of CBP to search and detain an individual for the limited purpose of determining whether he or she is or has been associated with known terrorists, so long as CBP is not violating the individual's other constitutional or statutory rights. Indeed, the customs laws provide sufficient authority for CBP to conduct the type of searches at issue here. *Cf.* 19 U.S.C. §1582 ("[A]ll persons coming into the United States from foreign countries shall be liable to detention and search by authorized officers or agents of the Government under [CBP regulations]."); 19 U.S.C. §1433(e) (providing that after arriving in the United States, a vehicle may "depart from the . . . place . . . of arrival; or discharge any passenger" only "in accordance with regulations prescribed by the Secretary [of Homeland Security]"); 8 U.S.C. §1225(b) (providing that an alien "shall be detained" unless he or she appears to the examining immigration officer to be "clearly and beyond a doubt entitled" to enter). Accordingly, the District Court was correct to conclude that the searches and detentions of plaintiffs were "entirely consistent with the CBP's statutory mandate. . . ."

III. The Searches and Detention of Plaintiffs Did Not Violate the Fourth Amendment

Plaintiffs' second claim is that CBP's searches were unreasonable in violation of the Fourth Amendment to the U.S. Constitution.

It is well established that the government has broad powers to conduct searches at the border even where, as here, there is no reasonable suspicion that the prospective entrant has committed a crime. *See, e.g.,* United States v. Flores-Montano, 541 U.S. 149, 153 (2004) ("Congress, since the beginning of our Government, has granted the Executive plenary authority to conduct routine searches and seizures at the border, without probable cause or a warrant. . . .") (internal quotation marks omitted); United States v. Montoya de Hernandez, 473 U.S. 531, 538, (1985) ("Routine searches of the persons and effects of entrants are not subject to any requirement of reasonable suspicion, probable cause, or warrant. . . ."); United States v. Ramsey, 431 U.S. 606, 616 (1977) ("[S]earches made at the border, pursuant to the longstanding right of the sovereign to protect itself by stopping and examining persons and property crossing into this country, are reasonable simply by virtue of the fact that they occur at the border. . . ."); United States v. Nieves, 609

F.2d 642, 645 (2d Cir. 1979) ("It long has been established that routine border searches, conducted for the purpose of controlling the movement of people and goods across our national boundaries, do not violate the Fourth Amendment's prohibition against unreasonable searches."). Accordingly, a suspicionless search at the border is permissible under the Fourth Amendment so long as it is considered to be "routine." *See, e.g.,* United States v. Irving, 452 F.3d 110, 123 (2d Cir. 2006).

The precise line between what is routine and what is not routine, however, has not been clearly delineated. On the one hand, it has been held that "[r]outine searches include those searches of outer clothing, luggage, a purse, wallet, pockets, or shoes which, unlike strip searches, do not substantially infringe on a traveler's privacy rights." *Id.* (citing United States v. Grotke, 702 F.2d 49, 51-52 (2d Cir. 1983)). By contrast, "more invasive searches, like strip searches, require reasonable suspicion." *Id.* The Supreme Court has stated that "non-routine" searches include "strip, body cavity, or involuntary x-ray searches." *Montoya de Hernandez,* 473 U.S. at 541 n.4. The determining factor is not how ordinary or commonplace a search is, but rather "the level of intrusion into a person's privacy." *Irving,* 452 F.3d at 123.

There is, of course, a good deal of distance between strip and body cavity searches near one end of the spectrum and a search of pockets or outer clothing near the other, and the searches at issue here fall somewhere in the middle. . . .

Plaintiffs focus on three aspects of the searches in question, which we address in turn. First, plaintiffs urge us to find that their treatment, when considered in its entirety, was not routine because of the combined effect of the various measures employed, including intrusive questioning, photographing, and fingerprinting. We are sympathetic to plaintiffs' argument because there arguably was a stigma associated with being subject to the IDSO procedures. In MacWade v. Kelly, 460 F.3d 260, 273 (2d Cir. 2006), we found that police searches of subway passengers' bags were "minimally intrusive" in part because the searches were conducted "out in the open, which reduces the fear and stigma that removal to a hidden area can cause. . . ." Here, plaintiffs were gathered into a separate building along with several other Muslims who had attended the RIS Conference – and all of these attendees were subject to a form of border processing normally reserved for suspected terrorists. As a result, it is not unreasonable for plaintiffs to have felt there was a stigma attached to the searches. *Cf.* United States v. Edwards, 498 F.2d 496, 500 (2d Cir. 1974) ("The search of carry-on baggage, *applied to everyone,* involves not the slightest stigma. More than a million

Americans subject themselves to it daily. . . .") (emphasis added and citation omitted).

On the other hand, none of the specific measures taken by CBP was more invasive than the types of searches at the border that courts have regularly held to be routine. Plaintiffs complain that they were required to answer intrusive questions about their activities at the conference, the content of the lectures they attended, and their reasons for attending. But these questions are not materially different than the types of questions border officers typically ask prospective entrants in an effort to determine the places they have visited and the purpose and duration of their trip. Likewise, pat-down searches have repeatedly been found to be routine, even when they were followed by the lifting of an applicant's shirt or the forced removal of shoes. The forcing open of plaintiffs' feet that we assume to have occurred here in at least two instances, while perhaps marginally more invasive than the lifting of a shirt, is not so invasive of plaintiffs' privacy as to be distinguishable from our holdings that pat-down searches are routine.

We also conclude that the fingerprinting and photographing of plaintiffs does not take the searches out of the realm of what is considered routine because, at least in the context of a border search, being fingerprinted (even forcibly) and photographed is not particularly invasive, especially considering that the photographs and fingerprints were used solely to verify plaintiffs' identities and then were discarded from the government's databases. *See* Davis v. Mississippi, 394 U.S. 721, 727 (1969) ("Fingerprinting involves none of the probing into an individual's private life and thoughts that marks an interrogation or search."); Nicholas v. Goord, 430 F.3d 652, 658 (2d Cir. 2005) (noting that the Supreme Court has suggested that fingerprinting is not entitled to Fourth Amendment protection and describing fingerprinting as a "non-intrusive means of obtaining physical evidence . . ."); *Montoya de Hernandez*, 473 U.S. at 539-40 ("[N]ot only is the expectation of privacy less at the border than in the interior, the Fourth Amendment balance between the interests of the Government and the privacy right of the individual is also struck much more favorably to the Government at the border.") (internal citation omitted).

Thus, each of the individual elements of the searches was routine. And while we leave open the possibility that in some circumstances the cumulative effect of several routine search methods could render an overall search non-routine, we do not find that to be the case here. While plaintiffs were undoubtedly made uncomfortable and angry by the searches, and they may understandably have felt stigmatized, their personal privacy was not invaded in the same way as it would have been had they been subject to a body cavity or strip search, or involuntary x-ray. Because the decisive factor in the analysis is invasiveness of privacy – not overall inconvenience – we find that CBP's searches of plaintiffs, considered in their entirety, were routine in the border context, albeit near the outer limits of what is permissible absent reasonable suspicion.

Plaintiffs' second argument is that the searches were not routine because CBP agents threatened to detain plaintiffs until they cooperated. We have not previously considered whether a threat of continued detention can turn an otherwise routine search into one requiring reasonable suspicion. However, as noted above, CBP has clear statutory authority to detain persons at the border in order to, *inter alia,* confirm their citizenship or ensure that they are not bringing illicit goods into the country. *See, e.g.,* 19 U.S.C. §1582; 19 U.S.C. §1433(e); 8 U.S.C. §1225(b). Thus, it would no doubt be considered routine for customs officials to continue to detain prospective entrants if, for example, they did not willingly turn over their passports or permit their vehicles to be searched. It is, quite reasonably, not the practice of CBP to allow prospective entrants who fail to comply with inspection to freely leave the checkpoint, as that would enable smugglers, terrorists, and others not entitled to enter the country to continuously try other checkpoints until they find one that provides a less rigorous screening. Thus, CBP's ability to threaten with extended detention those who do not comply with lawful screening measures is an important aspect of the "longstanding right of the sovereign to protect itself" at the border, and therefore is "reasonable simply by virtue of the fact that [it] occur[s] at the border. . . ." *Ramsey,* 431 U.S. at 616. In other words, border crossers cannot, by their own non-compliance, turn an otherwise routine search into a non-routine one.

Finally, plaintiffs argue that the duration of their detentions – between four and six hours – cannot be considered routine because U.S. citizens do not expect to be held at the border for that length of time. Plaintiffs rely on *United States v. Montoya de Hernandez,* in which the Supreme Court treated as non-routine the 16-hour detention of a woman whom customs officials suspected of smuggling drugs via her alimentary canal. 473 U.S. at 535, 540. Defendants, on the other hand, cite *United States v. Flores-Montano,* in which the Supreme Court held that a one-hour delay incident to a border search did not render that search non-routine because "[w]e think it clear that delays of one to two hours at international borders are to be expected." 541 U.S. at 155 n.3.

While the searches here fall between these two poles, we believe they are more akin to the one-hour delay in *Flores-Montano* than the overnight detention in *Montoya de Hernandez.* The Supreme Court noted in *Flores-Montano* that "no cases indicat[e] [that] the Fourth Amendment shields entrants from inconvenience or delay at the international border." 541 U.S. at 155 n.3. Moreover, the Supreme Court has "consistently rejected hard-and-fast time limits" in evaluating the reasonableness of border searches and has stressed that "'common sense and ordinary human experience must govern over rigid criteria.'" *Montoya de Hernandez,* 473 U.S. at 543 (quoting United States v. Sharpe, 470 U.S. 675, 685 (1985). In other words, we must consider "whether the detention of [the traveler] was reasonably related in scope to the circumstances which justified it initially." *Id.* at 542.

While a delay of four, five, or six hours is obviously of more serious magnitude than a delay of "one to two hours," "common sense and ordinary human experience" suggest that it may take up to six hours for CBP to complete the various steps at issue here, including vehicle searches, questioning, and identity verification, all of which we have already found to be routine. The additional four hours, while certainly inconvenient, thus cannot be considered an unexpected "level of intrusion into a person's privacy," *Irving,* 452 F.3d at 123, that by itself would render the searches non-routine. Accordingly, the searches and detention of plaintiffs were routine in the border context and thus did not violate the Fourth Amendment.

IV. Defendants' Actions Did Not Violate Plaintiffs' Right of Association

Plaintiffs next argue that the searches and detentions violated their First Amendment right of freedom of expressive association. Plaintiffs unquestionably had a protected right to express themselves through association at the RIS Conference. "[I]mplicit in the right to engage in activities protected by the First Amendment [is] a corresponding right to associate with others in pursuit of a wide variety of political, social, economic, educational, religious, and cultural ends." Roberts v. United States Jaycees, 468 U.S. 609, 622 (1984). As the Supreme Court observed in *Roberts,* the right of expressive association "is especially important in preserving political and cultural diversity and in shielding dissident expression from suppression by the majority." *Id.* Participation in the RIS Conference – a social, religious, and cultural gathering – falls squarely within the forms of associational activity protected by the First Amendment.

The first question we must answer, then, is whether and to what extent defendants' actions burdened that right. *See* Boy Scouts of Am. v. Dale, 530 U.S. 640, 657-59 (2000); Fighting Finest, Inc. v. Bratton, 95 F.3d 224, 228 (2d Cir. 1996). Mere incidental burdens on the right to associate do not violate the First Amendment; rather, "[t]o be cognizable, the interference with [plaintiffs'] associational rights must be "direct and substantial" or "significant." *Fighting Finest, Inc.,* 95 F.3d at 228 (quoting Lyng v. Int'l Union, 485 U.S. 360, 366, 367 & n.5 (1988)). . . .

. . . Government action can constitute a direct and substantial interference with associational rights even if there is no prior restraint and no clear chilling of future expressive activity. For example, when government action substantially penalizes members of a group for exercising their First Amendment rights, that penalty in itself can constitute a substantial burden, even if the government did not prevent the group from associating and regardless of any future chilling effect. . . .

Here, plaintiffs suffered a significant penalty, or disability, solely by virtue of associating at the RIS Conference: they were detained for a lengthy period of time, interrogated, fingerprinted, and photographed when others, who had not attended the conference, did not have to endure these measures. Moreover, even though some of the plaintiffs expressed a willingness to attend future RIS conferences, the prospect of being singled out for such extensive processing could reasonably deter others from associating at similar conferences. And contrary to the government's contention, the burden on plaintiffs was no less simply by virtue of the fact that they were not aware of the IDSO prior to going to the conference and therefore were not deterred from attending; First Amendment rights do not turn on whether their potential infringement came as a surprise. Thus, we find that the burden on plaintiffs' associational rights was sufficiently "significant" to implicate the protections of the First Amendment.[4]

Having found a cognizable burden, we must next determine the appropriate level of scrutiny to employ in evaluating defendants' actions.

---

4. Our conclusion that the searches constituted a significant or substantial burden on plaintiffs' First Amendment associational rights is unaltered by our holding that the searches were routine under the Fourth Amendment. As is clear from the above discussion, distinguishing between incidental and substantial burdens under the First Amendment requires a different analysis, applying different legal standards, than distinguishing what is and is not routine in the Fourth Amendment border context.

The District Court applied the test established in *Roberts v. United States Jaycees*: an infringement on associational rights is not unconstitutional so long as it "serve[s] compelling state interests, unrelated to the suppression of ideas, that cannot be achieved through means significantly less restrictive of associational freedoms." 468 U.S. at 623. Courts have regularly applied this test when evaluating associational claims, and we believe this test to be appropriate here.[5]

It is undisputed that the government's interest in protecting the nation from terrorism constitutes a compelling state interest unrelated to the suppression of ideas, and that the IDSO was instituted to serve this compelling state interest. The only question, therefore, is whether this interest could have been "achieved through means significantly less restrictive of [plaintiffs'] associational freedoms." *Roberts,* 468 U.S. at 623.

The government has established that it could not have been. As the District Court observed, "[i]nterception and detection at international border crossings is likely the most effective way to protect the United States from terrorists and instruments of terrorism."

Thus, when CBP officials received intelligence that gave them reason to believe that "certain individuals who were associated with terrorist organizations or activities . . . would be in attendance at the 2004 [RIS] conference," and that the conference "would serve as a possible meeting point for terrorists to exchange ideas and documents, coordinate operations, and raise funds intended for terrorist activities," CBP had

---

5. The author of this opinion, speaking for himself, does note, however, that because the infringement on association here occurred as part of a border search, a less rigorous form of scrutiny could potentially be warranted. The Supreme Court has pointed out on several occasions that "searches of persons or packages at the national border rest on different considerations and different rules of constitutional law from domestic regulations." *Montoya de Hernandez*, 473 U.S. at 537 (quoting *Ramsey*, 431 U.S. at 618-619); United States v. 12 200-Ft. Reels of Super 8mm. Film, 413 U.S. 123, 125 (1973). As the opinion has already explained, "the Fourth Amendment's balance of reasonableness is qualitatively different at the international border than in the interior" due to the government's "broad" and "comprehensive" powers "to protect the Nation by stopping and examining persons entering this country." *Montoya de Hernandez*, 473 U.S. at 537-38. It may also be true that the First Amendment's balance of interests is qualitatively different where, as here, the action being challenged is the government's attempt to exercise its broad authority to control who and what enters the country. We do not need to reach this issue because defendants' actions easily pass muster under *Roberts*.

ample justification to implement the IDSO, which was explicitly designed to detect and intercept potential terrorists from the conference who attempted to enter the United States. Importantly, the IDSO's reach was carefully circumscribed: it applied only to those conferences about which the government had specific intelligence regarding the possible congregation of suspected terrorists, it was limited to routine screening measures, and it was confined to those individuals, regardless of their religion, whom CBP could establish had attended the conferences in question.

Plaintiffs put forth two responses. First, they assert that *no* burden on their associational rights could be justified because "the First Amendment bars the government from penalizing mere participation in an expressive assembly, even if there is reason to believe that others associated with the assembly might be engaged in unlawful activity intended to undermine if not destroy the nation." For this extraordinary proposition, plaintiffs cite De Jonge v. Oregon, 299 U.S. 353 (1937), United States v. Robel, 389 U.S. 258 (1967), and Aptheker v. Sec'y of State, 378 U.S. 500 (1964).

These cases, however, are inapposite because they all involve categorical *prohibitions* on forms of association, as opposed to the indirect *burden* on association at issue here. In *De Jonge,* the Supreme Court struck down Oregon's criminal syndicalism statute, which made it a crime to speak at meetings of groups that advocate crime or sabotage. 299 U.S. at 357, 365. The Court emphasized that "[t]he holding of a meeting for peaceable political action cannot be proscribed," and held the statute unconstitutional because it made "mere participation in a peaceable assembly . . . the basis for a criminal charge." *Id.* at 365. Similarly, *Robel* involved a statute that made it unlawful for members of the Communist Party to work in a defense facility, 389 U.S. at 260-61, and *Aptheker* struck down a statute prohibiting members of the Communist Party from applying for or using passports, 378 U.S. at 515-16. Here, the government did not make attendance at or participation in the RIS Conference unlawful, and the purpose of the government's actions was not to prevent people from associating at the conference, but rather to prevent terrorists from entering the country. Defendants' actions are not *per se* unconstitutional simply because innocent U.S. citizens such as plaintiffs were subject to enhanced processing techniques and thus experienced an indirect burden on their right to associate.

Second, plaintiffs contend that CBP could have achieved its interest in preventing terrorists from entering the country in a manner that would have been less restrictive of plaintiffs' associational freedoms. According to plaintiffs, rather than instituting the IDSO, the government could have surveilled the individuals identified in the intelligence as being associated with terrorism, or stopped at the border only those conference attendees whom the government had reason to believe had personally interacted with suspected terrorists. These are plainly not viable alternatives. As defendants point out, the U.S. government cannot freely conduct surveillance on private individuals in Canada, and, given that approximately 13,000 people attended the RIS Conference, it is entirely unrealistic to expect the government to have been able to identify and keep track of all those who personally interacted with suspected terrorists who attended the conference. Indeed, the IDSO was necessary precisely because of the infeasibility of knowing who at the conference may have interacted, and potentially exchanged identification or travel documents, with suspected terrorists.

Plaintiffs also suggest that CBP could have instituted a graduated process of inspection such that only those conference attendees about whom the government had individualized suspicion of a terrorist link or other criminal activity would have been subject to fingerprinting and photographing. Plaintiffs place great emphasis on the fact that in February 2005 – two months after the searches at issue here – CBP modified its fingerprinting policy "to clarify that fingerprint checks should be run if there is at least one articulable fact concerning whether a traveler may lawfully enter the United States. . . ." . . .

Plaintiffs' argument fails for three reasons. First, CBP could have modified its fingerprinting policy for a host of reasons – such as political pressure or fear of litigation – unrelated to the policy's effectiveness in preventing terrorism. Second, even assuming that plaintiffs are correct about how the revised policy would be implemented, that does not mean it was unnecessary for CBP to fingerprint and photograph plaintiffs when they crossed the border in late 2004, especially given the nature of the intelligence the government received in advance of the RIS Conference. That intelligence gave rise to a reasonable concern that terrorists might use the conference to exchange "travel or identification documents such as passports or driver's licenses." In light of this concern, fingerprinting and photographing conference attendees was necessary to "ensure" that they were "who the[y] claim[ed] to be" – an objective that would not have been possible if CBP officials were limited to reviewing passports and other identification documents.

Finally, *Roberts* does not require the government to exhaust every possible means of furthering its interest; rather, the government must show only that its interest "cannot be achieved through means *significantly less restrictive* of associational freedoms." *Roberts,* 468 U.S. at 623 (emphasis added). Plaintiffs' argument supposes that it would have been acceptable for CBP to have segregated conference attendees into the secondary search area, rigorously searched and questioned them, and detained them for a considerable period of time while running their names through various government databases – so long as plaintiffs were not also fingerprinted and photographed absent individualized suspicion. We do not believe the extra hassle of being fingerprinted and photographed – for the sole purpose of having their identities verified – is a "significant[ ]" additional burden that turns an otherwise constitutional policy into one that is unconstitutional.

Thus, we agree with the District Court that the government has a compelling interest in protecting against terrorism, and that it could not have achieved that interest "through means significantly less restrictive of [plaintiffs'] associational freedoms." *Id.* We therefore affirm the District Court's grant of summary judgment on plaintiffs' freedom of association claim.

V. Defendants Did Not Violate Plaintiffs' Free Exercise Rights under RFRA or the First Amendment . . .

[The court held that the same strict scrutiny test applied to the plaintiffs' free exercise and Religious Freedom Restoration Act (RFRA) claims.]

Accordingly, the District Court was correct in finding that plaintiffs' claims under RFRA and the free exercise clause of the First Amendment fail.

CONCLUSION

In sum, we hold that, as a matter of law, defendants, in detaining and searching plaintiffs as they crossed the U.S.-Canada border following the RIS Conference, did not violate the Administrative Procedure Act or plaintiffs' rights under RFRA or the First or Fourth Amendments to the U.S. Constitution. We therefore AFFIRM the judgment of the District Court.

* * *

22

Organization and Coordination of Counterterrorism Investigations

A. EXECUTIVE AUTHORITY FOR NATIONAL SECURITY INVESTIGATIONS

Page 616. Replace the excerpt of Executive Order No. 12,333 with §§1.7(a), 2.3, 2.5, 2.6, 2.8, and 2.9 of the amended order, reproduced *supra* pp. 17-22.

Page 628. Replace the text of Note 3 with the following material.

Compare §§ 1.7(a) and 2.3(b) of amended Executive Order 12,333, *supra* pp. 17, 20, with 50 U.S.C. §403-4a(d)(1), part of the National Security Act of 1947, casebook p. 355. Does the amended order adequately respect the statutory mandate that the CIA not engage in "internal security functions"? The original Reagan order referred to the CIA's conduct of "counterintelligence activities within the United States in coordination with the FBI." Under the amended order, can the CIA still conduct such activities within the United States? If so, is this consistent with the National Security Act, and how are such activities regulated?

B. INFORMATION SHARING AND AGENCY REFORMS

Pages 634-635. Replace the carryover paragraph with the following material.

In addition to the 1947 Act, amended Executive Order No. 12,333, *supra* p. 9, explicitly charges the Director of National Intelligence (DNI) with developing guidelines for sharing of intelligence information by the intelligence community, subject to approval by the Attorney General. §1.3(a)(2). The DNI also "shall ensure, through appropriate policies and procedures, the deconfliction, coordination, and integration of all intelligence activities conducted by an intelligence Community element or funded by the National Intelligence Program." §1.3(b)(20). In accordance with these polices and procedures, the amended order directs the FBI to coordinate collection of foreign intelligence from human sources and counterintelligence activities within the United States, subject to approval by the Attorney General, and the CIA to coordinate them outside the United States. *Id.*

24

Civil Detention of Terrorist Suspects

Page 679. Insert the following case at the end of the chapter.

Iqbal v. Hasty

United States Court of Appeals, Second Circuit, 2007
490 F.3d 143
cert. granted, 2008 WL 336310 (U.S. Jun. 16, 2008) (No. 07-1015)

JON O. NEWMAN, Circuit Judge. These interlocutory appeals present several issues concerning the defense of qualified immunity in the aftermath of the events of 9/11. . . .

[Javaid Iqbal is a Muslim Pakistani who was arrested by agents of the FBI and the Immigration and Naturalization Service on November 2, 2001, and charged with conspiracy to defraud and identity fraud. Following his arrest, he was detained in the MDC's (Metropolitan Detention Center in Brooklyn) general prison population until January 8, 2002, when he was removed from the general prison population and assigned to a special section of the MDC known as the Administrative Maximum Special Housing Unit ("ADMAX SHU"), where he remained until he was reassigned to the general prison population at the end of July 2002. He alleged that he was arrested in the PENTTBOM investigation and detained as a person "of high interest" solely because of his race, religion, and national origin, and not because of any involvement in terrorism. The complaint further alleges that Attorney General John Ashcroft and FBI Director Robert Mueller approved a policy of holding detainees "of high interest" in highly restrictive conditions until they were "cleared" by the FBI. Iqbal further alleges that he was kept in solitary confinement.]

. . . Until March, [Iqbal alleges,] the lights in his cell were left on almost 24 hours a day, and MDC staff deliberately turned on air conditioning during the winter and heating during the summer. MDC staff left the Plaintiff in the open-air recreation area for hours when it was raining and then turned on the air conditioner when he returned to his cell. Whenever the Plaintiff was removed from his cell, he was handcuffed and shackled. The Plaintiff was not provided with adequate food and lost 40 pounds while in custody. MDC staff called him, among other things, a "terrorist" and a "Muslim killer."

The complaint further alleges that the Plaintiff was brutally beaten by MDC guards on two occasions: upon his transfer to the ADMAX SHU in January 2002 and again in March. Following the March beating, the Plaintiff was denied medical care for two weeks even though he was in excruciating pain. He was also subjected to daily strip and body-cavity searches. The March beating was prompted by the Plaintiff's protestations to a fourth consecutive strip and body-cavity search in the same room. MDC staff interfered with the Plaintiff's prayers, routinely confiscated his Koran, and refused to permit him to participate in Friday prayer services. They also interfered with the Plaintiff's communications with his defense attorney, for example, by disconnecting the phone if the Plaintiff complained about his conditions of confinement and delaying his receipt of legal mail for up to two months. . . .

[Iqbal pled guilty to non-terrorism charges, was sentenced, and eventually was removed to Pakistan. He brought this suit against his jailers, the Director of the FBI, and the Attorney General for damages based on violations of his constitutional and statutory rights as a result of the conditions of his confinement. Defendants moved to dismiss on grounds of qualified immunity. The lower court denied the motion, and this interlocutory appeal followed.] . . .

I. General Principles of Qualified Immunity . . .

. . . A defendant will be entitled to qualified immunity if either (1) his actions did not violate clearly established law or (2) it was objectively reasonable for him to believe that his actions did not violate clearly established law. . . .

. . . Several Defendants contend that even if the Plaintiff's complaint would survive a motion to dismiss in the face of a qualified immunity defense under normal circumstances, the post-9/11 context requires a different outcome. This argument is advanced on three fronts. First, some Defendants contend that the Government was entitled to take certain actions that might not have been lawful before 9/11 because the Government's interests assumed special weight in the post-9/11 context. Second, some Defendants contend that, even if the law was clearly established as to the existence of a right claimed to have been violated, it was not clearly established in the extraordinary circumstances of the 9/11 attack and its aftermath. Third, some Defendants contend that the post-9/11 context renders their actions objectively reasonable, an argument we do not reach in view of our disposition of their second contention.

We fully recognize the gravity of the situation that confronted investigative officials of the United States as a consequence of the 9/11 attack. We also recognize that some forms of governmental action are permitted in emergency situations that would exceed constitutional limits in normal times. *See* Home Building & Loan Association v. Blaisdell, 290 U.S. 398, 425-26 (1934) ("While emergency does not create power, emergency may furnish the occasion for the exercise of power."). But most of the rights that the Plaintiff contends were violated do not vary with surrounding circumstances, such as the right not to be subjected to needlessly harsh conditions of confinement, the right to be free from the use of excessive force, and the right not to be subjected to ethnic or religious discrimination. The strength of our system of constitutional rights derives from the steadfast protection of those rights in both normal and unusual times.

With some rights, for example, the right to be free from unreasonable searches, the existence of exigent circumstances might justify governmental action that would not otherwise be permitted. But, as we discuss below, the exigent circumstances of the post-9/11 context do not diminish the Plaintiff's right not to be needlessly harassed and mistreated in the confines of a prison cell by repeated strip and body-cavity searches. This and other rights, such as the right to be free from use of excessive force and not to be subjected to ethnic or religious discrimination, were all clearly established prior to 9/11, and they remained clearly established even in the aftermath of that horrific event. To whatever extent exigent circumstances might affect the lawfulness of the Defendants' actions or might have justified an objectively reasonable belief that their actions did not violate clearly established law, we consider the argument in connection with a particular claim.

With these general principles in mind, we turn to the Plaintiff's specific claims.

II. Procedural Due Process

The Plaintiff alleges that Ashcroft and Mueller, the FBI Defendants, the BOP [Bureau of Prisons] Defendants, and [former MDC Warden Dennis] Hasty adopted a policy under which he was deprived of a liberty interest without any of the procedural protections required by due process of law. . . .

(a) Has a Violation of a Procedural Due Process Right Been Adequately Pleaded? . . .

(i) *The Plaintiff's procedural due process right.*

. . . Under this Court's case law, the Plaintiff's confinement of more than six months fell in the intermediate range, thereby requiring inquiry into the conditions of his confinement, which he sufficiently alleges to have been severe. . . . [T]he conditions under which the Plaintiff alleges that he was confined – solitary confinement, repeated strip and body-cavity searches, beatings, exposure to excessive heat and cold, very limited exercise, and almost constant lighting – as well as the initially indefinite duration of confinement could be found to constitute atypical and significant hardships. The Plaintiff has alleged a protected liberty interest in avoiding more than six months' detention in the ADMAX SHU, especially in light of his status as a pretrial detainee. . . .

We recognize that in the post-9/11 context the third *Mathews* factor[1] – the gravity of the Government's interest – is appropriately accorded more weight than would otherwise be warranted. It might be that the combination of (1) the Plaintiff's interest in avoiding confinement under harsh conditions, (2) the risk of an erroneous determination of the need for such confinement, and (3) the Government's interest, accorded added weight in the post-9/11 context, would, on balance, lead to the conclusion that the Government need not have given the Plaintiff notice and a chance for rebuttal *before* placing him in the ADMAX SHU. However, once it became clear that the Plaintiff was going to be confined in the ADMAX SHU for an extended period of time, some process was required. We cannot say in the absence of a developed factual record whether the FBI's clearance procedure comported with the requirements

---

[1. The reference is to Mathews v. Eldridge, 424 U.S. 319 (1976). *See* casebook pp. 725 and 850 n.4, summarizing the *Mathews* balancing test.]

of the Due Process Clause as interpreted in *Mathews* and subsequent cases. The sparse record thus far developed provides no indication as to what security-related steps the Defendants were taking that might justify prolonged confinement. Nor does that record indicate in what respect providing the Plaintiff with some notice of the basis for his separation in the ADMAX SHU and affording some opportunity for rebuttal would have impaired national security interests or legitimate penological interests of the Government. The Government has not as yet had an opportunity to refute the Plaintiff's allegation that there was no evidence connecting him to terrorism. Accordingly, we cannot say whether the Government's national security interests rendered the clearance procedure sufficient to satisfy procedural due process requirements or whether more traditional procedural protections were required. Nevertheless, because we are required at this stage of the litigation to accept all of the Plaintiff's allegations as true and draw all reasonable inferences in his favor, we cannot say that the Plaintiff has failed to plead a viable claim under the procedural component of the Due Process Clause. . . .

(b) Was the Plaintiff's Right to Procedural Due Process Clearly Established?

Although we conclude that the Plaintiff has adequately pleaded a violation of a procedural due process right, we also conclude that in this case "officers of reasonable competence could [have] disagree[d]," Malley v. Briggs, 475 U.S. 335, 341 (1986), whether their conduct violated a clearly established procedural due process right. Accordingly, the Plaintiff's right to additional procedures was not clearly established with the level of specificity that is required to defeat a qualified immunity defense.

Several factors combine to create this lack of clarity in prior case law. First, some uncertainty exists in determining when administrative segregation procedures are required even in the ordinary criminal context. Our case law would require an officer in the Defendants' situation to consider various factors, including the length of the Plaintiff's confinement, the extent to which the conditions of confinement were atypical, the text of relevant BOP regulations, and the Plaintiff's status as a pretrial detainee. As noted above, no single factor is dispositive in this case, which concerns administrative segregation of approximately six months. Although the harshness of the conditions alleged weigh in favor of requiring procedural protections, an officer could reasonably note that the Plaintiff's six-month continued confinement was comparable to the duration of confinements in cases that we [have] characterized . . . as involving "relatively brief periods of confinement."

Second, uncertainty in existing case law is heightened by the fact that, even on the facts alleged in the complaint, which specified that the "of high interest" designation pertained to the Government's post-9/11 terrorism investigation, the investigation leading to the Plaintiff's separation from the general prison population could be reasonably understood by all of the Defendants to relate to matters of national security, rather than an ordinary criminal investigation. Prior to the instant case, neither the Supreme Court nor our Court had considered whether the Due Process Clause requires officials to provide ordinary administrative segregation hearings to persons detained under special conditions of confinement until cleared of connection with activities threatening national security.

Third, the BOP regulation on which the Plaintiff relies itself contains potentially relevant exceptions that undermine certainty as to established requirements of law. "Administrative detention is to be used only for short periods of time except . . . where there are exceptional circumstances, *ordinarily tied to security or complex investigative concerns,*" 28 C.F.R. §541.22(c)(1) (emphasis added), and inmates are entitled to "an administrative detention order detailing the reasons for placing an inmate in administrative detention . . . *provided institutional security is not compromised thereby,*" *id.* §541.22(b) (emphasis added).

In sum, these factors, taken together, would suffice to raise "a legitimate question" among Government officials as to whether the Due Process Clause required administrative segregation hearings or any procedures other than the FBI's clearance system. Accordingly, we will direct dismissal of the portions of the Plaintiff's complaint alleging violations of procedural due process rights.

III. Conditions of Confinement

[Defendant] Hasty contends that [District Court] Judge Gleeson should have dismissed the Plaintiff's conditions of confinement claims against him on the ground of qualified immunity because (1) the Plaintiff did not allege conditions amounting to a violation of substantive due process rights, (2) the Plaintiff failed to allege Hasty's deliberate indifference to the maintenance of the conditions of confinement, and (3) Hasty's actions were objectively reasonable under the circumstances.

Because the Plaintiff was a pretrial detainee during his detention in the ADMAX SHU, his challenge to the conditions of his confinement arises from the substantive component of the Due Process Clause of the Fifth Amendment and not from the cruel and unusual punishment standards of the Eighth Amendment. *See* Benjamin v. Fraser, 343 F.3d 35, 49 (2d Cir. 2003) ("*Benjamin II*"). Pretrial detainees have not been convicted of a crime and thus "may not be punished in any manner – neither cruelly and unusually nor otherwise." *Id.* at 49-50. Courts considering challenges to confinement brought by pretrial detainees must first consider whether the circumstances of the particular confinement render the confinement punitive; since some restraint is necessary to confine a pretrial detainee, not all uncomfortable conditions or restrictions are necessarily punitive. *Id.* at 50. In Bell v. Wolfish, [441 U.S. 520 (1979)], the seminal case on the substantive due process claims of pretrial detainees, the Supreme Court recognized the following factors as relevant to the determination of whether a condition of confinement is punitive:

> "Whether the sanction involves an affirmative disability or restraint, whether it has historically been regarded as a punishment, whether it comes into play only on a finding of *scienter,* whether its operation will promote the traditional aims of punishment – retribution and deterrence, whether the behavior to which it applies is already a crime, whether an alternative purpose to which it may rationally be connected is assignable for it, and whether it appears excessive in relation to the alternative purpose assigned. . . ."

441 U.S. at 537-38 (quoting [Kennedy v. Mendoza-Martinez, 372 U.S. 144, 168-169 (1963)]). A court may infer that a condition of confinement is intended as punishment if it is not reasonably related to a legitimate government objective.

The complaint alleges, among other things, that MDC staff placed the Plaintiff in solitary confinement, deliberately subjected him to extreme hot and cold temperatures, shackled him every time he left his cell, and repeatedly subjected him to strip and body-cavity searches, and that these conditions were intended to be, and were in fact, punitive. Applying *Wolfish,* Judge Gleeson found these allegations sufficient to state a substantive due process claim, observing that whether the conditions were reasonably related to legitimate government objectives could not be determined on a motion to dismiss. . . .

The Plaintiff has alleged the purposeful infliction of restraints that were punitive in nature. Accordingly, the District Court need not have considered whether a Defendant was "deliberately indifferent" in inflicting the restraints or whether the restraints constituted cruel and unusual punishment. The right of pretrial detainees to be free from punitive restraints was clearly established at the time of the events in question, and no reasonable officer could have thought that he could punish a pretrial detainee by subjecting him to the practices and conditions alleged by the Plaintiff. . . .

VII. Interference with Religious Practices

Hasty also argues that Judge Gleeson should have dismissed the Plaintiff's First Amendment claim against him on qualified immunity grounds because . . . the Plaintiff did not allege a violation of his First Amendment rights. . . .

Hasty's . . . argument is that Plaintiff has not alleged a violation of his First Amendment rights. He relies on O'Lone v. Estate of Shabazz, 482 U.S. 342 (1987), which applied *Turner*'s [Turner v. Safley, 482 U.S. 78 (1987)] "legitimate penological interests" test to First Amendment claims, *see id.* at 348-49. Though recognizing that a prison regulation precluded some Muslim prisoners from attending Friday prayers, the Supreme Court found the regulation justified under *Turner,* focusing on the officials' legitimate security objectives and the availability of other channels by which prisoners could exercise their religious rights. In the pending case, however, the Plaintiff alleges that he was not allowed to attend Friday prayers, that prison guards banged on his door when he tried to pray, and that his Koran was routinely confiscated. These allegations suffice to preclude a qualified immunity defense at this stage of the litigation. . . .

VIII. Racial and Religious Discrimination

The Defendants argue that they are entitled to qualified immunity on the Plaintiff's First Amendment claim of religious discrimination and Fifth Amendment claim of racial or ethnic discrimination on three grounds: (1) the Plaintiff has failed to state a violation of clearly established rights, (2) the Plaintiff's allegations of discriminatory intent are too conclusory, and (3) the Plaintiff has not alleged the personal involvement of Ashcroft and Mueller.

The arguments of Ashcroft and Mueller challenging the sufficiency of the Plaintiff's race, ethnic, and religious discrimination claims misunderstand his complaint. They contend that his "complaint amounts to an objection that most of those persons determined to be of high interest to the 9/11 investigation were Muslim or from certain Arab countries," which they justify by pointing out that the 9/11 hijackers were Muslims from Arab countries. However, what the Plaintiff is alleging is that he was deemed to be "of high interest," and accordingly was kept in the ADMAX SHU under harsh conditions, solely because of his race, ethnicity, and religion. The Plaintiff also alleges that "Defendants specifically targeted [him] for mistreatment because of [his] race, religion, and national origin." These allegations are sufficient to state a claim of animus-based discrimination that any "reasonably competent officer" would understand to have been illegal under prior case law. *See Malley,* 475 U.S. at 341. Accordingly, the Plaintiff's racial, ethnic, and religious discrimination claims cannot be dismissed on qualified immunity grounds at this stage of the litigation.

Hasty also argues that the Plaintiff has failed to state a claim of discrimination. Citing Reno v. American-Arab Anti-Discrimination Committee, 525 U.S. 471 (1999) ("*AAADC*"), he argues that the Equal Protection Clause does not apply in the context of proceedings to remove illegal aliens and that the Government can permissibly deem nationals of a particular country to be a special threat. In *AAADC,* the Supreme Court concluded that a provision of the Illegal Immigration Reform and Immigrant Responsibility Act of 1996, 8 U.S.C. §1252(g), deprived the federal courts of jurisdiction to consider an illegal alien's selective enforcement challenge to deportation. *See* 525 U.S. at 487. The Court rejected the argument that it nevertheless had jurisdiction to consider an alien's constitutional arguments, holding that "an alien unlawfully in this country has no constitutional right to assert selective enforcement as a defense against his deportation," *see id.* at 488, even when the Government deports the alien "for the additional reason that it believes him to be a member of an organization that supports terrorist activity," *id.* at 492. *AAADC* affords the Defendants no relief. The Plaintiff is not challenging his deportation or even his arrest on criminal charges. Moreover, *AAADC* does not stand for the proposition that the Government may subject members of a particular race, ethnicity, or religion to more restrictive conditions of confinement than members of other races, ethnic backgrounds, or religions. . . .

The Plaintiff's allegations suffice to state claims of racial, ethnic, and religious discrimination. He alleges in particular that the FBI Defendants classified him "of high interest" solely because of his race, ethnic background, and religion and not because of any evidence of involvement in terrorism. He offers additional factual support for this allegation, stating that "within the New York area, all Arab Muslim men arrested on criminal or immigration charges while the FBI was following an investigative lead into the September 11th attacks – however unrelated the arrestee was to the investigation – were immediately classified as 'of interest' to the post-September 11th investigation." We need not consider at this stage of the litigation whether these allegations are alone sufficient to state a clearly established constitutional violation under the circumstances presented because they are sufficient to state a violation when combined with the Plaintiff's allegation that, under the policy created and implemented by the Defendants, he was singled out for unnecessarily punitive conditions of confinement based on his racial, ethnic, and religious characteristics. . . .

Conclusion . . .

In sum, the serious allegations of gross mistreatment set forth in the complaint suffice, except as noted in this opinion, to defeat the Defendants' attempt to terminate the lawsuit at a preliminary stage, but, consistent with the important policies that justify the defense of qualified immunity, the defense may be reasserted in advance of trial after the carefully controlled and limited discovery that the District Court expects to supervise.

Affirmed in part, reversed in part, and remanded.

[Concurring opinion of JOSÉ A. CABRANES, J., omitted.]

25

Suspending the Great Writ

C. AVAILABILITY OF THE WRIT TO NONRESIDENT ALIENS

Page 702. Add these materials after Note 8.

Boumediene v. Bush

United States Supreme Court, 2008
128 S. Ct. 2229

JUSTICE KENNEDY delivered the opinion of the Court. Petitioners are aliens designated as enemy combatants and detained at the United States Naval Station at Guantanamo Bay, Cuba. There are others detained there, also aliens, who are not parties to this suit.

Petitioners present a question not resolved by our earlier cases relating to the detention of aliens at Guantanamo: whether they have the constitutional privilege of habeas corpus, a privilege not to be withdrawn except in conformance with the Suspension Clause, Art. I, §9, cl. 2. We hold these petitioners do have the habeas corpus privilege. Congress has enacted a statute, the Detainee Treatment Act of 2005 (DTA), 119 Stat. 2739, that provides certain procedures for review of the detainees' status. We hold that those procedures are not an adequate and effective substitute for habeas corpus. Therefore, §7 of the Military Commissions Act of 2006 (MCA), 28 U.S.C.A. §2241(e) (Supp. 2007), operates as an unconstitutional suspension of the writ. We do not address whether the President has authority to detain these petitioners nor do we hold that the writ must issue. These and other questions regarding the legality of the detention are to be resolved in the first instance by the District Court.

I . . .

Interpreting the AUMF [Authorization for Use of Military Force, Pub. L. No. 107-40 (2001), casebook p. 100], the Department of Defense ordered the detention of these petitioners, and they were transferred to Guantanamo. Some of these individuals were apprehended on the battlefield in Afghanistan, others in places as far away from there as Bosnia and Gambia. All are foreign nationals, but none is a citizen of a nation now at war with the United States. Each denies he is a member of the al Qaeda terrorist network that carried out the September 11 attacks or of the Taliban regime that provided sanctuary for al Qaeda. Each petitioner appeared before a separate CSRT [Combatant Status Review Tribunal, *see* casebook p. 700, Note 3]; was determined to be an enemy combatant; and has sought a writ of habeas corpus in the United States District Court for the District of Columbia.

[These initial petitions culminated in the Supreme Court's decision in Rasul v. Bush, 524 U.S. 466 (2004), extending *statutory* habeas corpus jurisdiction to Guantanamo. The Court there did not reach the question of *constitutional* habeas corpus jurisdiction, which is presented in the instant cases.] . . .

II

As a threshold matter, we must decide whether MCA §7 denies the federal courts jurisdiction to hear habeas corpus actions pending at the time of its enactment. We hold the statute does deny that jurisdiction, so that, if the statute is valid, petitioners' cases must be dismissed.

As amended by the terms of the MCA, §2241(e) now provides:

> (1) No court, justice, or judge shall have jurisdiction to hear or consider an application for a writ of habeas corpus filed by or on behalf of an alien detained by the United States who has been determined by the United States to have been properly detained as an enemy combatant or is awaiting such determination.
>
> (2) Except as provided in [§1005(e)(2) and (e)(3) of the DTA] no court, justice, or judge shall have jurisdiction to hear or consider any other action against the United States or its agents relating to any aspect of the detention, transfer, treatment, trial, or conditions of confinement of an alien who is or was detained by the United States and has been determined by the United States to have been properly detained as an enemy combatant or is awaiting such determination. . . .

III

In deciding the constitutional questions now presented we must determine whether petitioners are barred from seeking the writ or invoking the protections of the Suspension Clause either because of their status, *i.e.,* petitioners' designation by the Executive Branch as enemy combatants, or their physical location, *i.e.,* their presence at Guantanamo Bay. The Government contends that noncitizens designated as enemy combatants and detained in territory located outside our Nation's borders have no constitutional rights and no privilege of habeas corpus. Petitioners contend they do have cognizable constitutional rights and that Congress, in seeking to eliminate recourse to habeas corpus as a means to assert those rights, acted in violation of the Suspension Clause.

We begin with a brief account of the history and origins of the writ. Our account proceeds from two propositions. First, protection for the privilege of habeas corpus was one of the few safeguards of liberty specified in a Constitution that, at the outset, had no Bill of Rights. In the system conceived by the Framers the writ had a centrality that must inform proper interpretation of the Suspension Clause. Second, to the extent there were settled precedents or legal commentaries in 1789 regarding the extraterritorial scope of the writ or its application to enemy aliens, those authorities can be instructive for the present cases.

A

The Framers viewed freedom from unlawful restraint as a fundamental precept of liberty, and they understood the writ of habeas corpus as a vital instrument to secure that freedom. Experience taught, however, that the common-law writ all too often had been insufficient to guard against the abuse of monarchial power. That history counseled the necessity for specific language in the Constitution to secure the writ and ensure its place in our legal system. . . .

This history was known to the Framers. It no doubt confirmed their view that pendular swings to and away from individual liberty were endemic to undivided, uncontrolled power. The Framers' inherent distrust of governmental power was the driving force behind the constitutional plan that allocated powers among three independent branches. This design serves not only to make Government accountable but also to secure individual liberty. Because the Constitution's separation-of-powers structure, like the substantive guarantees of the Fifth and Fourteenth Amendments, see Yick Wo v. Hopkins, 118 U.S.

356, 374 (1886), protects persons as well as citizens, foreign nationals who have the privilege of litigating in our courts can seek to enforce separation-of-powers principles, see, *e.g.,* INS v. Chadha, 462 U.S. 919, 958-959 (1983).

That the Framers considered the writ a vital instrument for the protection of individual liberty is evident from the care taken to specify the limited grounds for its suspension: "The Privilege of the Writ of Habeas Corpus shall not be suspended, unless when in Cases of Rebellion or Invasion the public Safety may require it." Art. I, §9, cl. 2; see Amar, Of Sovereignty and Federalism, 96 Yale L.J. 1425, 1509 n.329 (1987) ("[T]he non-suspension clause is the original Constitution's most explicit reference to remedies"). . . .

In our own system the Suspension Clause is designed to protect against these cyclical abuses. The Clause protects the rights of the detained by a means consistent with the essential design of the Constitution. It ensures that, except during periods of formal suspension, the Judiciary will have a time-tested device, the writ, to maintain the "delicate balance of governance" that is itself the surest safeguard of liberty. See *Hamdi* [v. Rumsfeld, 542 U.S. 507 (2004)], at 536 (plurality opinion). The Clause protects the rights of the detained by affirming the duty and authority of the Judiciary to call the jailer to account. The separation-of-powers doctrine, and the history that influenced its design, therefore must inform the reach and purpose of the Suspension Clause.

B

The broad historical narrative of the writ and its function is central to our analysis, but we seek guidance as well from founding-era authorities addressing the specific question before us: whether foreign nationals, apprehended and detained in distant countries during a time of serious threats to our Nation's security, may assert the privilege of the writ and seek its protection. The Court has been careful not to foreclose the possibility that the protections of the Suspension Clause have expanded along with post-1789 developments that define the present scope of the writ. See INS v. St. Cyr, 533 U.S. 289, 300-301 (2001). But the analysis may begin with precedents as of 1789, for the Court has said that "at the absolute minimum" the Clause protects the writ as it existed when the Constitution was drafted and ratified. *Id*., at 301.

To support their arguments, the parties in these cases have examined historical sources to construct a view of the common-law writ as it existed in 1789 – as have *amici* whose expertise in legal history the

Court has relied upon in the past. The Government argues the common-law writ ran only to those territories over which the Crown was sovereign. Petitioners argue that jurisdiction followed the King's officers. Diligent search by all parties reveals no certain conclusions. In none of the cases cited do we find that a common-law court would or would not have granted, or refused to hear for lack of jurisdiction, a petition for a writ of habeas corpus brought by a prisoner deemed an enemy combatant, under a standard like the one the Department of Defense has used in these cases, and when held in a territory, like Guantanamo, over which the Government has total military and civil control. . . .

. . . Recent scholarship points to the inherent shortcomings in the historical record. And given the unique status of Guantanamo Bay and the particular dangers of terrorism in the modern age, the common-law courts simply may not have confronted cases with close parallels to this one. We decline, therefore, to infer too much, one way or the other, from the lack of historical evidence on point.

IV

Drawing from its position that at common law the writ ran only to territories over which the Crown was sovereign, the Government says the Suspension Clause affords petitioners no rights because the United States does not claim sovereignty over the place of detention.

Guantanamo Bay is not formally part of the United States. See DTA §1005(g), 119 Stat. 2743. And under the terms of the lease between the United States and Cuba, Cuba retains "ultimate sovereignty" over the territory while the United States exercises "complete jurisdiction and control." See Lease of Lands for Coaling and Naval Stations, Feb. 23, 1903, U.S.-Cuba, Art. III, T.S. No. 418 (hereinafter 1903 Lease Agreement); *Rasul,* 542 U.S., at 471. Under the terms of the 1934 Treaty, however, Cuba effectively has no rights as a sovereign until the parties agree to modification of the 1903 Lease Agreement or the United States abandons the base. See Treaty Defining Relations with Cuba, May 29, 1934, U.S.-Cuba, Art. III, 48 Stat. 1683, T.S. No. 866.

The United States contends, nevertheless, that Guantanamo is not within its sovereign control. This was the Government's position well before the events of September 11, 2001. And in other contexts the Court has held that questions of sovereignty are for the political branches to decide. Even if this were a treaty interpretation case that did not involve a political question, the President's construction of the lease agreement would be entitled to great respect.

We therefore do not question the Government's position that Cuba, not the United States, maintains sovereignty, in the legal and technical sense of the term, over Guantanamo Bay. But this does not end the analysis. Our cases do not hold it is improper for us to inquire into the objective degree of control the Nation asserts over foreign territory. . . .

A

The Court has discussed the issue of the Constitution's extraterritorial application on many occasions. These decisions undermine the Government's argument that, at least as applied to noncitizens, the Constitution necessarily stops where *de jure* sovereignty ends.

[The Court reviewed cases, including the *Insular Cases* and Reid v. Covert, 345 U.S. 1 (1957), as standing for the proposition that "whether a constitutional provision has extraterritorial effect depends upon the 'particular circumstances, the practical necessities, and the possible alternatives which Congress had before it' and, in particular, whether judicial enforcement of the provision would be 'impracticable and anomalous.'" (quoting Justice Harlan in *Reid*).] . . .

Practical considerations weighed heavily as well in Johnson v. Eisentrager, 339 U.S. 763 (1950), where the Court addressed whether habeas corpus jurisdiction extended to enemy aliens who had been convicted of violating the laws of war. The prisoners were detained at Landsberg Prison in Germany during the Allied Powers' postwar occupation. The Court stressed the difficulties of ordering the Government to produce the prisoners in a habeas corpus proceeding. It "would require allocation of shipping space, guarding personnel, billeting and rations" and would damage the prestige of military commanders at a sensitive time. *Id.,* at 779. In considering these factors the Court sought to balance the constraints of military occupation with constitutional necessities. *Id.,* at 769-779; see *Rasul,* 542 U.S., at 475-476 (discussing the factors relevant to *Eisentrager*'s constitutional holding); 542 U.S., at 486 (KENNEDY, J., concurring in judgment) (same).

True, the Court in *Eisentrager* denied access to the writ, and it noted the prisoners "at no relevant time were within any territory over which the United States is sovereign, and [that] the scenes of their offense, their capture, their trial and their punishment were all beyond the territorial jurisdiction of any court of the United States." 339 U.S., at 778. The Government seizes upon this language as proof positive that the

Eisentrager Court adopted a formalistic, sovereignty-based test for determining the reach of the Suspension Clause. We reject this reading for three reasons.

First, we do not accept the idea that the above-quoted passage from *Eisentrager* is the only authoritative language in the opinion and that all the rest is dicta. The Court's further determinations, based on practical considerations, were integral to Part II of its opinion and came before the decision announced its holding. See 339 U.S., at 781.

. . . Even if we assume the *Eisentrager* Court considered the United States' lack of formal legal sovereignty over Landsberg Prison as the decisive factor in that case, its holding is not inconsistent with a functional approach to questions of extraterritoriality. The formal legal status of a given territory affects, at least to some extent, the political branches' control over that territory. *De jure* sovereignty is a factor that bears upon which constitutional guarantees apply there.

Third, if the Government's reading of *Eisentrager* were correct, the opinion would have marked not only a change in, but a complete repudiation of, the *Insular Cases*' (and later *Reid*'s) functional approach to questions of extraterritoriality. We cannot accept the Government's view. Nothing in *Eisentrager* says that *de jure* sovereignty is or has ever been the only relevant consideration in determining the geographic reach of the Constitution or of habeas corpus. Were that the case, there would be considerable tension between *Eisentrager,* on the one hand, and the *Insular Cases* and *Reid,* on the other. Our cases need not be read to conflict in this manner. A constricted reading of *Eisentrager* overlooks what we see as a common thread uniting the *Insular Cases*, *Eisentrager,* and *Reid:* the idea that questions of extraterritoriality turn on objective factors and practical concerns, not formalism.

B

The Government's formal sovereignty-based test raises troubling separation-of-powers concerns as well. The political history of Guantanamo illustrates the deficiencies of this approach. The United States has maintained complete and uninterrupted control of the bay for over 100 years. . . . The necessary implication of the argument is that by surrendering formal sovereignty over any unincorporated territory to a third party, while at the same time entering into a lease that grants total control over the territory back to the United States, it would be possible for the political branches to govern without legal constraint.

Our basic charter cannot be contracted away like this. The

Constitution grants Congress and the President the power to acquire, dispose of, and govern territory, not the power to decide when and where its terms apply. Even when the United States acts outside its borders, its powers are not "absolute and unlimited" but are subject "to such restrictions as are expressed in the Constitution." Murphy v. Ramsey, 114 U.S. 15, 44 (1885). Abstaining from questions involving formal sovereignty and territorial governance is one thing. To hold the political branches have the power to switch the Constitution on or off at will is quite another. The former position reflects this Court's recognition that certain matters requiring political judgments are best left to the political branches. The latter would permit a striking anomaly in our tripartite system of government, leading to a regime in which Congress and the President, not this Court, say "what the law is." Marbury v. Madison, 1 Cranch 137, 177 (1803).

These concerns have particular bearing upon the Suspension Clause question in the cases now before us, for the writ of habeas corpus is itself an indispensable mechanism for monitoring the separation of powers. The test for determining the scope of this provision must not be subject to manipulation by those whose power it is designed to restrain.

C

As we recognized in *Rasul,* 542 U.S., at 476; *id.,* at 487 (KENNEDY, J., concurring in judgment), the outlines of a framework for determining the reach of the Suspension Clause are suggested by the factors the Court relied upon in *Eisentrager*. In addition to the practical concerns discussed above, the *Eisentrager* Court found relevant that each petitioner:

> "(a) is an enemy alien; (b) has never been or resided in the United States; (c) was captured outside of our territory and there held in military custody as a prisoner of war; (d) was tried and convicted by a Military Commission sitting outside the United States; (e) for offenses against laws of war committed outside the United States; (f) and is at all times imprisoned outside the United States." 339 U.S., at 777.

Based on this language from *Eisentrager,* and the reasoning in our other extraterritoriality opinions, we conclude that at least three factors are relevant in determining the reach of the Suspension Clause: (1) the citizenship and status of the detainee and the adequacy of the process through which that status determination was made; (2) the nature of the sites where apprehension and then detention took place; and (3) the practical obstacles inherent in resolving the prisoner's entitlement to the writ.

Applying this framework, we note at the onset that the status of these detainees is a matter of dispute. The petitioners, like those in *Eisentrager,* are not American citizens. But the petitioners in *Eisentrager* did not contest, it seems, the Court's assertion that they were "enemy alien[s]." In the instant cases, by contrast, the detainees deny they are enemy combatants. They have been afforded some process in CSRT proceedings to determine their status; but, unlike in *Eisentrager,* there has been no trial by military commission for violations of the laws of war. The difference is not trivial. The records from the *Eisentrager* trials suggest that, well before the petitioners brought their case to this Court, there had been a rigorous adversarial process to test the legality of their detention. The *Eisentrager* petitioners were charged by a bill of particulars that made detailed factual allegations against them. To rebut the accusations, they were entitled to representation by counsel, allowed to introduce evidence on their own behalf, and permitted to cross-examine the prosecution's witnesses.

In comparison, the procedural protections afforded to the detainees in the CSRT hearings are far more limited, and, we conclude, fall well short of the procedures and adversarial mechanisms that would eliminate the need for habeas corpus review. Although the detainee is assigned a "Personal Representative" to assist him during CSRT proceedings, the Secretary of the Navy's memorandum makes clear that person is not the detainee's lawyer or even his "advocate." The Government's evidence is accorded a presumption of validity. The detainee is allowed to present "reasonably available" evidence, but his ability to rebut the Government's evidence against him is limited by the circumstances of his confinement and his lack of counsel at this stage. And although the detainee can seek review of his status determination in the Court of Appeals, that review process cannot cure all defects in the earlier proceedings. See Part V, *infra*.

As to the second factor relevant to this analysis, the detainees here are similarly situated to the *Eisentrager* petitioners in that the sites of their apprehension and detention are technically outside the sovereign territory of the United States. As noted earlier, this is a factor that weighs against finding they have rights under the Suspension Clause. But there are critical differences between Landsberg Prison, circa 1950, and the United States Naval Station at Guantanamo Bay in 2008. Unlike its present control over the naval station, the United States' control over the prison in Germany was neither absolute nor indefinite. Like all parts of occupied Germany, the prison was under the jurisdiction of the combined Allied Forces. The United States was therefore answerable to its Allies for all activities occurring there. The Court's holding in *Eisentrager* was thus consistent with the *Insular Cases*, where it had held there was no need to extend full constitutional protections to territories the United States did not intend to govern indefinitely. Guantanamo Bay, on the other hand, is no transient possession. In every practical sense Guantanamo is not abroad; it is within the constant jurisdiction of the United States.

As to the third factor, we recognize, as the Court did in *Eisentrager,* that there are costs to holding the Suspension Clause applicable in a case of military detention abroad. Habeas corpus proceedings may require expenditure of funds by the Government and may divert the attention of military personnel from other pressing tasks. While we are sensitive to these concerns, we do not find them dispositive. Compliance with any judicial process requires some incremental expenditure of resources. Yet civilian courts and the Armed Forces have functioned along side each other at various points in our history. See, *e.g.,* Duncan v. Kahanamoku, 327 U.S. 304 (1946); Ex parte Milligan, 4 Wall. 2 (1866). The Government presents no credible arguments that the military mission at Guantanamo would be compromised if habeas corpus courts had jurisdiction to hear the detainees' claims. And in light of the plenary control the United States asserts over the base, none are apparent to us.

The situation in *Eisentrager* was far different, given the historical context and nature of the military's mission in post-War Germany. When hostilities in the European Theater came to an end, the United States became responsible for an occupation zone encompassing over 57,000 square miles with a population of 18 million. In addition to supervising massive reconstruction and aid efforts the American forces stationed in Germany faced potential security threats from a defeated enemy. In retrospect the post-War occupation may seem uneventful. But at the time *Eisentrager* was decided, the Court was right to be concerned about judicial interference with the military's efforts to contain "enemy elements, guerilla fighters, and 'were-wolves.'" 339 U.S., at 784.

Similar threats are not apparent here; nor does the Government argue that they are. The United States Naval Station at Guantanamo Bay consists of 45 square miles of land and water. The base has been used, at various points, to house migrants and refugees temporarily. At present, however, other than the detainees themselves, the only long-term residents are American military personnel, their families, and a small number of workers. The detainees have been deemed enemies of the United States. At present, dangerous as they may be if released, they are contained in a secure prison facility located on an isolated and heavily fortified military base.

There is no indication, furthermore, that adjudicating a habeas corpus petition would cause friction with the host government. No Cuban court has jurisdiction over American military personnel at Guantanamo or the enemy combatants detained there. While obligated to abide by the terms of the lease, the United States is, for all practical purposes, answerable to no other sovereign for its acts on the base. Were that not the case, or if the detention facility were located in an active theater of war, arguments that issuing the writ would be "impracticable or anomalous" would have more weight. See *Reid,* 354 U.S., at 74 (HARLAN, J., concurring in result). Under the facts presented here, however, there are few practical barriers to the running of the writ. To the extent barriers arise, habeas corpus procedures likely can be modified to address them.

It is true that before today the Court has never held that noncitizens detained by our Government in territory over which another country maintains *de jure* sovereignty have any rights under our Constitution. But the cases before us lack any precise historical parallel. They involve individuals detained by executive order for the duration of a conflict that, if measured from September 11, 2001, to the present, is already among the longest wars in American history. The detainees, moreover, are held in a territory that, while technically not part of the United States, is under the complete and total control of our Government. Under these circumstances the lack of a precedent on point is no barrier to our holding.

We hold that Art. I, §9, cl. 2, of the Constitution has full effect at Guantanamo Bay. If the privilege of habeas corpus is to be denied to the detainees now before us, Congress must act in accordance with the requirements of the Suspension Clause. Cf. *Hamdi,* 542 U.S., at 564 (SCALIA, J., dissenting) ("[I]ndefinite imprisonment on reasonable suspicion is not an available option of treatment for those accused of aiding the enemy, absent a suspension of the writ"). This Court may not impose a *de facto* suspension by abstaining from these controversies. The MCA does not purport to be a formal suspension of the writ; and the Government, in its submissions to us, has not argued that it is. Petitioners, therefore, are entitled to the privilege of habeas corpus to challenge the legality of their detention.

V

In light of this holding the question becomes whether the statute stripping jurisdiction to issue the writ avoids the Suspension Clause mandate because Congress has provided adequate substitute procedures for habeas corpus. The Government submits there has been compliance with the Suspension Clause because the DTA review process in the Court of Appeals, see DTA §1005(e), provides an adequate substitute. Congress has granted that court jurisdiction to consider

> "(i) whether the status determination of the [CSRT] . . . was consistent with the standards and procedures specified by the Secretary of Defense . . . and (ii) to the extent the Constitution and laws of the United States are applicable, whether the use of such standards and procedures to make the determination is consistent with the Constitution and laws of the United States." §1005(e)(2)(C), 119 Stat. 2742. . . .

A

Our case law does not contain extensive discussion of standards defining suspension of the writ or of circumstances under which suspension has occurred. This simply confirms the care Congress has taken throughout our Nation's history to preserve the writ and its function. Indeed, most of the major legislative enactments pertaining to habeas corpus have acted not to contract the writ's protection but to expand it or to hasten resolution of prisoners' claims. . . .

. . . [Unlike those statutes], here we confront statutes, the DTA and the MCA, that were intended to circumscribe habeas review. Congress' purpose is evident not only from the unequivocal nature of MCA §7's jurisdiction-stripping language, 28 U.S.C.A. §2241(e)(1) (Supp. 2007) ("No court, justice, or judge shall have jurisdiction to hear or consider an application for a writ of habeas corpus . . ."), but also from a comparison of the DTA to the statutes at issue in [cases construing habeas-strengthening statutes]. . . . When Congress has intended to replace traditional habeas corpus with habeas-like substitutes, . . . it has granted to the courts broad remedial powers to secure the historic office of the writ. . . .

In contrast, the DTA's jurisdictional grant is quite limited. The Court of Appeals has jurisdiction not to inquire into the legality of the detention generally but only to assess whether the CSRT complied with the "standards and procedures specified by the Secretary of Defense" and whether those standards and procedures are lawful. DTA

§1005(e)(2)(C), 119 Stat. 2742. If Congress had envisioned DTA review as coextensive with traditional habeas corpus, it would not have drafted the statute in this manner. . . . [M]oreover, there has been no effort to preserve habeas corpus review as an avenue of last resort. No saving clause exists in either the MCA or the DTA. And MCA §7 eliminates habeas review for these petitioners. . . .

To the extent any doubt remains about Congress' intent, the legislative history confirms what the plain text strongly suggests: In passing the DTA Congress did not intend to create a process that differs from traditional habeas corpus process in name only. It intended to create a more limited procedure. See, *e.g.,*151 Cong. Rec. S14263 (Dec. 21, 2005) (statement of Sen. Graham) (noting that the DTA "extinguish[es] these habeas and other actions in order to effect a transfer of jurisdiction over these cases to the DC Circuit Court" and agreeing that the bill "create[s] in their place a very limited judicial review of certain military administrative decisions"); *id.,* at S14268 (statement of Sen. Kyl) ("It is important to note that the limited judicial review authorized by paragraphs 2 and 3 of subsection (e) [of DTA §1005] are not habeas-corpus review. It is a limited judicial review of its own nature").

It is against this background that we must interpret the DTA and assess its adequacy as a substitute for habeas corpus. . . .

B

We do not endeavor to offer a comprehensive summary of the requisites for an adequate substitute for habeas corpus. We do consider it uncontroversial, however, that the privilege of habeas corpus entitles the prisoner to a meaningful opportunity to demonstrate that he is being held pursuant to "the erroneous application or interpretation" of relevant law. *St. Cyr,* 533 U.S., at 302. And the habeas court must have the power to order the conditional release of an individual unlawfully detained – though release need not be the exclusive remedy and is not the appropriate one in every case in which the writ is granted. These are the easily identified attributes of any constitutionally adequate habeas corpus proceeding. But, depending on the circumstances, more may be required.

Indeed, common-law habeas corpus was, above all, an adaptable remedy. Its precise application and scope changed depending upon the circumstances. It appears the common-law habeas court's role was most extensive in cases of pretrial and noncriminal detention, where there had been little or no previous judicial review of the cause for detention. Notably, the black-letter rule that prisoners could not controvert facts in the jailer's return was not followed (or at least not with consistency) in such cases.

There is evidence from 19th-century American sources indicating that, even in States that accorded strong res judicata effect to prior adjudications, habeas courts in this country routinely allowed prisoners to introduce exculpatory evidence that was either unknown or previously unavailable to the prisoner. . . .

The idea that the necessary scope of habeas review in part depends upon the rigor of any earlier proceedings accords with our test for procedural adequacy in the due process context. See Mathews v. Eldridge, 424 U.S. 319, 335 (1976) (noting that the Due Process Clause requires an assessment of, *inter alia,* "the risk of an erroneous deprivation of [a liberty interest;] and the probable value, if any, of additional or substitute procedural safeguards"). . . .

Accordingly, where relief is sought from a sentence that resulted from the judgment of a court of record, . . . considerable deference is owed to the court that ordered confinement. Likewise in those cases the prisoner should exhaust adequate alternative remedies before filing for the writ in federal court. Both aspects of federal habeas corpus review are justified because it can be assumed that, in the usual course, a court of record provides defendants with a fair, adversary proceeding. . . . The present cases fall outside these categories, however; for here the detention is by executive order.

Where a person is detained by executive order, rather than, say, after being tried and convicted in a court, the need for collateral review is most pressing. A criminal conviction in the usual course occurs after a judicial hearing before a tribunal disinterested in the outcome and committed to procedures designed to ensure its own independence. These dynamics are not inherent in executive detention orders or executive review procedures. In this context the need for habeas corpus is more urgent. The intended duration of the detention and the reasons for it bear upon the precise scope of the inquiry. Habeas corpus proceedings need not resemble a criminal trial, even when the detention is by executive order. But the writ must be effective. The habeas court must have sufficient authority to conduct a meaningful review of both the cause for detention and the Executive's power to detain.

To determine the necessary scope of habeas corpus review, therefore, we must assess the CSRT process, the mechanism through which petitioners' designation as enemy combatants became final. Whether one characterizes the CSRT process as direct review of the Executive's battlefield determination that the detainee is an enemy combatant – as the parties have and as we do – or as the first step in the collateral review of a battlefield determination makes no difference in a proper analysis of whether the procedures Congress put in place are an adequate substitute for habeas corpus. What matters is the sum total of procedural protections afforded to the detainee at all stages, direct and collateral.

Petitioners identify what they see as myriad deficiencies in the CSRTs. The most relevant for our purposes are the constraints upon the detainee's ability to rebut the factual basis for the Government's assertion that he is an enemy combatant. As already noted, at the CSRT stage the detainee has limited means to find or present evidence to challenge the Government's case against him. He does not have the assistance of counsel and may not be aware of the most critical allegations that the Government relied upon to order his detention. See App. to Pet. for Cert. in No. 06-1196, at 156, ¶F(8) (noting that the detainee can access only the "unclassified portion of the Government Information"). The detainee can confront witnesses that testify during the CSRT proceedings. *Id.,* at 144, ¶g(8). But given that there are in effect no limits on the admission of hearsay evidence – the only requirement is that the tribunal deem the evidence "relevant and helpful," *ibid.,* ¶g(9) – the detainee's opportunity to question witnesses is likely to be more theoretical than real. . . .

Even if we were to assume that the CSRTs satisfy due process standards, it would not end our inquiry. Habeas corpus is a collateral process that exists, in Justice Holmes' words, to "cu[t] through all forms and g[o] to the very tissue of the structure. It comes in from the outside, not in subordination to the proceedings, and although every form may have been preserved opens the inquiry whether they have been more than an empty shell." Frank v. Mangum, 237 U.S. 309, 346 (1915) (dissenting opinion). Even when the procedures authorizing detention are structurally sound, the Suspension Clause remains applicable and the writ relevant. See 2 Chambers, Course of Lectures on English Law 1767-1773, at 6 ("Liberty may be violated either by arbitrary *imprisonment* without law or the appearance of law, or by a lawful magistrate for an unlawful reason"). . . .

Although we make no judgment as to whether the CSRTs, as currently constituted, satisfy due process standards, we agree with petitioners that, even when all the parties involved in this process act with diligence and in good faith, there is considerable risk of error in the tribunal's findings of fact. This is a risk inherent in any process that, in the words of the former Chief Judge of the Court of Appeals, is "closed and accusatorial." See [Bismullah v. Gates, 514 F.3d 1291, 1296 (D.C. Cir. 2008)] (Ginsburg, C.J., concurring in denial of rehearing en banc). And given that the consequence of error may be detention of persons for the duration of hostilities that may last a generation or more, this is a risk too significant to ignore.

For the writ of habeas corpus, or its substitute, to function as an effective and proper remedy in this context, the court that conducts the habeas proceeding must have the means to correct errors that occurred during the CSRT proceedings. This includes some authority to assess the sufficiency of the Government's evidence against the detainee. It also must have the authority to admit and consider relevant exculpatory evidence that was not introduced during the earlier proceeding. . . .

The extent of the showing required of the Government in these cases is a matter to be determined. We need not explore it further at this stage. We do hold that when the judicial power to issue habeas corpus properly is invoked the judicial officer must have adequate authority to make a determination in light of the relevant law and facts and to formulate and issue appropriate orders for relief, including, if necessary, an order directing the prisoner's release.

C

We now consider whether the DTA allows the Court of Appeals to conduct a proceeding meeting these standards. "[W]e are obligated to construe the statute to avoid [constitutional] problems" if it is "'fairly possible'" to do so. *St. Cyr*, 533 U.S., at 299-300 (quoting Crowell v. Benson, 285 U.S. 22, 62 (1932)). There are limits to this principle, however. The canon of constitutional avoidance does not supplant traditional modes of statutory interpretation. See Clark v. Martinez, 543 U.S. 371, 385 (2005) ("The canon of constitutional avoidance comes into play only when, after the application of ordinary textual analysis, the statute is found to be susceptible of more than one construction; and the canon functions as *a means of choosing between them*"). We cannot ignore the text and purpose of a statute in order to save it.

The DTA does not explicitly empower the Court of Appeals to order the applicant in a DTA review proceeding released should the court find that the standards and procedures used at his CSRT hearing were insufficient to justify detention. This is troubling. Yet, for present purposes, we can assume congressional silence permits a constitutionally required remedy. . . .

The absence of a release remedy and specific language allowing AUMF challenges are not the only constitutional infirmities from which the statute potentially suffers, however. The more difficult question is whether the DTA permits the Court of Appeals to make requisite findings of fact. The DTA enables petitioners to request "review" of their CSRT determination in the Court of Appeals, DTA §1005(e)(2)(B)(i), 119 Stat. 2742; but the "Scope of Review" provision confines the Court of Appeals' role to reviewing whether the CSRT followed the "standards and procedures" issued by the Department of Defense and assessing whether those "standards and procedures" are lawful. §1005(e)(C), *ibid.* Among these standards is "the requirement that the conclusion of the Tribunal be supported by a preponderance of the evidence . . . allowing a rebuttable presumption in favor of the Government's evidence." §1005(e)(C)(i), *ibid.*

Assuming the DTA can be construed to allow the Court of Appeals to review or correct the CSRT's factual determinations, as opposed to merely certifying that the tribunal applied the correct standard of proof, we see no way to construe the statute to allow what is also constitutionally required in this context: an opportunity for the detainee to present relevant exculpatory evidence that was not made part of the record in the earlier proceedings.

On its face the statute allows the Court of Appeals to consider no evidence outside the CSRT record. . . .

By foreclosing consideration of evidence not presented or reasonably available to the detainee at the CSRT proceedings, the DTA disadvantages the detainee by limiting the scope of collateral review to a record that may not be accurate or complete. In other contexts, *e.g.*, in post-trial habeas cases where the prisoner already has had a full and fair opportunity to develop the factual predicate of his claims, similar limitations on the scope of habeas review may be appropriate. In this context, however, where the underlying detention proceedings lack the necessary adversarial character, the detainee cannot be held responsible for all deficiencies in the record. . . .

We do not imply DTA review would be a constitutionally sufficient replacement for habeas corpus but for these limitations on the detainee's ability to present exculpatory evidence. For even if it were possible, as a textual matter, to read into the statute each of the necessary procedures we have identified, we could not overlook the cumulative effect of our doing so. To hold that the detainees at Guantanamo may, under the DTA, challenge the President's legal authority to detain them, contest the CSRT's findings of fact, supplement the record on review with exculpatory evidence, and request an order of release would come close to reinstating the §2241 habeas corpus process Congress sought to deny them. The language of the statute, read in light of Congress' reasons for enacting it, cannot bear this interpretation. Petitioners have met their burden of establishing that the DTA review process is, on its face, an inadequate substitute for habeas corpus.

Although we do not hold that an adequate substitute must duplicate §2241 in all respects, it suffices that the Government has not established that the detainees' access to the statutory review provisions at issue is an adequate substitute for the writ of habeas corpus. MCA §7 thus effects an unconstitutional suspension of the writ. In view of our holding we need not discuss the reach of the writ with respect to claims of unlawful conditions of treatment or confinement.

VI

A

In light of our conclusion that there is no jurisdictional bar to the District Court's entertaining petitioners' claims the question remains whether there are prudential barriers to habeas corpus review under these circumstances.

The Government argues petitioners must seek review of their CSRT determinations in the Court of Appeals before they can proceed with their habeas corpus actions in the District Court. . . .

The real risks, the real threats, of terrorist attacks are constant and not likely soon to abate. The ways to disrupt our life and laws are so many and unforeseen that the Court should not attempt even some general catalogue of crises that might occur. Certain principles are apparent, however. Practical considerations and exigent circumstances inform the definition and reach of the law's writs, including habeas corpus. The cases and our tradition reflect this precept.

In cases involving foreign citizens detained abroad by the Executive, it likely would be both an impractical and unprecedented extension of judicial power to assume that habeas corpus would be available at the moment the prisoner is taken into custody. If and when habeas corpus jurisdiction applies, as it does in these cases, then proper deference can be accorded to reasonable procedures for screening and initial detention under lawful and proper conditions of confinement and treatment for a reasonable period of time. Domestic exigencies, furthermore, might also impose such onerous burdens on the Government that here, too, the

Judicial Branch would be required to devise sensible rules for staying habeas corpus proceedings until the Government can comply with its requirements in a responsible way. Cf. Ex parte Milligan, 4 Wall., at 127 ("If, in foreign invasion or civil war, the courts are actually closed, and it is impossible to administer criminal justice according to law, *then,* on the theatre of active military operations, where war really prevails, there is a necessity to furnish a substitute for the civil authority, thus overthrown, to preserve the safety of the army and society; and as no power is left but the military, it is allowed to govern by martial rule until the laws can have their free course"). Here, as is true with detainees apprehended abroad, a relevant consideration in determining the courts' role is whether there are suitable alternative processes in place to protect against the arbitrary exercise of governmental power.

The cases before us, however, do not involve detainees who have been held for a short period of time while awaiting their CSRT determinations. Were that the case, or were it probable that the Court of Appeals could complete a prompt review of their applications, the case for requiring temporary abstention or exhaustion of alternative remedies would be much stronger. These qualifications no longer pertain here. In some of these cases six years have elapsed without the judicial oversight that habeas corpus or an adequate substitute demands. And there has been no showing that the Executive faces such onerous burdens that it cannot respond to habeas corpus actions. To require these detainees to complete DTA review before proceeding with their habeas corpus actions would be to require additional months, if not years, of delay. The first DTA review applications were filed over a year ago, but no decisions on the merits have been issued. While some delay in fashioning new procedures is unavoidable, the costs of delay can no longer be borne by those who are held in custody. The detainees in these cases are entitled to a prompt habeas corpus hearing.

Our decision today holds only that the petitioners before us are entitled to seek the writ; that the DTA review procedures are an inadequate substitute for habeas corpus; and that the petitioners in these cases need not exhaust the review procedures in the Court of Appeals before proceeding with their habeas actions in the District Court. The only law we identify as unconstitutional is MCA §7, 28 U.S.C.A. §2241(e) (Supp. 2007). Accordingly, both the DTA and the CSRT process remain intact. Our holding with regard to exhaustion should not be read to imply that a habeas court should intervene the moment an enemy combatant steps foot in a territory where the writ runs. The Executive is entitled to a reasonable period of time to determine a detainee's status before a court entertains that detainee's habeas corpus petition. The CSRT process is the mechanism Congress and the President set up to deal with these issues. Except in cases of undue delay, federal courts should refrain from entertaining an enemy combatant's habeas corpus petition at least until after the Department, acting via the CSRT, has had a chance to review his status.

B

Although we hold that the DTA is not an adequate and effective substitute for habeas corpus, it does not follow that a habeas corpus court may disregard the dangers the detention in these cases was intended to prevent. . . . [T]he Suspension Clause does not resist innovation in the field of habeas corpus. Certain accommodations can be made to reduce the burden habeas corpus proceedings will place on the military without impermissibly diluting the protections of the writ.

In the DTA Congress sought to consolidate review of petitioners' claims in the Court of Appeals. Channeling future cases to one district court would no doubt reduce administrative burdens on the Government. This is a legitimate objective that might be advanced even without an amendment to §2241. If, in a future case, a detainee files a habeas petition in another judicial district in which a proper respondent can be served, see Rumsfeld v. Padilla, 542 U.S. 426, 435-436 (2004), the Government can move for change of venue to the court that will hear these petitioners' cases, the United States District Court for the District of Columbia.

Another of Congress' reasons for vesting exclusive jurisdiction in the Court of Appeals, perhaps, was to avoid the widespread dissemination of classified information. The Government has raised similar concerns here and elsewhere. We make no attempt to anticipate all of the evidentiary and access-to-counsel issues that will arise during the course of the detainees' habeas corpus proceedings. We recognize, however, that the Government has a legitimate interest in protecting sources and methods of intelligence gathering; and we expect that the District Court will use its discretion to accommodate this interest to the greatest extent possible. Cf. United States v. Reynolds, 345 U.S. 1, 10 (1953) (recognizing an evidentiary privilege in a civil damages case where "there is a reasonable danger that compulsion of the evidence will expose military matters which, in the interest of national security, should not be divulged").

These and the other remaining questions are within the expertise and competence of the District Court to address in the first instance.

* * *

In considering both the procedural and substantive standards used to impose detention to prevent acts of terrorism, proper deference must be accorded to the political branches. See United States v. Curtiss-Wright Export Corp., 299 U.S. 304, 320 (1936). Unlike the President and some designated Members of Congress, neither the Members of this Court nor most federal judges begin the day with briefings that may describe new and serious threats to our Nation and its people. The law must accord the Executive substantial authority to apprehend and detain those who pose a real danger to our security.

Officials charged with daily operational responsibility for our security may consider a judicial discourse on the history of the Habeas Corpus Act of 1679 and like matters to be far removed from the Nation's present, urgent concerns. Established legal doctrine, however, must be consulted for its teaching. Remote in time it may be; irrelevant to the present it is not. Security depends upon a sophisticated intelligence apparatus and the ability of our Armed Forces to act and to interdict. There are further considerations, however. Security subsists, too, in fidelity to freedom's first principles. Chief among these are freedom from arbitrary and unlawful restraint and the personal liberty that is secured by adherence to the separation of powers. It is from these principles that the judicial authority to consider petitions for habeas corpus relief derives.

Our opinion does not undermine the Executive's powers as Commander in Chief. On the contrary, the exercise of those powers is vindicated, not eroded, when confirmed by the Judicial Branch. Within the Constitution's separation-of-powers structure, few exercises of judicial power are as legitimate or as necessary as the responsibility to hear challenges to the authority of the Executive to imprison a person. Some of these petitioners have been in custody for six years with no definitive judicial determination as to the legality of their detention. Their access to the writ is a necessity to determine the lawfulness of their status, even if, in the end, they do not obtain the relief they seek.

Because our Nation's past military conflicts have been of limited duration, it has been possible to leave the outer boundaries of war powers undefined. If, as some fear, terrorism continues to pose dangerous threats to us for years to come, the Court might not have this luxury. This result is not inevitable, however. The political branches, consistent with their independent obligations to interpret and uphold the Constitution, can engage in a genuine debate about how best to preserve constitutional values while protecting the Nation from terrorism. Cf. *Hamdan* [v. Rumsfeld, 548 U.S. 557 (2006)], at 636 (BREYER, J., concurring) ("[J]udicial insistence upon that consultation does not weaken our Nation's ability to deal with danger. To the contrary, that insistence strengthens the Nation's ability to determine – through democratic means – how best to do so").

It bears repeating that our opinion does not address the content of the law that governs petitioners' detention. That is a matter yet to be determined. We hold that petitioners may invoke the fundamental procedural protections of habeas corpus. The laws and Constitution are designed to survive, and remain in force, in extraordinary times. Liberty and security can be reconciled; and in our system they are reconciled within the framework of the law. The Framers decided that habeas corpus, a right of first importance, must be a part of that framework, a part of that law.

The determination by the Court of Appeals that the Suspension Clause and its protections are inapplicable to petitioners was in error. The judgment of the Court of Appeals is reversed. The cases are remanded to the Court of Appeals with instructions that it remand the cases to the District Court for proceedings consistent with this opinion.

It is so ordered.

JUSTICE SOUTER, with whom JUSTICE GINSBURG and JUSTICE BREYER join, concurring. . . . A . . . fact insufficiently appreciated by the dissents is the length of the disputed imprisonments, some of the prisoners represented here today having been locked up for six years. Hence the hollow ring when the dissenters suggest that the Court is somehow precipitating the judiciary into reviewing claims that the military (subject to appeal to the Court of Appeals for the District of Columbia Circuit) could handle within some reasonable period of time. These suggestions of judicial haste are all the more out of place given the Court's realistic acknowledgment that in periods of exigency the tempo of any habeas review must reflect the immediate peril facing the country.

It is in fact the very lapse of four years from the time *Rasul* put everyone on notice that habeas process was available to Guantanamo prisoners, and the lapse of six years since some of these prisoners were captured and incarcerated, that stand at odds with the repeated suggestions of the dissenters that these cases should be seen as a judicial victory in a contest for power between the Court and the political branches. The several answers to the charge of triumphalism might start with a basic fact of Anglo-American constitutional history: that the power, first of the Crown and now of the Executive Branch of the United States, is necessarily limited by habeas corpus jurisdiction to enquire into the legality of executive detention. And one could explain that in this Court's exercise of responsibility to preserve habeas corpus something much more significant is involved than pulling and hauling between the judicial and political branches. Instead, though, it is enough to repeat that some of these petitioners have spent six years behind bars. After six years of sustained executive detentions in Guantanamo, subject to habeas jurisdiction but without any actual habeas scrutiny, today's decision is no judicial victory, but an act of perseverance in trying to make habeas review, and the obligation of the courts to provide it, mean something of value both to prisoners and to the Nation.

CHIEF JUSTICE ROBERTS, with whom JUSTICE SCALIA, JUSTICE THOMAS, and JUSTICE ALITO join, dissenting. Today the Court strikes down as inadequate the most generous set of procedural protections ever afforded aliens detained by this country as enemy combatants. The political branches crafted these procedures amidst an ongoing military conflict, after much careful investigation and thorough debate. The Court rejects them today out of hand, without bothering to say what due process rights the detainees possess, without explaining how the statute fails to vindicate those rights, and before a single petitioner has even attempted to avail himself of the law's operation. And to what effect? The majority merely replaces a review system designed by the people's representatives with a set of shapeless procedures to be defined by federal courts at some future date. One cannot help but think, after surveying the modest practical results of the majority's ambitious opinion, that this decision is not really about the detainees at all, but about control of federal policy regarding enemy combatants. . . .

. . . The important point for me, however, is that the Court should have resolved these cases on other grounds. Habeas is most fundamentally a procedural right, a mechanism for contesting the legality of executive detention. The critical threshold question in these cases, prior to any inquiry about the writ's scope, is whether the system the political branches designed protects whatever rights the detainees may possess. If so, there is no need for any additional process, whether called "habeas" or something else. . . .

I . . .

The political branches created a two-part, collateral review procedure for testing the legality of the prisoners' detention: It begins with a hearing before a Combatant Status Review Tribunal (CSRT) followed by review in the D.C. Circuit. As part of that review, Congress authorized the D.C. Circuit to decide whether the CSRT proceedings are consistent with "the Constitution and laws of the United States." DTA §1005(e)(2)(C), 119 Stat. 2742. No petitioner, however, has invoked the D.C. Circuit review the statute specifies. As a consequence, that court has had no occasion to decide whether the CSRT hearings, followed by review in the Court of Appeals, vindicate whatever constitutional and statutory rights petitioners may possess.

Remarkably, this Court does not require petitioners to exhaust their remedies under the statute; it does not wait to see whether those remedies will prove sufficient to protect petitioners' rights. Instead, it not only denies the D.C. Circuit the opportunity to assess the statute's remedies, it refuses to do so itself: the majority expressly declines to decide whether the CSRT procedures, coupled with Article III review, satisfy due process. . . .

. . . If the majority were truly concerned about delay, it would have required petitioners to use the DTA process that has been available to them for 2 1/2 years, with its Article III review in the D.C. Circuit. That system might well have provided petitioners all the relief to which they are entitled long before the Court's newly installed habeas review could hope to do so.[1] . . .

---

1. In light of the foregoing, the concurrence is wrong to suggest that I "insufficiently appreciat[e]" the issue of delay in these cases. This Court issued its decisions in Rasul v. Bush, 542 U.S. 466, and Hamdi v. Rumsfeld 542 U.S. 507, in 2004. The concurrence makes it sound as if the political branches have done nothing in the interim. In fact, Congress responded 18 months later by enacting the DTA. Congress cannot be faulted for taking that time to consider how best to accommodate both the detainees' interests and the need to keep the American people safe. Since the DTA became law, petitioners have steadfastly refused to avail themselves of the statute's review mechanisms. It is unfair to complain that the DTA system involves too much delay when petitioners have consistently refused to use it, preferring to litigate instead. Today's decision obligating district courts to craft new procedures to replace those in the DTA will only prolong the process – and delay relief.

II . . .

. . . After much hemming and hawing, the majority appears to concede that the DTA provides an Article III court competent to order release. The only issue in dispute is the process the Guantanamo prisoners are entitled to use to test the legality of their detention. . . .

A . . .

. . . [T]he *Hamdi* plurality concluded that [two-layered] . . . review would be enough to satisfy due process, even for citizens. Congress followed the Court's lead, only to find itself the victim of a constitutional bait and switch.

Hamdi merits scant attention from the Court – a remarkable omission, as *Hamdi* bears directly on the issues before us. The majority attempts to dismiss *Hamdi*'s relevance by arguing that because the availability of §2241 federal habeas was never in doubt in that case, "the Court had no occasion to define the necessary scope of habeas review . . . in the context of enemy combatant detentions." Hardly. *Hamdi* was all about the scope of habeas review in the context of enemy combatant detentions. The petitioner, an American citizen held within the United States as an enemy combatant, invoked the writ to challenge his detention. After "a careful examination both of the writ . . . and of the Due Process Clause," this Court enunciated the "basic process" the Constitution entitled Hamdi to expect from a habeas court under §2241. That process consisted of the right to "receive notice of the factual basis for his classification, and a fair opportunity to rebut the Government's factual assertions before a neutral decisionmaker." In light of the Government's national security responsibilities, the plurality found the process could be "tailored to alleviate [the] uncommon potential to burden the Executive at a time of ongoing military conflict." For example, the Government could rely on hearsay and could claim a presumption in favor of its own evidence.

Hamdi further suggested that this "basic process" on collateral review could be provided by a military tribunal. It pointed to prisoner-of-war tribunals as a model that would satisfy the Constitution's requirements. Only "[i]n the *absence* of such process" before a military tribunal, the Court held, would Article III courts need to conduct full-dress habeas proceedings to "ensure that the minimum requirements of due process are achieved." *Ibid.* (emphasis added). And even then, the petitioner would be entitled to no more process than he would have received from a properly constituted military review panel, given his limited due process rights and the Government's weighty interests.

Contrary to the majority, *Hamdi* is of pressing relevance because it establishes the procedures American *citizens* detained as enemy combatants can expect from a habeas court proceeding under §2241. The DTA system of military tribunal hearings followed by Article III review looks a lot like the procedure *Hamdi* blessed. If nothing else, it is plain from the design of the DTA that Congress, the President, and this Nation's military leaders have made a good-faith effort to follow our precedent.

The Court, however, will not take "yes" for an answer. . . .

B . . .

By virtue of its refusal to allow the D.C. Circuit to assess petitioners' statutory remedies, and by virtue of its own refusal to consider, at the outset, the fit between those remedies and due process, the majority now finds itself in the position of evaluating whether the DTA system is an adequate substitute for habeas review without knowing what rights either habeas or the DTA is supposed to protect. . . .

For my part, I will assume that any due process rights petitioners may possess are no greater than those of American citizens detained as enemy combatants. It is worth noting again that the *Hamdi* controlling opinion said the Constitution guarantees citizen detainees only "basic" procedural rights, and that the process for securing those rights can "be tailored to alleviate [the] uncommon potential to burden the Executive at a time of ongoing military conflict." The majority, however, objects that "the procedural protections afforded to the detainees in the CSRT hearings are . . . limited." But the evidentiary and other limitations the Court complains of reflect the nature of the issue in contest, namely, the status of aliens captured by our Armed Forces abroad and alleged to be enemy combatants. Contrary to the repeated suggestions of the majority, DTA review need not parallel the habeas privileges enjoyed by noncombatant American citizens, as set out in 28 U.S.C. §2241 (2000 ed. and Supp. V). It need only provide process adequate for noncitizens detained as alleged combatants. . . .

III . . .

The majority rests its decision on abstract and hypothetical concerns. Step back and consider what, in the real world, Congress and the

Executive have actually granted aliens captured by our Armed Forces overseas and found to be enemy combatants:

- The right to hear the bases of the charges against them, including a summary of any classified evidence.
- The ability to challenge the bases of their detention before military tribunals modeled after Geneva Convention procedures. Some 38 detainees have been released as a result of this process.
- The right, before the CSRT, to testify, introduce evidence, call witnesses, question those the Government calls, and secure release, if and when appropriate.
- The right to the aid of a personal representative in arranging and presenting their cases before a CSRT.
- Before the D.C. Circuit, the right to employ counsel, challenge the factual record, contest the lower tribunal's legal determinations, ensure compliance with the Constitution and laws, and secure release, if any errors below establish their entitlement to such relief.

In sum, the DTA satisfies the majority's own criteria for assessing adequacy. This statutory scheme provides the combatants held at Guantanamo greater procedural protections than have ever been afforded alleged enemy detainees – whether citizens or aliens – in our national history. . . .

I respectfully dissent.

JUSTICE SCALIA, with whom THE CHIEF JUSTICE, JUSTICE THOMAS, and JUSTICE ALITO join, dissenting. . . . Contrary to my usual practice, . . . I think it appropriate to begin with a description of the disastrous consequences of what the Court has done today.

I

America is at war with radical Islamists. . . .

The game of bait-and-switch that today's opinion plays upon the Nation's Commander in Chief will make the war harder on us. It will almost certainly cause more Americans to be killed. That consequence would be tolerable if necessary to preserve a time-honored legal principle vital to our constitutional Republic. But it is this Court's blatant *abandonment* of such a principle that produces the decision today. The President relied on our settled precedent in Johnson v. Eisentrager, 339 U.S. 763 (1950), when he established the prison at Guantanamo Bay for enemy aliens. Citing that case, the President's Office of Legal Counsel advised him "that the great weight of legal authority indicates that a federal district court could not properly exercise habeas jurisdiction over an alien detained at [Guantanamo Bay]." Memorandum from Patrick F. Philbin and John C. Yoo, Deputy Assistant Attorneys General, Office of Legal Counsel, to William J. Haynes II, General Counsel, Dept. of Defense (Dec. 28, 2001). Had the law been otherwise, the military surely would not have transported prisoners there, but would have kept them in Afghanistan, transferred them to another of our foreign military bases, or turned them over to allies for detention. Those other facilities might well have been worse for the detainees themselves.

In the long term, then, the Court's decision today accomplishes little, except perhaps to reduce the well-being of enemy combatants that the Court ostensibly seeks to protect. In the short term, however, the decision is devastating. At least 30 of those prisoners hitherto released from Guantanamo Bay have returned to the battlefield. Some have been captured or killed. But others have succeeded in carrying on their atrocities against innocent civilians. . . .

These, mind you, were detainees whom *the military* had concluded were not enemy combatants. Their return to the kill illustrates the incredible difficulty of assessing who is and who is not an enemy combatant in a foreign theater of operations where the environment does not lend itself to rigorous evidence collection. Astoundingly, the Court today raises the bar, requiring military officials to appear before civilian courts and defend their decisions under procedural and evidentiary rules that go beyond what Congress has specified. As THE CHIEF JUSTICE's dissent makes clear, we have no idea what those procedural and evidentiary rules are, but they will be determined by civil courts and (in the Court's contemplation at least) will be more detainee-friendly than those now applied, since otherwise there would no reason to hold the congressionally prescribed procedures unconstitutional. If they impose a higher standard of proof (from foreign battlefields) than the current procedures require, the number of the enemy returned to combat will obviously increase.

But even when the military has evidence that it can bring forward, it is often foolhardy to release that evidence to the attorneys representing our enemies. And one escalation of procedures that the Court *is* clear about is affording the detainees increased access to witnesses (perhaps troops serving in Afghanistan?) and to classified information. During the 1995 prosecution of Omar Abdel Rahman, federal prosecutors gave the names of 200 unindicted co-conspirators to the "Blind Sheik's" defense lawyers; that information was in the hands of Osama Bin Laden within two weeks. In another case, trial testimony revealed to the enemy that the United States had been monitoring their cellular network, whereupon they promptly stopped using it, enabling more of them to evade capture and continue their atrocities. . . .

. . . The Court today decrees that no good reason to accept the judgment of the other two branches is "apparent." "The Government," it declares, "presents no credible arguments that the military mission at Guantanamo would be compromised if habeas corpus courts had jurisdiction to hear the detainees' claims." What competence does the Court have to second-guess the judgment of Congress and the President on such a point? None whatever. But the Court blunders in nonetheless. Henceforth, as today's opinion makes unnervingly clear, how to handle enemy prisoners in this war will ultimately lie with the branch that knows least about the national security concerns that the subject entails.

II

A . . .

. . . The Court admits that it cannot determine whether the writ historically extended to aliens held abroad, and it concedes (necessarily) that Guantanamo Bay lies outside the sovereign territory of the United States. Together, these two concessions establish that it is (in the Court's view) perfectly ambiguous whether the common-law writ would have provided a remedy for these petitioners. If that is so, the Court has no basis to strike down the Military Commissions Act, and must leave undisturbed the considered judgment of the coequal branches.

How, then, does the Court weave a clear constitutional prohibition out of pure interpretive equipoise? The Court resorts to "fundamental separation-of-powers principles" to interpret the Suspension Clause. According to the Court, because "the writ of habeas corpus is itself an indispensable mechanism for monitoring the separation of powers," the test of its extraterritorial reach "must not be subject to manipulation by those whose power it is designed to restrain."

That approach distorts the nature of the separation of powers and its role in the constitutional structure. The "fundamental separation-of-powers principles" that the Constitution embodies are to be derived not from some judicially imagined matrix, but from the sum total of the individual separation-of-powers provisions that the Constitution sets forth. Only by considering them one-by-one does the full shape of the

Constitution's separation-of-powers principles emerge. It is nonsensical to interpret those provisions themselves in light of some general "separation-of-powers principles" dreamed up by the Court. Rather, they must be interpreted to mean what they were understood to mean when the people ratified them. And if the understood scope of the writ of habeas corpus was "designed to restrain" (as the Court says) the actions of the Executive, the understood *limits* upon that scope were (as the Court seems not to grasp) just as much "designed to restrain" the incursions of the Third Branch. "Manipulation" of the territorial reach of the writ by the Judiciary poses just as much a threat to the proper separation of powers as "manipulation" by the Executive. As I will show below, manipulation is what is afoot here. The understood limits upon the writ deny our jurisdiction over the habeas petitions brought by these enemy aliens, and entrust the President with the crucial wartime determinations about their status and continued confinement.

B

The Court purports to derive from our precedents a "functional" test for the extraterritorial reach of the writ, which shows that the Military Commissions Act unconstitutionally restricts the scope of habeas. That is remarkable because the most pertinent of those precedents, Johnson v. Eisentrager, 339 U.S. 763, conclusively establishes the opposite. . . .

The Court would have us believe that *Eisentrager* rested on "[p]ractical considerations," such as the "difficulties of ordering the Government to produce the prisoners in a habeas corpus proceeding." Formal sovereignty, says the Court, is merely one consideration "that bears upon which constitutional guarantees apply" in a given location. This is a sheer rewriting of the case. *Eisentrager* mentioned practical concerns, to be sure – but not for the purpose of determining *under what circumstances* American courts could issue writs of habeas corpus for aliens abroad. It cited them to support *its holding* that the Constitution does not empower courts to issue writs of habeas corpus to aliens abroad *in any circumstances*. . . .

. . . *Eisentrager* nowhere mentions a "functional" test, and the notion that it is based upon such a principle is patently false. . . .

The category of prisoner comparable to these detainees are not the *Eisentrager* criminal defendants, but the more than 400,000 prisoners of war detained in the United States alone during World War II. Not a single one was accorded the right to have his detention validated by a habeas corpus action in federal court – and that despite the fact that they were present on U.S. soil. The Court's analysis produces a crazy result: Whereas those convicted and sentenced to death for war crimes are without judicial remedy, all enemy combatants detained during a war, at least insofar as they are confined in an area away from the battlefield over which the United States exercises "absolute and indefinite" control, may seek a writ of habeas corpus in federal court. And, as an even more bizarre implication from the Court's reasoning, those prisoners whom the military plans to try by full-dress Commission at a future date may file habeas petitions and secure release before their trials take place. . . .

III

Putting aside the conclusive precedent of *Eisentrager,* it is clear that the original understanding of the Suspension Clause was that habeas corpus was not available to aliens abroad, as Judge Randolph's thorough opinion for the court below detailed. . . .

. . . [*A*]*ll* available historical evidence points to the conclusion that the writ would not have been available at common law for aliens captured and held outside the sovereign territory of the Crown. Despite three opening briefs, three reply briefs, and support from a legion of *amici,* petitioners have failed to identify a single case in the history of Anglo-American law that supports their claim to jurisdiction. The Court finds it significant that there is no recorded case *denying* jurisdiction to such prisoners either. But a case standing for the remarkable proposition that the writ could issue to a foreign land would surely have been reported, whereas a case denying such a writ for lack of jurisdiction would likely not. At a minimum, the absence of a reported case either way leaves unrefuted the voluminous commentary stating that habeas was confined to the dominions of the Crown.

What history teaches is confirmed by the nature of the limitations that the Constitution places upon suspension of the common-law writ. It can be suspended only "in Cases of Rebellion or Invasion." Art. I, §9, cl. 2. The latter case (invasion) is plainly limited to the territory of the United States; and while it is conceivable that a rebellion could be mounted by American citizens abroad, surely the overwhelming majority of its occurrences would be domestic. If the extraterritorial scope of habeas turned on flexible, "functional" considerations, as the Court holds, why would the Constitution limit its suspension almost entirely to instances of domestic crisis? Surely there is an even greater justification for suspension in foreign lands where the United States might hold prisoners of war during an ongoing conflict. And correspondingly, there is less threat to liberty when the Government suspends the writ's (supposed) application in foreign lands, where even on the most extreme view prisoners are entitled to fewer constitutional rights. It makes no sense, therefore, for the Constitution generally to forbid suspension of the writ abroad if indeed the writ has application there. . . .

The Nation will live to regret what the Court has done today. I dissent.

Page 702. Insert the following material after Note 8.

D. AVAILABILITY OF THE WRIT TO U.S. CITIZENS ABROAD

Munaf v. Geren

United States Supreme Court, 2008
128 S. Ct. 2207

CHIEF JUSTICE ROBERTS delivered the opinion of the Court. The Multinational Force-Iraq (MNF-I) is an international coalition force operating in Iraq composed of 26 different nations, including the United States. The force operates under the unified command of United States military officers, at the request of the Iraqi Government, and in accordance with United Nations (U.N.) Security Council Resolutions. Pursuant to the U.N. mandate, MNF-I forces detain individuals alleged to have committed hostile or warlike acts in Iraq, pending investigation and prosecution in Iraqi courts under Iraqi law.

These consolidated cases concern the availability of habeas corpus relief arising from the MNF-I's detention of American citizens who voluntarily traveled to Iraq and are alleged to have committed crimes there. We are confronted with two questions. *First,* do United States courts have jurisdiction over habeas corpus petitions filed on behalf of American citizens challenging their detention in Iraq by the MNF-I? *Second,* if such jurisdiction exists, may district courts exercise that jurisdiction to enjoin the MNF-I from transferring such individuals to Iraqi custody or allowing them to be tried before Iraqi courts?

We conclude that the habeas statute extends to American citizens held overseas by American forces operating subject to an American chain of command, even when those forces are acting as part of a multinational coalition. Under circumstances such as those presented here, however, habeas corpus provides petitioners with no relief.

I . . .

MNF-I forces . . . detain individuals who pose a threat to the security of Iraq. The Government of Iraq retains ultimate responsibility for the arrest and imprisonment of individuals who violate its laws, but because many of Iraq's prison facilities have been destroyed, the MNF-I agreed to maintain physical custody of many such individuals during Iraqi criminal proceedings. . . . An American military unit . . . oversees detention operations and facilities in Iraq, including those located at Camp Cropper, the detention facility currently housing Shawqi Omar and Mohammad Munaf (hereinafter petitioners). . . .

A

Petitioner Shawqi Omar, an American-Jordanian citizen, voluntarily traveled to Iraq in 2002. In October 2004, Omar was captured and detained in Iraq by U.S. military forces operating as part of the MNF-I during a raid of his Baghdad home. Omar is believed to have provided aid to Abu Musab al-Zarqawi – the late leader of al Qaeda in Iraq – by facilitating his group's connection with other terrorist groups, bringing foreign fighters into Iraq, and planning and executing kidnappings in Iraq. . . .

Following Omar's arrest, a three-member MNF-I Tribunal composed of American military officers concluded that Omar posed a threat to the security of Iraq and designated him a "security internee." The tribunal also found that Omar had committed hostile and warlike acts, and that he was an enemy combatant in the war on terrorism. . . .

. . . At all times since his capture, Omar has remained in the custody of the United States military operating as part of the MNF-I.

Omar's wife and son filed a next-friend petition for a writ of habeas corpus on Omar's behalf in the District Court for the District of Columbia. After the Department of Justice informed Omar that the MNF-I had decided to refer him to the Central Criminal Court of Iraq (CCCI) for criminal proceedings, his attorney sought and obtained a preliminary injunction barring Omar's "remov[al] . . . from United States or MNF-I custody." . . . The United States appealed and the Court of Appeals for the District of Columbia Circuit affirmed. . . .

B

Petitioner Munaf, a citizen of both Iraq and the United States, voluntarily traveled to Iraq with several Romanian journalists. He was to serve as the journalists' translator and guide. Shortly after arriving in Iraq, the group was kidnapped and held captive for two months. After the journalists were freed, MNF-I forces detained Munaf based on their belief that he had orchestrated the kidnappings.

A three-judge MNF-I Tribunal . . . found that Munaf posed a serious threat to Iraqi security, designated him a "security internee," and referred his case to the CCCI for criminal investigation and prosecution.

During his CCCI trial, Munaf admitted on camera and in writing that he had facilitated the kidnapping of the Romanian journalists. . . . Later in the proceedings, Munaf recanted his confession, but the CCCI nonetheless found him guilty of kidnapping. On appeal, the Iraqi Court of Cassation vacated Munaf's conviction and remanded his case to the CCCI for further investigation. The Court of Cassation directed that Munaf was to "remain in custody pending the outcome" of further criminal proceedings.

Meanwhile, Munaf's sister filed a next-friend petition for a writ of habeas corpus in the District Court for the District of Columbia. The District Court dismissed the petition for lack of jurisdiction . . . .

The Court of Appeals for the District of Columbia Circuit affirmed. . . .

II

The Solicitor General argues that the federal courts lack jurisdiction over the detainees' habeas petitions because the American forces holding Omar and Munaf operate as part of a multinational force. The habeas statute provides that a federal district court may entertain a habeas application by a person held "in custody under or by color of the authority of the United States," or "in custody in violation of the Constitution or laws or treaties of the United States." 28 U.S.C. §§2241(c)(1), (3). MNF-I forces, the argument goes, "are not operating solely under United States authority, but rather 'as the agent of' a multi-national force." Omar and Munaf are thus held pursuant to international authority, not "the authority of the United States," §2241(c)(1), and they are therefore not within the reach of the habeas statute.

The United States acknowledges that Omar and Munaf are American citizens held overseas in the immediate "physical custody" of American soldiers who answer only to an American chain of command. . . .

We think these concessions [mark] the end of the jurisdictional inquiry. The Government's argument – that the federal courts have no jurisdiction over American citizens held by American forces operating as multinational agents – is not easily reconciled with the text of §2241(c)(1). An individual is held "in custody" by the United States when the United States official charged with his detention has "the power to produce" him. Wales v. Whitney, 114 U.S. 564, 574 (1885). The disjunctive "or" in §2241(c)(1) makes clear that actual custody by the United States suffices for jurisdiction, even if that custody could be viewed as "under . . . color of" another authority, such as the MNF-I.

The Government's primary contention is that the District Courts lack jurisdiction in these cases because of this Court's decision in *Hirota* [v. MacArthur, 338 U.S. 197 (1948) (*per curiam*)]. That slip of a case cannot bear the weight the Government would place on it. In *Hirota,* Japanese citizens sought permission to file habeas corpus applications directly in this Court. The petitioners were noncitizens detained in Japan. They had been convicted and sentenced by the International Military Tribunal for the Far East – an international tribunal established by General Douglas MacArthur acting, as the Court put it, in his capacity as "the agent of the Allied Powers." 338 U.S., at 198. Although those familiar with the history of the period would appreciate the possibility of confusion over who General MacArthur took orders from, the Court concluded that the sentencing tribunal was "not a tribunal of the United States." *Ibid*. The Court then held that, "[u]nder the foregoing circumstances," United States courts had "no power or authority to review, to affirm, set aside or annul the judgments and sentences" imposed by that tribunal. *Ibid*. Accordingly, the Court denied petitioners leave to file their habeas corpus applications, without further legal analysis. *Ibid*.

The Government argues that the multinational character of the MNF-I, like the multinational character of the tribunal at issue in *Hirota,* means that it too is not a United States entity subject to habeas. . . .

The Court in *Hirota,* however, may have found it significant, in considering the nature of the tribunal established by General MacArthur, that the Solicitor General expressly contended that General MacArthur, as pertinent, was not subject to United States authority. . . . Here, in contrast, the Government acknowledges that our military commanders do answer to the President.

Even if the Government is correct that the international authority at issue in *Hirota* is no different from the international authority at issue here, the present "circumstances" differ in another respect. These cases concern American citizens while *Hirota* did not, and the Court has indicated that habeas jurisdiction can depend on citizenship. See Johnson v. Eisentrager, 339 U.S. 763, 781 (1950); Rasul v. Bush, 542 U.S. 466, 486 (2004) (KENNEDY, J., concurring in judgment). "Under the foregoing circumstances," we decline to extend our holding in *Hirota* to preclude American citizens held overseas by American soldiers subject to a United States chain of command from filing habeas petitions.

III

We now turn to the question whether United States district courts may exercise their habeas jurisdiction to enjoin our Armed Forces from transferring individuals detained within another sovereign's territory to that sovereign's government for criminal prosecution. The nature of that question requires us to proceed "with the circumspection appropriate when this Court is adjudicating issues inevitably entangled in the conduct of our international relations." Romero v. International Terminal Operating Co., 358 U.S. 354, 383 (1959). Here there is the further consideration that those issues arise in the context of ongoing military operations conducted by American Forces overseas. We therefore approach these questions cognizant that "courts traditionally have been reluctant to intrude upon the authority of the Executive in military and national security affairs." Department of Navy v. Egan, 484 U.S. 518, 530 (1988). . . .

Our authority to address the merits of the habeas petitioners' claims is clear. Review of a preliminary injunction "is not confined to the act of granting the injunctio[n], but extends as well to determining whether there is any insuperable objection, in point of jurisdiction or merits, to the maintenance of [the] bill, and, if so, to directing a final decree dismissing it." City and County of Denver v. New York Trust Co., 229 U.S. 123, 136 (1913). . . .

Given that the present cases involve habeas petitions that implicate sensitive foreign policy issues in the context of ongoing military operations, reaching the merits is the wisest course. See Youngstown Sheet & Tube Co. v. Sawyer, 343 U.S. 579, 584-585 (1952) (finding the case ripe for merits review on appeal from stay of preliminary injunction). For the reasons we explain below, the relief sought by the habeas petitioners makes clear under our precedents that the power of the writ ought not to be exercised. Because the Government is entitled to judgment as a matter of law, it is appropriate for us to terminate the litigation now.

IV

The habeas petitioners argue that the writ should be granted in their cases because they have "a legally enforceable right" not to be transferred to Iraqi authority for criminal proceedings under both the Due Process Clause and the Foreign Affairs Reform and Restructuring Act of 1998 (FARR Act), div. G, 112 Stat. 2681-761, and because they are innocent civilians who have been unlawfully detained by the United States in violation of the Due Process Clause. With respect to the transfer claim, petitioners request an injunction prohibiting the United States from transferring them to Iraqi custody. With respect to the unlawful detention claim, petitioners seek "release" – but only to the extent that release would not result in "unlawful" transfer to Iraqi custody. Both of these requests would interfere with Iraq's sovereign right to "punish offenses against its laws committed within its borders." *Wilson* [v. Girard, 354 U.S. 524 (1957)], at 529. We accordingly hold that the detainees' claims do not state grounds upon which habeas relief may be granted, that the habeas petitions should have been promptly dismissed, and that no injunction should have been entered.

A

Habeas corpus is "governed by equitable principles." Fay v. Noia, 372 U.S. 391, 438 (1963). We have therefore recognized that "prudential concerns," Withrow v. Williams, 507 U.S. 680, 686 (1993), such as comity and the orderly administration of criminal justice, may "require a federal court to forgo the exercise of its habeas corpus power," Francis v. Henderson, 425 U.S. 536, 539 (1976).

The principle that a habeas court is "not bound in every case" to issue the writ, Ex parte Royall, 117 U.S. 241, 251 (1886), follows from the precatory language of the habeas statute, and from its common-law origins. The habeas statute provides only that a writ of habeas corpus "*may* be granted," §2241(a) (emphasis added), and directs federal courts to "dispose of [habeas petitions] as law and justice require," §2243. Likewise, the writ did not issue in England "as of mere course," but rather required the petitioner to demonstrate why the "extraordinary power of the crown" should be exercised, 3 W. Blackstone, Commentaries on the Laws of England 132 (1768); even then, courts were directed to "do as to justice shall appertain," 1 *id.,* at 131 (1765). The question, therefore, even where a habeas court has the power to issue the writ, is "whether this be a case in which [that power] ought to be exercised." Ex parte Watkins, 3 Pet. 193, 201 (1830) (MARSHALL, C.J.).

At the outset, the nature of the relief sought by the habeas petitioners suggests that habeas is not appropriate in these cases. Habeas is at its core a remedy for unlawful executive detention. Hamdi v. Rumsfeld, 542 U.S. 507, 536 (2004) (plurality opinion). The typical remedy for such detention is, of course, release. But here the last thing petitioners want is simple release; that would expose them to apprehension by Iraqi authorities for criminal prosecution – precisely what petitioners went to federal court to avoid. At the end of the day, what petitioners are really after is a court order requiring the United States to shelter them from the sovereign government seeking to have them answer for alleged crimes committed within that sovereign's borders. . . .

. . . [O]ur cases make clear that Iraq has a sovereign right to prosecute Omar and Munaf for crimes committed on its soil. As Chief Justice Marshall explained nearly two centuries ago, "[t]he jurisdiction of the nation within its own territory is necessarily exclusive and absolute." Schooner Exchange v. McFaddon, 7 Cranch 116, 136 (1812).

This is true with respect to American citizens who travel abroad and commit crimes in another nation whether or not the pertinent criminal process comes with all the rights guaranteed by our Constitution. "When an American citizen commits a crime in a foreign country he cannot complain if required to submit to such modes of trial and to such punishment as the laws of that country may prescribe for its own people." Neely v. Henkel, 180 U.S. 109, 123 (1901).

The habeas petitioners nonetheless argue that the Due Process Clause includes a "[f]reedom from unlawful transfer" that is "protected *wherever* the government seizes a citizen." We disagree. Not only have we long recognized the principle that a nation state reigns sovereign within its own territory, we have twice applied that principle to reject claims that the Constitution precludes the Executive from transferring a prisoner to a foreign country for prosecution in an allegedly unconstitutional trial.

[The Court here cites the cases of *Wilson*, *supra*, involving a U.S. soldier who caused the death of a Japanese woman in Japan, and *Neely*, *supra*, in which a petitioner accused of violating Cuban law sought to block his extradition to Cuba.] . . .

In the present cases, the habeas petitioners concede that Iraq has the sovereign authority to prosecute them for alleged violations of its law, yet nonetheless request an injunction prohibiting the United States from transferring them to Iraqi custody. But as the foregoing cases make clear, habeas is not a means of compelling the United States to harbor fugitives from the criminal justice system of a sovereign with undoubted authority to prosecute them. . . .

While the Iraqi Government is ultimately "responsible for [the] arrest, detention and imprisonment" of individuals who violate its laws, S.C. Res. 1790, Annex I, ¶4, p. 6, U.N. Doc. S/RES/1790 (Dec. 18, 2007), the MNF-I maintains physical custody of individuals like Munaf and Omar while their cases are being heard by the CCCI. . . . MNF-I detention is an integral part of the Iraqi system of criminal justice. MNF-I forces augment the Iraqi Government's peacekeeping efforts by functioning, in essence, as its jailor. Any requirement that the MNF-I release a detainee would, in effect, impose a release order on the Iraqi Government. . . .

To allow United States courts to intervene in an ongoing foreign criminal proceeding and pass judgment on its legitimacy seems at least as great an intrusion as the plainly barred collateral review of foreign convictions. See Banco Nacional de Cuba v. Sabbatino, 376 U.S. 398, 417-418 (1964).

There is of course even more at issue here: Neither *Neely* nor *Wilson* concerned individuals captured and detained within an ally's territory during ongoing hostilities involving our troops. *Neely* involved a charge of embezzlement; *Wilson* the peacetime actions of a serviceman. Yet in those cases we held that the Constitution allows the Executive to transfer American citizens to foreign authorities for criminal prosecution. It would be passing strange to hold that the Executive lacks that same authority where, as here, the detainees were captured by our Armed Forces for engaging in serious hostile acts against an ally in what the Government refers to as "an active theater of combat."

Such a conclusion would implicate not only concerns about interfering with a sovereign's recognized prerogative to apply its criminal law to those alleged to have committed crimes within its borders, but also concerns about unwarranted judicial intrusion into the Executive's ability to conduct military operations abroad. Our constitutional framework "requires that the judiciary be as scrupulous not to interfere with legitimate Army matters as the Army must be scrupulous not to intervene in judicial matters." Orloff v. Willoughby, 345 U.S. 83, 94 (1953). Those who commit crimes within a sovereign's territory may be transferred to that sovereign's government for prosecution; there is hardly an exception to that rule when the crime at issue is not embezzlement but unlawful insurgency directed against an ally during ongoing hostilities involving our troops.

B

Petitioners contend that these general principles are trumped in their cases because their transfer to Iraqi custody is likely to result in torture. . . . Such allegations are of course a matter of serious concern, but in the present context that concern is to be addressed by the political branches, not the judiciary.

This conclusion is reflected in the cases already cited. Even with respect to claims that detainees would be denied constitutional rights if transferred, we have recognized that it is for the political branches, not the judiciary, to assess practices in foreign countries and to determine national policy in light of those assessments. Thus, the Court in *Neely* concluded that an American citizen who "commits a crime in a foreign country" "cannot complain if required to submit to such modes of trial and to such punishment as the laws of that country may prescribe for its own people," but went on to explain that this was true "unless a different mode be provided for by treaty stipulation between that country and the United States." 180 U.S., at 123. Diplomacy was the means of addressing the petitioner's concerns. . . .

The Executive Branch may, of course, decline to surrender a detainee for many reasons, including humanitarian ones. Petitioners here allege only the possibility of mistreatment in a prison facility; this is not a more extreme case in which the Executive has determined that a detainee is likely to be tortured but decides to transfer him anyway. Indeed, the Solicitor General states that it is the policy of the United States *not* to transfer an individual in circumstances where torture is likely to result. . . .

The Judiciary is not suited to second-guess such determinations – determinations that would require federal courts to pass judgment on foreign justice systems and undermine the Government's ability to speak with one voice in this area. See The Federalist No. 42, p. 279 (J. Cooke ed. 1961) (J. Madison) ("If we are to be one nation in any respect, it clearly ought to be in respect to other nations"). In contrast, the political branches are well situated to consider sensitive foreign policy issues, such as whether there is a serious prospect of torture at the hands of an ally, and what to do about it if there is. . . .

For all the reasons given above, petitioners state no claim in their habeas petitions for which relief can be granted, and those petitions should have been promptly dismissed. . . .

It is so ordered.

JUSTICE SOUTER, with whom JUSTICE GINSBURG and JUSTICE BREYER join, concurring. The Court holds that "[u]nder circumstances such as those presented here, . . . habeas corpus provides petitioners with no relief." The Court's opinion makes clear that those circumstances include the following: (1) Omar and Munaf "voluntarily traveled to Iraq." They are being held (2) in the "territory" of (3) an "all[y]" of the United States, (4) by our troops, (5) "during ongoing hostilities" that (6) "involv[e] our troops." (7) The government of a foreign sovereign, Iraq, has decided to prosecute them "for crimes committed on its soil." And (8) "the State Department has determined that . . . the department that would have authority over Munaf and Omar . . . as well as its prison and detention facilities have generally met internationally accepted standards for basic prisoner needs." Because I consider these circumstances essential to the Court's holding, I join its opinion.

The Court accordingly reserves judgment on an "extreme case in which the Executive has determined that a detainee [in U.S. custody] is likely to be tortured but decides to transfer him anyway." I would add that nothing in today's opinion should be read as foreclosing relief for a citizen of the United States who resists transfer, say, from the American military to a foreign government for prosecution in a case of that sort, and I would extend the caveat to a case in which the probability of torture is well documented, even if the Executive fails to acknowledge it. Although the Court rightly points out that any likelihood of extreme mistreatment at the receiving government's hands is a proper matter for the political branches to consider, if the political branches did favor transfer it would be in order to ask whether substantive due process bars the Government from consigning its own people to torture. And although the Court points out that habeas is aimed at securing release, not protective detention, habeas would not be the only avenue open to an objecting prisoner; "where federally protected rights [are threatened], it has been the rule from the beginning that courts will be alert to adjust their remedies so as to grant the necessary relief," Bell v. Hood, 327 U.S. 678, 684 (1946).

* * *

26

Military Detention

B. WARTIME DETENTION OF COMBATANTS BEFORE 9/11

Page 720. Insert the following case after Note 5.

Johnson v. Eisentrager

United States Supreme Court, 1950
339 U.S. 763

Mr. Justice JACKSON delivered the opinion of the Court. The ultimate question in this case is one of jurisdiction of civil courts of the United States *vis-à-vis* military authorities in dealing with enemy aliens overseas. . . .

[U.S. armed forces captured 21 German nationals in service of German armed forces in China. A U.S. military commission sitting in China tried and convicted them of violating laws of war, namely, engaging in, permitting, or ordering continued military activity against the United States after the surrender of Germany and before the surrender of Japan. After conviction, their sentences were reviewed and approved by military reviewing authority. They were then repatriated to the U.S.-run Landsberg Prison in Germany to serve their sentences.

They filed a petition for a writ of habeas corpus in the District of Columbia, naming the Secretary of Defense, among others, and asserting that their trial, conviction, and imprisonment violated Articles I and III of the Constitution, the Fifth Amendment, and provisions of the Geneva Convention governing the treatment of prisoners of war.]

We are cited to no instance where a court, in this or any other country where the writ is known, has issued it on behalf of an alien enemy who, at no relevant time and in no stage of his captivity, has been within its territorial jurisdiction. Nothing in the text of the Constitution extends such a right, nor does anything in our statutes. . . .

I.

Modern American law has come a long way since the time when outbreak of war made every enemy national an outlaw, subject to both public and private slaughter, cruelty and plunder. But even by the most magnanimous view, our law does not abolish inherent distinctions recognized throughout the civilized world between citizens and aliens, nor between aliens of friendly and of enemy allegiance, nor between resident enemy aliens who have submitted themselves to our laws and nonresident enemy aliens who at all times have remained with, and adhered to, enemy governments.

With the citizen we are now little concerned, except to set his case apart as untouched by this decision and to take measure of the difference between his status and that of all categories of aliens. . . .

The alien, to whom the United States has been traditionally hospitable, has been accorded a generous and ascending scale of rights as he increases his identity with our society. Mere lawful presence in the country creates an implied assurance of safe conduct and gives him certain rights . . . .

But, in extending constitutional protections beyond the citizenry, the Court has been at pains to point out that it was the alien's presence within its territorial jurisdiction that gave the Judiciary power to act. In the pioneer case of Yick Wo v. Hopkins, the Court said of the Fourteenth Amendment, "These provisions are universal in their application, to all persons within the territorial jurisdiction, without regard to any differences of race, of color, or of nationality; * * *." 118 U.S. 356, 369. . . .

Since most cases involving aliens afford this ground of jurisdiction, and the civil and property rights of immigrants or transients of foreign nationality so nearly approach equivalence to those of citizens, courts in peace time have little occasion to inquire whether litigants before them are alien or citizen.

It is war that exposes the relative vulnerability of the alien's status. The security and protection enjoyed while the nation of his allegiance remains in amity with the United States are greatly impaired when his nation takes up arms against us. While his lot is far more humane and endurable than the experience of our citizens in some enemy lands, it is still not a happy one. But disabilities this country lays upon the alien who becomes also an enemy are imposed temporarily as an incident of war and not as an incident of alienage. . . .

. . . [T]he nonresident enemy alien, especially one who has remained in the service of the enemy, does not have even this qualified access to our courts, for he neither has comparable claims upon our institutions nor could his use of them fail to be helpful to the enemy. Our law on this subject first emerged about 1813 when the Supreme Court of the State of New York had occasion, in a series of cases, to examine the foremost authorities of the Continent and of England. It concluded the rule of the common law and the law of nations to be that alien enemies resident in the country of the enemy could not maintain an action in its courts during the period of hostilities. This Court has recognized that rule, and it continues to be the law throughout this country and in England.

II.

The foregoing demonstrates how much further we must go if we are to invest these enemy aliens, resident, captured and imprisoned abroad, with standing to demand access to our courts.

We are here confronted with a decision whose basic premise is that these prisoners are entitled, as a constitutional right, to sue in some court of the United States for a writ of habeas corpus. To support that assumption we must hold that a prisoner of our military authorities is constitutionally entitled to the writ, even though he (a) is an enemy alien; (b) has never been or resided in the United States; (c) was captured outside of our territory and there held in military custody as a prisoner of war; (d) was tried and convicted by a Military Commission sitting outside the United States; (e) for offenses against laws of war committed outside the United States; (f) and is at all times imprisoned outside the United States.

We have pointed out that the privilege of litigation has been extended to aliens, whether friendly or enemy, only because permitting their presence in the country implied protection. No such basis can be invoked here, for these prisoners at no relevant time were within any territory over which the United States is sovereign, and the scenes of their offense, their capture, their trial and their punishment were all beyond the territorial jurisdiction of any court of the United States.

Another reason for a limited opening of our courts to resident aliens is that among them are many of friendly personal disposition to whom the status of enemy is only one imputed by law. But these prisoners were actual enemies, active in the hostile service of an enemy power. . . .

A basic consideration in habeas corpus practice is that the prisoner will be produced before the court. This is the crux of the statutory scheme established by the Congress; indeed, it is inherent in the very term "habeas corpus." . . . To grant the writ to these prisoners might mean that our army must transport them across the seas for hearing. This would require allocation of shipping space, guarding personnel, billeting and rations. It might also require transportation for whatever witnesses the prisoners desired to call as well as transportation for those necessary to defend legality of the sentence. The writ, since it is held to be a matter of right, would be equally available to enemies during active hostilities as in the present twilight between war and peace. Such trials would hamper the war effort and bring aid and comfort to the enemy. They would diminish the prestige of our commanders, not only with enemies but with wavering neutrals. It would be difficult to devise more effective fettering of a field commander than to allow the very enemies he is ordered to reduce to submission to call him to account in his own civil courts and divert his efforts and attention from the military offensive abroad to the legal defensive at home. Nor is it unlikely that the result of such enemy litigiousness would be a conflict between judicial and military opinion highly comforting to enemies of the United States. . . .

III.

The Court of Appeals dispensed with all requirement of territorial jurisdiction based on place of residence, captivity, trial, offense, or confinement. It could not predicate relief upon any intraterritorial contact of these prisoners with our laws or institutions. Instead, it gave our Constitution an extraterritorial application to embrace our enemies in arms. Right to the writ, it reasoned, is a subsidiary procedural right that follows from possession of substantive constitutional rights. These prisoners, it considered, are invested with a right of personal liberty by our Constitution and therefore must have the right to the remedial writ. The court stated the steps in its own reasoning as follows: "First. The Fifth Amendment, by its terms, applies to 'any person.' Second. Action of Government officials in violation of the Constitution is void. This is the ultimate essence of the present controversy. Third. A basic and inherent function of the judicial branch of a government built upon a constitution is to set aside void action by government officials, and so to restrict executive action to the confines of the constitution. In our jurisprudence, no Government action which is void under the Constitution is exempt from judicial power. Fourth. The writ of habeas corpus is the established, time-honored process in our law for testing the authority of one who deprives another of his liberty, – 'the best and only sufficient defense of personal freedom.' * * *" 174 F.2d 961, 963-964. . . .

When we analyze the claim prisoners are asserting and the court below sustained, it amounts to a right not to be tried at all for an offense against our armed forces. If the Fifth Amendment protects them from military trial, the Sixth Amendment as clearly prohibits their trial by civil courts. The latter requires in all criminal prosecutions that "the accused" be tried "by an impartial jury of the State and district wherein the crime shall have been committed, which district shall have been previously ascertained by law." And if the Fifth be held to embrace these prisoners because it uses the inclusive term "no person," the Sixth must, for it applies to all "accused." No suggestion is advanced by the court below or by prisoners of any constitutional method by which any violations of the laws of war endangering the United States forces could be reached or punished, if it were not by a Military Commission in the theatre where the offense was committed. . . .

If this Amendment invests enemy aliens in unlawful hostile action against us with immunity from military trial, it puts them in a more protected position than our own soldiers. American citizens conscripted into the military service are thereby stripped of their Fifth Amendment rights and as members of the military establishment are subject to its discipline, including military trials for offenses against aliens or Americans. . . .

If the Fifth Amendment confers its rights on all the world except Americans engaged in defending it, the same must be true of the companion civil-rights Amendments, for none of them is limited by its express terms, territorially or as to persons. Such a construction would mean that during military occupation irreconcilable enemy elements, guerrilla fighters, and "were-wolves" [German nationals trained to conduct terrorist activities in postwar Germany] could require the American Judiciary to assure them freedoms of speech, press, and assembly as in the First Amendment, right to bear arms as in the Second, security against "unreasonable" searches and seizures as in the Fourth, as well as rights to jury trial as in the Fifth and Sixth Amendments.

Such extraterritorial application of organic law would have been so significant an innovation in the practice of governments that, if intended or apprehended, it could scarcely have failed to excite contemporary comment. Not one word can be cited. No decision of this Court supports such a view. None of the learned commentators on our Constitution has ever hinted at it. The practice of every modern government is opposed to it.

We hold that the Constitution does not confer a right of personal security or an immunity from military trial and punishment upon an alien enemy engaged in the hostile service of a government at war with the United States. . . .

V. . . .

Since in the present application we find no basis for invoking federal judicial power in any district, we need not debate as to where, if the case were otherwise, the petition should be filed.

For reasons stated, the judgment of the Court of Appeals is reversed and the judgment of the District Court dismissing the petition is affirmed.

Reversed.

Mr. Justice BLACK, with whom Mr. Justice DOUGLAS and Mr. Justice BURTON concur, dissenting. . . . In Parts I, II, and III of its opinion, the Court apparently holds that no American court can even consider the jurisdiction of the military tribunal to convict and sentence these prisoners for the alleged crime. . . . [T]his holding . . . is based on the facts that (1) they were enemy aliens who were belligerents when captured, and (2) they were captured, tried, and imprisoned outside our realm, never having been in the United States.

The contention that enemy alien belligerents have no standing whatever to contest conviction for war crimes by habeas corpus proceedings has twice been emphatically rejected by a unanimous Court [citing Ex parte Quirin and In re Yamashita]. . . . That we went on to deny the requested writ [in both cases] in no way detracts from the clear holding that habeas corpus jurisdiction is available even to belligerent aliens convicted by a military tribunal for an offense committed in actual acts of warfare.

. . . Does a prisoner's right to test legality of a sentence then depend on where the Government chooses to imprison him? Certainly the *Quirin* and *Yamashita* opinions lend no support to that conclusion, for in upholding jurisdiction they place no reliance whatever on territorial location. The Court is fashioning wholly indefensible doctrine if it permits the executive branch, by deciding where its prisoners will be tried and imprisoned, to deprive all federal courts of their power to protect against a federal executive's illegal incarcerations.

If the opinion thus means, and it apparently does, that these petitioners are deprived of the privilege of habeas corpus solely because they were convicted and imprisoned overseas, the Court is adopting a broad and dangerous principle. . . .

. . . It has always been recognized that actual warfare can be conducted successfully only if those in command are left the most ample independence in the theatre of operations. Our Constitution is not so impractical or inflexible that it unduly restricts such necessary independence. It would be fantastic to suggest that alien enemies could hail our military leaders into judicial tribunals to account for their day to day activities on the battlefront. Active fighting forces must be free to fight while hostilities are in progress. But that undisputable axiom has no bearing on this case or the general problem from which it arises. . . .

The question here involves a far narrower issue. Springing from recognition that our government is composed of three separate and independent branches, it is whether the judiciary has power in habeas corpus proceedings to test the legality of criminal sentences imposed by the executive through military tribunals in a country which we have occupied for years. . . .

Though the scope of habeas corpus review of military tribunal sentences is narrow, I think it should not be denied to these petitioners and others like them. We control that part of Germany we occupy. These prisoners were convicted by our own military tribunals under our own Articles of War, years after hostilities had ceased. However illegal their sentences might be, they can expect no relief from German courts or any other branch of the German Government we permit to function. Only our own courts can inquire into the legality of their imprisonment. Perhaps, as some nations believe, there is merit in leaving the administration of criminal laws to executive and military agencies completely free from judicial scrutiny. Our Constitution has emphatically expressed a contrary policy. . . .

. . . Our nation proclaims a belief in the dignity of human beings as such, no matter what their nationality or where they happen to live. Habeas corpus, as an instrument to protect against illegal imprisonment, is written into the Constitution. Its use by courts cannot in my judgment be constitutionally abridged by Executive or by Congress. I would hold that our courts can exercise it whenever any United States official illegally imprisons any person in any land we govern. . . .

D. MILITARY DETENTION OF ALIEN ENEMY COMBATANTS AFTER 9/11

Page 758. Insert the following case after Note 4.

Al-Marri v. Pucciarelli

United States Court of Appeals, Fourth Circuit (en banc), 2008
2008 WL 2736787 (July 15, 2008)

PER CURIAM: Ali Saleh Kahlah al-Marri filed a petition for a writ of habeas corpus challenging his military detention as an enemy combatant. After the district court denied all relief, al-Marri noted this appeal. A divided panel of this court reversed the judgment of the district court and ordered that al-Marri's military detention cease. *See* Al-Marri v. Wright, 487 F.3d 160 (4th Cir. 2007).

Subsequently, this court vacated that judgment and considered the case *en banc.* The parties present two principal issues for our consideration: (1) assuming the Government's allegations about al-Marri are true, whether Congress has empowered the President to detain al-Marri as an enemy combatant; and (2) assuming Congress has empowered the President to detain al-Marri as an enemy combatant provided the Government's allegations against him are true, whether al-Marri has been afforded sufficient process to challenge his designation as an enemy combatant.

Having considered the briefs and arguments of the parties, the *en banc* court now holds: (1) by a 5 to 4 vote (Chief Judge Williams and Judges Wilkinson, Niemeyer, Traxler, and Duncan voting in the affirmative; Judges Michael, Motz, King, and Gregory voting in the negative), that, if the Government's allegations about al-Marri are true, Congress has empowered the President to detain him as an enemy combatant; and (2) by a 5 to 4 vote (Judges Michael, Motz, Traxler, King, and Gregory voting in the affirmative; Chief Judge Williams and Judges Wilkinson, Niemeyer, and Duncan voting in the negative), that, assuming Congress has empowered the President to detain al-Marri as an enemy combatant provided the Government's allegations against him are true, al-Marri has not been afforded sufficient process to challenge his designation as an enemy combatant.

Accordingly, the judgment of the district court is reversed and remanded for further proceedings consistent with the opinions that follow.

DIANA GRIBBON MOTZ, CIRCUIT JUDGE, concurring in the judgment: For over two centuries of growth and struggle, peace and war, the Constitution has secured our freedom through the guarantee that, in the United States, no one will be deprived of liberty without due process of law. Yet more than five years ago, military authorities seized Ali Saleh Kahlah al-Marri, an alien lawfully residing here. He has been held by the military ever since – without criminal charge or process. He has been so held, despite the fact that he was initially taken from his home in Peoria, Illinois, by civilian authorities and imprisoned awaiting trial for purported domestic crimes. He has been so held, although the Government has never alleged that he is a member of any nation's military, has fought alongside any nation's armed forces, or has borne arms against the United States anywhere in the world. And he has been so held, without acknowledgment of the protection afforded by the Constitution, solely because the Executive believes that his indefinite military detention – or even the indefinite military detention of a similarly situated American citizen – is proper.

While criminal proceedings were underway against al-Marri, the President ordered the military to seize and detain him indefinitely as an enemy combatant. Since that order, issued in June of 2003, al-Marri has been imprisoned without charge in a military jail in South Carolina. Al-Marri petitions for a writ of habeas corpus to secure his release from military imprisonment. The Government defends this detention, asserting that al-Marri associated with al Qaeda and "prepar[ed] for acts of international terrorism." It maintains that the President has both statutory and inherent constitutional authority to subject to indefinite military detention al-Marri or anyone else who associates with al Qaeda and "prepare[s]" for such acts. If the Government accurately describes al-Marri's conduct, he has committed grave crimes, but a majority of the *en banc* court holds, as the panel did, that the judgment of the district court must be reversed.

We would also grant al-Marri habeas relief. Even assuming the truth of the Government's allegations, they provide no basis for treating al-Marri as an enemy combatant or as anything other than a civilian. This does not mean that al-Marri, or similarly situated American citizens, would have to be freed. Like others accused of terrorist activity in this country, from the Oklahoma City bombers to the convicted September 11th conspirator, they could be tried on criminal charges and, if convicted, punished severely. But the Government would not be able to subject them to indefinite military detention.

With regret, we recognize that this view does not command a

majority of the court. Our colleagues hold that the President can order the military to seize from his home and indefinitely detain anyone in this country – including an American citizen – even though he has never affiliated with an enemy nation, fought alongside any nation's armed forces, or borne arms against the United States anywhere in the world. We cannot agree that in a broad and general statute, Congress silently authorized a detention power that so vastly exceeds all traditional bounds. No existing law permits this extraordinary exercise of executive power. Even in times of national peril, we must follow the law, lest this country cease to be a nation of laws. For "[l]iberty and security can be reconciled; and in our system they are reconciled within the framework of the law." Boumediene v. Bush*,* 553 U.S. ----, ----, slip op. at 70 (June 12, 2008).

Although our preferred disposition does not command a majority of the court, a majority does refuse to affirm the judgment of the district court. . . . In this case, that means that we join in a judgment reversing and remanding for evidentiary proceedings to determine whether al-Marri actually is an enemy combatant and so subject to military detention. Although we believe that Congress in the . . . AUMF [Authorization for Use of Military Force, Pub. L. No. 107-40 (2001), casebook p. 100] has not authorized al-Marri's military detention, the evidentiary proceedings envisioned by Judge Traxler will at least place the burden on the Government to make an initial showing that "the normal due process protections available to all within this country" are impractical or unduly burdensome in al-Marri's case and that the hearsay declaration that constitutes the Government's only evidence against al-Marri is "the most reliable available evidence" supporting the Government's allegations. . . .

I.

Al-Marri, a citizen of Qatar, lawfully entered the United States with his wife and children on September 10, 2001, to pursue a master's degree at Bradley University in Peoria, Illinois, where he had obtained a bachelor's degree in 1991. The following day, terrorists hijacked four commercial airliners and used them to kill and inflict grievous injury on thousands of Americans. Three months later, on December 12, 2001, FBI agents arrested al-Marri at his home in Peoria as a material witness in the Government's investigation of the September 11th attacks. Al-Marri was imprisoned in civilian jails in Peoria and then New York City.

In February 2002, al-Marri was charged in the Southern District of New York with the possession of unauthorized or counterfeit credit card numbers with the intent to defraud. A year later, in January 2003, he was charged in a second, six-count indictment with two counts of making a false statement to the FBI, three counts of making a false statement on a bank application, and one count of using another person's identification for the purpose of influencing the action of a federally insured financial institution. Al-Marri pleaded not guilty to all of these charges. In May 2003, a federal district court in New York dismissed the charges against al-Marri for lack of venue.

The Government then returned al-Marri to Peoria, and he was re-indicted in the Central District of Illinois on the same seven counts, to which he again pleaded not guilty. The district court set a July 21, 2003, trial date. On Friday, June 20, 2003, the court scheduled a hearing on pre-trial motions, including a motion to suppress evidence against al-Marri assertedly obtained by torture. On the following Monday, June 23, before that hearing could be held, the Government moved *ex parte* to dismiss the indictment based on an order signed that morning by the President.

In the order, President George W. Bush stated that he "DETERMINE[D] for the United States of America that" al-Marri: (1) is an enemy combatant; (2) is closely associated with al Qaeda; (3) "engaged in conduct that constituted hostile and war-like acts, including conduct in preparation for acts of international terrorism"; (4) "possesses intelligence . . . that . . . would aid U.S. efforts to prevent attacks by al Qaeda"; and (5) "represents a continuing, present, and grave danger to the national security of the United States." The President determined that al-Marri's detention by the military was "necessary to prevent him from aiding al Qaeda" and thus ordered the Attorney General to surrender al-Marri to the Secretary of Defense and further directed the Secretary of Defense to "detain him as an enemy combatant."

The federal district court in Illinois granted the Government's motion to dismiss the criminal indictment against al-Marri. In accordance with the President's order, al-Marri was then transferred to military custody and brought to the Naval Consolidated Brig in South Carolina.

Since that time (that is, for five years) the military has held al-Marri as an enemy combatant, without charge and without any indication when this confinement will end. For the first sixteen months of his military confinement, the Government did not permit al-Marri any communication with the outside world, including his attorneys, his wife, and his children. . . .

[Al-Marri's lawyer filed a petition for a writ of habeas corpus on his behalf. The government responded with a declaration of Jeffrey N. Rapp, Director of the Joint Intelligence Task Force for Combating Terrorism, as support for the President's order for military detention.] . . .

The Rapp Declaration asserts that al-Marri: (1) is "closely associated with al Qaeda, an international terrorist organization with which the United States is at war"; (2) trained at an al Qaeda terrorist training camp in Afghanistan sometime between 1996 and 1998; (3) in the summer of 2001, was introduced to Osama Bin Laden by Khalid Shaykh Muhammed; (4) at that time, volunteered for a "martyr mission" on behalf of al Qaeda; (5) was ordered to enter the United States sometime before September 11, 2001, to serve as a "sleeper agent" to facilitate terrorist activities and explore disrupting this country's financial system through computer hacking; (6) in the summer of 2001, met with terrorist financier Mustafa Ahmed al-Hawsawi, who gave al-Marri money, including funds to buy a laptop; (7) gathered technical information about poisonous chemicals on his laptop; (8) undertook efforts to obtain false identification, credit cards, and banking information, including stolen credit card numbers; (9) communicated with known terrorists, including Khalid Shaykh Muhammed and al-Hawsawi, by phone and e-mail; and (10) saved information about jihad, the September 11th attacks, and Bin Laden on his laptop computer.

The Rapp Declaration does *not* assert that al-Marri: (1) is a citizen, or affiliate of the armed forces, of any nation at war with the United States; (2) was seized on, near, or having escaped from a battlefield on which the armed forces of the United States or its allies were engaged in combat; (3) was ever in Afghanistan during the armed conflict between the United States and the Taliban there; or (4) directly participated in any hostilities against United States or allied armed forces. . . .

II. . . .

A. . . .

[Judge Motz found that as a lawfully admitted alien with a substantial connection to the United States, al-Marri was entitled to due process before he could be deprived of his liberty. But she also acknowledged that in Hamdi v. Rumsfeld, 542 U.S. 507 (2004), the Supreme Court found that Congress had constitutionally authorized the President to order the military detention, without the criminal process ordinarily required by the Due Process Clause, of persons who qualify as "enemy combatants."]

These principles thus form the legal framework for consideration of the issues before us. Both parties recognize that it does not violate the Due Process Clause for the President to order the military to seize and detain individuals who "qualify" as enemy combatants for the duration of a war. They disagree, however, as to whether the evidence the Government has proffered, even assuming its accuracy, establishes that al-Marri fits within the "legal category of enemy combatant." The Government principally contends that its evidence establishes this, and therefore the AUMF grants the President *statutory* authority to detain al-Marri as an enemy combatant. Alternatively, the Government asserts that the President has inherent *constitutional* authority to order al-Marri's indefinite military detention. Al-Marri maintains that the proffered evidence does not establish that he fits within the "legal category of enemy combatant," *id.*, and so the AUMF does not authorize the President to order the military to seize and detain him, and that the President has no inherent constitutional authority to order this detention. We now turn to these contentions.

B.

The Government's primary argument is that the AUMF, as construed by precedent and considered against "the legal background against which [it] was enacted," i.e., constitutional and law-of-war principles, empowers the President to order the military to seize and detain al-Marri as an enemy combatant. The AUMF provides:

> . . . the President is authorized to use all necessary and appropriate force against those nations, organizations, or persons he determines planned, authorized, committed, or aided the terrorist attacks that occurred on September 11, 2001, or harbored such organizations or persons, in order to prevent any future acts of international terrorism against the United States by such nations, organizations or persons.

§2(a), 115 Stat. 224. . . .

1.

Tellingly, the Deputy Solicitor General conceded at oral argument before the *en banc* court that the AUMF only authorizes detention of enemy combatants. Thus, the Government does *not* argue that the broad language of the AUMF authorizes the President to subject to indefinite military detention anyone he believes to have aided any "nation[ ], organization [ ], or person[ ]" related to the September 11th attacks. *See* §2(a), 115 Stat. 224. Such an interpretation would lead to absurd results that Congress could not have intended.

Under that reading of the AUMF, the President would be able to subject to indefinite military detention anyone, including an American citizen, whom the President believed was associated with any organization that the President believed in some way "planned, authorized, committed, or aided" the September 11th attacks, so long as the President believed this to be "necessary and appropriate" to prevent future acts of terrorism.

Under such an interpretation of the AUMF, if some money from a nonprofit charity that feeds Afghan orphans made its way to al Qaeda, the President could subject to indefinite military detention any donor to that charity. Similarly, this interpretation of the AUMF would allow the President to detain indefinitely any employee or shareholder of an American corporation that built equipment used by the September 11th terrorists; or allow the President to order the military seizure and detention of an American-citizen physician who treated a member of al Qaeda. . . .

2.

. . . [T]he Government wisely limits its argument. It relies only on the scope of the AUMF as construed by precedent and considered in light of "the legal background against which [it] was enacted." Specifically, the Government contends that "[t]he Supreme Court's and this Court's prior construction of the AUMF govern[s] this case and compel[s] the conclusion that the President is authorized to detain al-Marri as an enemy combatant."

i.

The precedent interpreting the AUMF on which the Government relies for this argument consists of two cases: the Supreme Court's opinion in *Hamdi,* 542 U.S. 507, and our opinion in Padilla v. Hanft, 423 F.3d 386 (4th Cir. 2005). The "legal background" for the AUMF, which the Government cites, consists of two cases from earlier conflicts, Ex Parte Quirin, 317 U.S. 1 (1942) (World War II), and Ex Parte Milligan, 71 U.S. (4 Wall.) 2 (1866) (U.S. Civil War), as well as constitutional and law-of-war principles.

With respect to the latter, we note that American courts have often been reluctant to follow international law in resolving domestic disputes. In the present context, however, they, like the Government here, have relied on the law of war-treaty obligations including the Hague and Geneva Conventions and customary principles developed alongside them. The law of war provides clear rules for determining an individual's status during an international armed conflict, distinguishing between "combatants" (members of a nation's military, militia, or other armed forces, and those who fight alongside them) and "civilians" (all other persons).[11] *See, e.g.,* Geneva Convention Relative to the Treatment of Prisoners of War (Third Geneva Convention) arts. 2, 4, 5, Aug. 12, 1949, 6 U.S.T. 3316, 75 U.N.T.S. 135; Geneva Convention Relative to the Protection of Civilian Persons in Time of War (Fourth Geneva Convention) art. 4, Aug. 12, 1949, 6 U.S.T. 3516, 75 U.N.T.S. 287. American courts have repeatedly looked to these careful distinctions made in the law of war in identifying which individuals fit within the "legal category" of "enemy combatant" under our Constitution. *See, e.g., Hamdi,* 542 U.S. at 518; *Quirin,* 317 U.S. at 30-31 & n.7; *Milligan,* 71 U.S. at 121-22; *Padilla,* 423 F.3d at 391. . . .

In *Hamdi,* the Supreme Court looked to precedent and the law of war to determine whether the AUMF authorized the President to detain as an enemy combatant an American citizen captured while engaging in battle against American and allied armed forces in Afghanistan as part of the Taliban. In support of that detention, the Government offered evidence

---

11. Thus, "civilian" is a term of art in the law of war, not signifying an innocent person, but rather someone in a certain legal category who is *not* subject to *military* seizure or detention. So, too, a "combatant" is by no means always a wrongdoer, but rather a member of a different "legal category" who *is* subject to *military* seizure and detention. *Hamdi,* 542 U.S. at 522 n.1. For example, our brave soldiers fighting in Germany during World War II were "combatants" under the law of war, and viewed from Germany's perspective they were "enemy combatants." While civilians are subject to trial and punishment in civilian courts for all crimes committed during wartime in the country in which they are captured and held, combatant status protects an individual from trial and punishment by the capturing nation, unless the combatant has violated the law of war. *See id.* at 518; *Quirin,* 317 U.S. at 28-31. Nations in international conflicts can summarily remove the adversary's "combatants," i.e., the "enemy combatants," from the battlefield and detain them for the duration of such conflicts, but no such provision is made for "civilians." *Hamdi,* 542 U.S. at 518; *Quirin,* 317 U.S. at 28-31.

that Yaser Esam Hamdi "affiliated with a Taliban military unit and received weapons training," "took up arms with the Taliban," "engaged in armed conflict against the United States" in Afghanistan, and, when captured on the battlefield, "surrender[ed] his Kalishnikov assault rifle." Hamdi's detention was upheld because, in fighting against the United States on the battlefield in Afghanistan with the Taliban, the *de facto* government of Afghanistan at the time, Hamdi bore arms with the army of an enemy nation and so, under the law of war, was an enemy combatant.

The *Hamdi* Court expressly recognized that the AUMF did not explicitly provide for detention. It concluded, however, "in light of" the law-of-war principles applicable to Hamdi's battlefield capture, that this was "of no moment" in the case before it. As the plurality explained, "[b]ecause detention to prevent a combatant's *return to the battlefield* is a fundamental incident of waging war, in permitting the use of 'necessary and appropriate force,' Congress has clearly and unmistakably authorized detention in the *narrow circumstances considered here.*" Thus, the *Hamdi* Court reached the following limited holding: "the AUMF is explicit congressional authorization for the detention of individuals in the *narrow category* we describe," that is, individuals who were "part of or supporting forces hostile to the United States or coalition partners in Afghanistan and who engaged in an armed conflict against the United States there." The plurality explained that its opinion "only finds legislative authority to detain under the AUMF once it is sufficiently clear that the individual *is,* in fact, an enemy combatant." The plurality also cautioned that "[i]f the practical circumstances of a given conflict" differed from those of the traditional conflicts that informed the law of war, the understanding that the AUMF authorizes detention "may unravel."

In *Padilla,* a panel of this court similarly held that the AUMF authorized the President to detain as an enemy combatant an American citizen who "was armed and present in a combat zone" in Afghanistan as part of Taliban forces during the conflict there with the United States. The Government had not been able to capture Jose Padilla until he came to the border of the United States, but, because the Government presented evidence that Padilla "took up arms against United States forces in [Afghanistan] in the same way and to the same extent as did Hamdi," we concluded that he "unquestionably qualifies as an 'enemy combatant' as that term was defined for the purposes of the controlling opinion in *Hamdi.*" We too invoked the law of war, upholding Padilla's detention because we understood "the plurality's *reasoning* in *Hamdi* to be that the AUMF authorizes the President to detain all those who qualify as 'enemy combatants' within the meaning of the law of war." We also noted that Padilla's detention, like Hamdi's, was permissible "'to prevent a *combatant's return to the battlefield* . . . a fundamental incident of waging war.'". . .

Hamdi and *Padilla* ground their holdings on this central teaching from *Quirin,* i.e., enemy combatant status rests on an individual's affiliation during wartime with the "military arm of the enemy government." *Quirin,* 317 U.S. at 37-38; *Hamdi,* 542 U.S. at 519; *Padilla,* 423 F.3d at 391. In *Quirin,* that enemy government was the German Reich; in *Hamdi* and *Padilla,* it was the Taliban government of Afghanistan.

Hamdi and *Padilla* also rely on this principle from *Quirin* to distinguish (but not disavow) *Milligan.* In *Milligan,* the Court rejected the Government's impassioned contention that a presidential order and the "laws and usages of war," 71 U.S. at 121-22, justified exercising military jurisdiction over Lamdin Milligan, an Indiana resident, during the Civil War. The Government alleged that Milligan had communicated with the enemy, had conspired to "seize munitions of war," and had "join[ed] and aid[ed] . . . a secret" enemy organization "for the purpose of overthrowing the Government and duly constituted authorities of the United States." *Id.* at 6. The Court recognized that Milligan had committed "an enormous crime" during "a period of war" and at a place "within . . . the theatre of military operations, and which had been and was constantly threatened to be invaded by the enemy." *Id.* at 7, 130. But it found no support in the "laws and usages of war" for subjecting Milligan to military jurisdiction as a combatant, for although he was a "dangerous enem[y]" of the nation, he was a civilian and had to be treated as such. *Id.* at 121-22, 130.

Quirin, Hamdi, and *Padilla* all emphasize that *Milligan's* teaching – that our Constitution does not permit the Government to subject *civilians* within the United States to military jurisdiction – remains good law. The *Quirin* Court explained that while the petitioners before it were affiliated with the armed forces of an enemy nation and so were enemy belligerents, Milligan was a "non-belligerent" and so "not subject to the law of war." 317 U.S. at 45. The *Hamdi* plurality similarly took care to note that *Milligan* "turned in large part on the fact that Milligan was not a prisoner of war" (i.e., combatant) and suggested that "[h]ad Milligan been captured while he was assisting Confederate soldiers by carrying a rifle against Union troops on a Confederate battlefield, the holding of the Court might well have been different." 542 U.S. at 522. And in *Padilla,* we reaffirmed that "*Milligan* does not extend to enemy combatants" and so "is inapposite here because Padilla, unlike Milligan, associated with, and has taken up arms against the forces of the United States on behalf of, an enemy of the United States." 423 F.3d at 396-97. Thus, although *Hamdi, Quirin,* and *Padilla* distinguish *Milligan,* they recognize that its core holding remains the law of the land. That is, civilians within this country (even "dangerous enemies" like Milligan who perpetrate "enormous crime[s]" on behalf of "secret" enemy organizations bent on "overthrowing the Government" of this country) may not be subjected to military control and deprived of constitutional rights.

In sum, the holdings of *Hamdi* and *Padilla* share two characteristics: (1) they look to law-of-war principles to determine who fits within the "legal category" of enemy combatant; and (2) following the law of war, they rest enemy combatant status on affiliation with the military arm of an enemy nation.

ii.

In view of the holdings in *Hamdi* and *Padilla,* we find it remarkable that the Government contends that they "compel the conclusion" that the President may detain al-Marri as an enemy combatant. For unlike Hamdi and Padilla, al-Marri is not alleged to have been part of a Taliban unit, not alleged to have stood alongside the Taliban or the armed forces of any other enemy nation, not alleged to have been on the battlefield during the war in Afghanistan, not alleged to have even been in Afghanistan during the armed conflict there, and not alleged to have engaged in combat with United States forces anywhere in the world. *See* Rapp Declaration (alleging none of these facts, but instead that "[a]l-Marri engaged in conduct in preparation for acts of international terrorism intended to cause injury or adverse effects on the United States"). Indeed, unlike Hamdi and Padilla, al-Marri had been imprisoned in the United States by civil authorities on criminal charges for more than a year before being seized by the military and indefinitely confined in a Navy brig as an enemy combatant.

In place of the "classic wartime detention" that the Government argued justified Hamdi's detention as an enemy combatant, or the "classic battlefield" detention it maintained justified Padilla's, here the Government argues that al-Marri's seizure and indefinite detention by the military in this country are justified "because he engaged in, and continues to pose a very real threat of carrying out, . . . acts of international terrorism." And instead of seeking judicial deference to decisions of "military officers who are engaged in the serious work of waging battle," *Hamdi,* 542 U.S. at 531-32, the Government asks us to defer to the "multi-agency evaluation process" of government bureaucrats in Washington made eighteen months after al-Marri was taken into custody. Neither the holding in *Hamdi* nor that in *Padilla* supports the Government's contentions here. . . .

. . . Instead, the *Hamdi* plurality emphasized the narrowness of its holding, 542 U.S. at 509, 516-19, and the "limited category" of individuals controlled by that holding, *id.* at 518. In *Padilla,* we similarly saw no need to embrace a broader construction of the AUMF than that adopted by the Supreme Court in *Hamdi.* Indeed, the Government itself *principally* argued that Padilla was an enemy combatant because he, like Hamdi, "engaged in armed conflict" alongside the Taliban "against our forces in Afghanistan."

Thus, the Government is mistaken in its representation that *Hamdi* and *Padilla* "recognized" "[t]he President's authority to detain 'enemy combatants' during the current conflict with al Qaeda." *Hamdi* and *Padilla* evidence no sympathy for the view that the AUMF permits indefinite military detention beyond the "limited category" of people covered by the "narrow circumstances" of those cases. Therefore the Government's argument – that *Hamdi* and *Padilla* "compels the conclusion" that the AUMF authorizes the President "to detain al-Marri as an enemy combatant" – fails.

3. . . .

i.

. . . [T]he Supreme Court's most recent terrorism cases – *Hamdan* [v. Rumsfeld, 548 U.S. 557, 126 S. Ct. 2749 (2006)] and *Boumediene* – provide no support for the dissenters' position. In *Hamdan,* the Court held that because the conflict between the United States and al Qaeda in Afghanistan is not "between nations," it is a "'conflict not of an international character'" – and so is governed by Common Article 3 of the Geneva Conventions.

Common Article 3 and other Geneva Convention provisions applying to non-international conflicts (in contrast to those applying to international conflicts) simply do *not* recognize the "legal category" of enemy combatant. *See* Third Geneva Convention, art. 3, 6 U.S.T. at 3318. As the International Committee of the Red Cross – the official codifier of the Geneva Conventions – explains, "an 'enemy combatant' is a person who, either lawfully or unlawfully, engages in hostilities for the opposing side in an *international* armed conflict"; in contrast, "[i]n non-international armed conflict combatant status *does not exist.*" Int'l Comm. of the Red Cross, Official Statement: The Relevance of IHL in the Context of Terrorism, at 1, 3 (Feb. 21, 2005), http://www.icrc.org/Web/Eng/siteeng0.nsf/htmlall/terrorismihl-210705 (emphasis added).

Perhaps for this reason, our dissenting colleagues and the Government ignore *Hamdan*'s holding that the conflict with al Qaeda in Afghanistan is a non-international conflict and ignore the fact that, in such conflicts, the legal category of enemy combatant does not exist. . . .

. . . Furthermore, in *Boumediene,* the Court demonstrated no more sympathy for the Government's position than it had in any of the other recent terrorism cases. Rather, the Court expressly held that persons designated by the Executive "as enemy combatants" and held by United States forces at Guantanamo Bay must be afforded "the fundamental procedural protections of habeas corpus" guaranteed by our Constitution, even though they were foreign nationals who had been seized in foreign lands. The Court explained that "[t]he laws and Constitution are designed to survive, and remain in force, in extraordinary times."

Moreover, even were the Supreme Court ultimately to approve the detention of Boumediene, Hamdan, and those like them, that would not bolster the view that the Government can militarily detain al-Marri as an enemy combatant. Because the legal status of enemy combatant does not exist in non-international conflicts, the law of war leaves the detention of persons in such conflicts to the applicable law of the detaining country. In al-Marri's case, the applicable law is our Constitution. Under our Constitution, even if the Supreme Court should hold that the Government may detain indefinitely Boumediene, Hamdan, and others like them, who were captured *outside* the United States and lack substantial and voluntary connections to this country, that holding would provide no support for approving al-Marri's military detention. For not only was al-Marri seized and detained *within* the United States, he also has substantial connections to the United States and so plainly is protected by the Due Process Clause.

ii. . . .

We recognize the understandable instincts of those who wish to treat domestic terrorists as "combatants" in a "global war on terror." Allegations of criminal activity in association with a terrorist organization, however, do not permit the Government to transform a civilian into an enemy combatant subject to indefinite military detention, just as allegations of murder in association with others while in military service do not permit the Government to transform a civilian into a soldier subject to trial by court martial. *See* United States ex rel. Toth v. Quarles, 350 U.S. 11, 23 (1955) (holding that ex-servicemen, "like other civilians, are entitled to have the benefit of safeguards afforded those tried in the regular courts authorized by Article III of the Constitution").

To be sure, enemy combatants may commit crimes just as civilians may. When an enemy combatant violates the law of war, that conduct will render the person an "unlawful" enemy combatant, subject not only to detention but also to military trial and punishment. *Quirin,* 317 U.S. at 31. But merely engaging in unlawful behavior does not make one an enemy combatant. *Quirin* illustrates these distinctions well. The *Quirin* petitioners were first enemy combatants – associating themselves with the military arm of the German government with which the United States was at war. They became *unlawful* enemy combatants when they violated the law of war by "without uniform com[ing] secretly through the lines for the purpose of waging war." *Id.* By doing so, in addition to being subject to military detention for the duration of the conflict as enemy combatants, they also became "subject to trial and punishment by military tribunals for acts which render their belligerency illegal." *Id.* Had the *Quirin* petitioners never "secretly and without uniform" passed our "military lines," *id.*, they still would have been enemy combatants, subject to military detention, but would not have been *unlawful* enemy combatants subject to military trial and punishment.

Neither *Quirin* nor any other precedent even suggests, as our dissenting colleagues seem to believe, that individuals with constitutional rights, unaffiliated with the military arm of any enemy government, can be subjected to military jurisdiction and deprived of those rights solely on the basis of their conduct on behalf of a terrorist organization.[18] In

---

18. The distinction between organizations and nations is not without rationale. The law of war does not classify persons affiliated with terrorist organizations as enemy combatants for fear that doing so would immunize them from prosecution and punishment by civilian authorities in the capturing country. *See, e.g.,* Message from the President of the United States Transmitting the Protocol II Additional to the 1949 Geneva Conventions, and Relating to the Protection of Victims of Non-international Armed Conflicts, S. Treaty Doc. No. 100-2, at IV (1987) (explaining President Reagan's recommendation against ratifying a treaty provision that "would grant combatant status to irregular forces" and so "give recognition and protection to terrorist groups"). Moreover,

fact, *Milligan* rejected the Government's attempt to do just this. There, the Court acknowledged that Milligan's conduct – "joining and aiding" a "secret political organization, armed to oppose the laws, and seek[ing] by stealthy means to introduce the enemies of the country into peaceful communities, there to . . . overthrow the power of the United States" – made him and his co-conspirators "dangerous enemies to their country." 71 U.S. at 6, 130. But the Government did not allege that Milligan took orders from any enemy government or took up arms against this country on the battlefield. And so the Court held that the Government could not subject Milligan to trial by military tribunal or treat him as an enemy combatant subject to military detention as a prisoner of war. Milligan was an "enem[y] of the country" and associated with an organization seeking to "overthrow[ ] the Government" of this country, but he was still a civilian and had to be treated as one. *Id.* . . .

iii. . . .

. . . [B]ecause the AUMF contains only a broad grant of war powers and lacks any specific language authorizing detention, the *Hamdi* plurality explained that its opinion "only finds legislative authority to detain under the AUMF once it is sufficiently clear that the individual *is*, in fact, an enemy combatant." 542 U.S. at 523 (emphasis added). Although the military detention of enemy combatants like Hamdi is certainly "a fundamental incident of waging war," *id.* at 519, the military

---

a rule permitting indefinite military detention of members of a "terrorist" organization as enemy combatants, in addition to being contrary to controlling precedent, *Milligan,* 71 U.S. at 130, could well endanger citizens of this country or our allies. For example, a nation could employ this rule to treat American members of an environmental group, which it regards as a terrorist organization, as enemy combatants and so subject those Americans to indefinite military detention. Under definitions as nebulous as the ones proposed by our dissenting colleagues, these fears are hardly "completely unfounded." Foreign leaders who have already designated members of these environmental organizations "terrorists" might well, applying the dissents' definitions, conclude that those individuals are enemy combatants and thus detain them indefinitely without criminal process. *See* Hiroko Tabuchi, *Japanese Are Hunting Humpbacks,* Record (N.N.J.), Nov. 18, 2007, at A10 (reporting that some Japanese leaders regard activists for Greenpeace, an organization with 2.8 million members, as terrorists); Amanda Hodge, *Japan Warship "Sent to Help Whalers"*, Australian, Jan. 2, 2006, at 3 (same).

detention of civilians like al-Marri just as certainly is not.

Even assuming the Constitution permitted Congress to grant the President such an awesome and unprecedented power, if Congress intended to grant this authority, it could and would have said so explicitly. The AUMF lacks the particularly clear statement from Congress that would, at a minimum, be necessary to authorize the indefinite military detention of *civilians* as enemy combatants. *See, e.g.,* Greene v. McElroy, 360 U.S. 474, 508 (1959) (rejecting Government argument that executive orders and statutes permitted deprivation of liberty rights absent "explicit authorization"); Duncan v. Kahanamoku, 327 U.S. 304, 324 (1946) (rejecting Government argument that statute authorized trial of civilians by military tribunals because Congress could not have intended "to exceed the boundaries between military and civilian power, in which our people have always believed"); Ex Parte Endo, 323 U.S. 283, 300 (1944) (rejecting Government argument that a "wartime" executive order and statute permitted detention of citizen of Japanese heritage when neither "use[d] the language of detention"); Brown v. United States, 12 U.S. (8 Cranch) 110, 128-29 (1814) (rejecting Government argument that declaration of war authorized confiscation of enemy property because it did not clearly "declare[ ]" the legislature's "will"). We are exceedingly reluctant to infer a grant of authority that is so far afield from anything recognized by precedent or law-of-war principles, especially given the serious constitutional concerns it would raise. . . .

C.

Thus, we turn to the Government's final contention. The Government summarily argues that even if the AUMF does not authorize al-Marri's seizure and indefinite detention as an enemy combatant, the President has "inherent constitutional authority" to order the military to seize and detain al-Marri. According to the Government, the President's "war-making powers" afford him "inherent" authority to subject persons legally residing in this country and protected by our Constitution to military arrest and detention, without the benefit of any criminal process, if the President believes these individuals have "engaged in conduct in preparation for acts of international terrorism." *See* Rapp Declaration. Given that the Government has now acknowledged that aliens lawfully residing in the United States have the same due process rights as United States citizens, this is a breathtaking claim – and one that no member of the court embraces. . . .

1.

In contrast to the AUMF, which is silent on the detention of asserted alien terrorists captured and held within the United States, in the Patriot Act, enacted shortly after the AUMF, Congress carefully stated how it wished the Government to handle aliens believed to be terrorists who were seized and held within the United States. The Patriot Act provides the Executive with broad powers to deal with "terrorist aliens," but it *explicitly prohibits* their indefinite detention.

Section 412 of the Patriot Act, entitled "Mandatory Detention of Suspected Terrorists," permits the short-term "[d]etention of [t]errorist [a]liens." Patriot Act §412(a). The statute authorizes the Attorney General to detain any alien whom he "has reasonable grounds to believe": (1) "seeks to enter the United States" to "violate any law of the United States relating to espionage or sabotage" or to use "force, violence, or other unlawful means" in opposition to the government of the United States; (2) "has engaged in a terrorist activity"; or (3) is "likely to engage after entry in any terrorist activity," has "incited terrorist activity," is a "representative" or "member" of a "terrorist organization," is a "representative" of a "group that endorses or espouses terrorist activity," or "has received military-type training" from a terrorist organization. *Id.*; 8 U.S.C.A. §1182(a)(3)(A)-(B) (West 2007); *see also* 8 U.S.C.A. §1227(a)(4)(A)(i), (a)(4)(A)(iii), (a)(4)(B) (West 2007). In addition, the Patriot Act authorizes the Attorney General to detain any other alien who "is engaged in any other activity that endangers the national security of the United States." Patriot Act §412(a). In particular, the Patriot Act permits the Attorney General to "take into custody" any "terrorist aliens" based only on the Attorney General's "belie[fs]" as to the aliens' threat, with *no* process or evidentiary hearing, and judicial review available only through petition for habeas corpus. *Id.*

Recognizing the breadth of this grant of power, however, Congress also imposed strict limits in the Patriot Act on the duration of the detention of such "terrorist aliens" within the United States. Thus, the Patriot Act expressly prohibits unlimited "indefinite detention"; instead it requires the Attorney General either to begin "removal proceedings" or to "charge the alien with a criminal offense" "not later than 7 days after the commencement of such detention." *Id.* If a terrorist alien's removal "is unlikely for the reasonably foreseeable future," he "may be detained for additional periods of up to six months" if his release "will threaten the national security of the United States." *Id.* But no provision of the Patriot Act allows for unlimited indefinite detention. Moreover, the

Attorney General must provide the legislature with reports on the use of this detention authority every six months, which must include the number of aliens detained, the grounds for their detention, and the length of the detention. *Id.* §412(c).

Therefore, the Patriot Act establishes a specific method for the Government to detain aliens affiliated with terrorist organizations who the Government believes have come to the United States to endanger our national security, conduct espionage and sabotage, use force and violence to overthrow the government, engage in terrorist activity, or are likely to engage in any terrorist activity. Congress could not have better described the Government's allegations against al-Marri – *and* Congress decreed that individuals so described are *not* to be detained indefinitely, but only for a limited time, and only by civilian authorities, prior to deportation or criminal prosecution.

In sum, Congress has carefully prescribed the process by which it wishes to permit detention of "terrorist aliens" within the United States, and it has expressly prohibited the indefinite detention the President seeks here. The Government's argument that the President may indefinitely detain al-Marri is thus contrary to Congress's expressed will. "When the President takes measures incompatible with the expressed or implied will of Congress, his power is at its lowest ebb, for then he can rely only upon his own constitutional powers minus any constitutional powers of Congress over the matter." *Youngstown* [Sheet & Tube Co. v. Sawyer, 343 U.S. 579 (1952),] at 637 (Jackson, J., concurring). As the Supreme Court has recently explained, "[w]hether or not the President has independent power . . . he may not disregard limitations that Congress has, in proper exercise of its own war powers, placed on his powers." *Hamdan,* 126 S. Ct. at 2774 n.23 (citing *Youngstown,* 343 U.S. at 637 (Jackson, J., concurring)). In such cases, "Presidential claim[s]" to power "must be scrutinized with caution, for what is at stake is the equilibrium established by our constitutional system." *Youngstown,* 343 U.S. at 638 (Jackson, J., concurring). . . .

3.

In light of al-Marri's due process rights under our Constitution and Congress's express prohibition in the Patriot Act on the indefinite detention of those civilians arrested as "terrorist aliens" within this country, we can only conclude that, in the case at hand, the President claims power that far exceeds that granted him by the Constitution.

We do not question the President's wartime authority over enemy combatants, but absent suspension of the writ of habeas corpus, the Constitution simply does not provide the President the power to exercise military authority over civilians within the United States. *See Toth,* 350 U.S. at 14 ("[A]ssertion of military authority over civilians cannot rest on the President's power as commander-in-chief."). The President cannot eliminate constitutional protections with the stroke of a pen by proclaiming a civilian, even a criminal civilian, an enemy combatant subject to indefinite military detention. Put simply, the Constitution does not empower the President to order the military to seize civilians residing within the United States and detain them indefinitely without criminal process, and this is so even if he calls them "enemy combatants."

A "well-established purpose of the Founders" was "to keep the military strictly within its proper sphere, subordinate to civil authority." *Reid* [v. Covert, 354 U.S. 1, 30 (1957)]. In the Declaration of Independence, our forefathers lodged the complaint that the King of Great Britain had "affected to render the Military independent of and superior to the Civil power" and objected that the King had "depriv[ed] us in many cases, of the benefits of Trial by Jury." *The Declaration of Independence* paras. 14, 20 (U.S. 1776). Thus, a resolute conviction that civilian authority should govern the military animated the framing of the Constitution. As Alexander Hamilton, no foe of executive power, observed, the President's Commander-in-Chief powers "amount to nothing more than the supreme command and direction of the military and naval forces." The Federalist No. 69, at 386 (Alexander Hamilton) (Clinton Rossiter ed., 1961). "That military powers of the Commander in Chief were not to supersede representative government of *internal affairs* seems obvious from the Constitution and from elementary American history." *Youngstown,* 343 U.S. at 644 (Jackson, J., concurring) (emphasis added). For this reason, in *Youngstown,* the Supreme Court rejected the President's claim to "inherent power" to use the military even to seize property within the United States, despite the Government's argument that the refusal would "endanger the well-being and safety of the Nation." *Id.* at 584 (majority opinion). . . .

To sanction such presidential authority to order the military to seize and indefinitely detain civilians, even if the President calls them "enemy combatants," would have disastrous consequences for the Constitution – and the country. For a court to uphold a claim to such extraordinary power would do more than render lifeless the Suspension Clause, the Due Process Clause, and the rights to criminal process in the Fourth, Fifth, Sixth, and Eighth Amendments; it would effectively undermine all of the freedoms guaranteed by the Constitution. It is that power – were a court to recognize it – that could lead all our laws "to go unexecuted, and the government itself to go to pieces." We refuse to recognize a claim to power that would so alter the constitutional foundations of our Republic.

III.

Because we find that neither the AUMF nor the President's inherent authority permits the military to detain al-Marri indefinitely as an enemy combatant, we would not reach the question of whether the Government has afforded al-Marri sufficient process to challenge his designation as an enemy combatant. We would simply reverse the judgment of the district court and remand the case with instructions to issue a writ of habeas corpus directing the Secretary of Defense to release al-Marri from military custody within a reasonable period of time to be set by the district court. Pursuant to this directive, the Government could transfer al-Marri to civilian authorities to face criminal charges, initiate deportation proceedings against him, hold him as a material witness in connection with grand jury proceedings, or detain him for a limited time pursuant to the Patriot Act, but military detention of al-Marri would have to cease.

This disposition, however, does not command a majority of the *en banc* court. Accordingly, to give practical effect to the conclusions of the majority of the court who reject the Government's position, we join in ordering remand on the terms closest to those we would impose. We believe that it is unnecessary to litigate whether al-Marri is an enemy combatant, but joining in remand for the evidentiary proceedings outlined by Judge Traxler will at least place the burden on the Government to make an initial showing that normal due process protections are unduly burdensome and that the Rapp declaration is "the most reliable available evidence," supporting the Government's allegations before it may order al-Marri's military detention. Therefore, we concur in the per curiam opinion reversing and remanding for evidentiary proceedings to determine whether al-Marri actually is an enemy combatant subject to military detention.

Judges Michael, King, and Gregory have authorized me to indicate that they join in this opinion.

TRAXLER, Circuit Judge, concurring in the judgment: . . . I agree with my colleagues who hold that the AUMF . . . grants the President the power to detain enemy combatants in the war against al Qaeda, including belligerents who enter our country for the purpose of committing hostile and war-like acts such as those carried out by the al Qaeda operatives on 9/11. And, I agree that the allegations made by the government against al-Marri, if true, would place him within this category and permit the President to militarily detain him.

However, I depart from my dissenting colleagues on the issue of whether al-Marri has been afforded a fair opportunity to challenge the factual basis for his designation as an enemy combatant. Because the process afforded al-Marri by the district court to challenge the factual basis for his designation as an enemy combatant did not meet the minimal requirements of due process guaranteed by the Fifth Amendment, I would reverse the district court's dismissal of al-Marri's habeas petition and remand for further evidentiary proceedings on the issue of whether al-Marri is, in fact, an enemy combatant subject to military detention . . . .

II. The Authority to Detain. . . .

B.

Like my colleagues, I agree that neither *Hamdi* nor *Padilla* compels the conclusion that the AUMF authorized the President to detain al-Marri as an enemy combatant, although they do provide guidance. I disagree, however, that *Ex Parte Milligan,* 71 U.S. (4 Wall.) 2 (1866), compels the opposite conclusion. Having carefully considered these cases, as well as the Supreme Court's decision in *Quirin,* I am of the opinion that the AUMF also grants the President the authority to detain enemy combatants who associate themselves "with al Qaeda, an entity with which the United States is at war," and "travel[ ] to the United States for the avowed purpose of further prosecuting that war on American soil, against American citizens and targets," even though the government cannot establish that the combatant also "took up arms on behalf of that enemy and against our country in a *foreign* combat zone of that war." *Padilla,* 423 F.3d at 389 (emphasis added).

1. . . .

In my opinion . . . there is no doubt that individuals who are dispatched here by al Qaeda, the organization known to have carried out the 9/11 attacks upon our country, as sleeper agents and terrorist operatives charged with the task of committing additional attacks upon our homeland "are [also] individuals Congress sought to target in passing the AUMF." *Hamdi,* 542 U.S. at 518. Citing the right of the United States "to protect United States citizens *both at home and abroad,*" the AUMF authorized the President's use of "all necessary and appropriate force against" the nations *and organizations* that "planned, authorized, committed, or aided" the 9/11 attacks, "or harbored such organizations or persons, in order to prevent any future acts of international terrorism against the United States." 115 Stat. 224. Clearly, Congress was not merely authorizing military retaliation against a reigning foreign government known to have *supported* the enemy force that attacked us in our homeland, but was also authorizing military action against al Qaeda operatives who, like the 9/11 hijackers, were sent by the al Qaeda organization to the United States to conduct additional terror operations here.

As persuasively pointed out by the government, it was the 9/11 attacks which triggered the passage of the AUMF. The al Qaeda operatives who successfully carried out those attacks entered this country under false pretenses for the purpose of carrying out al Qaeda orders and, while finalizing the preparations for these attacks, maintained a facade of peaceful residence until the very moment they boarded the commercial airliners that they used as weapons. The hijackers never engaged in combat operations against our forces on a foreign battlefield. Yet al-Marri would have us rule that when Congress authorized the President to deal militarily with those responsible for the 9/11 attacks upon our country, it did not intend to authorize the President to deal militarily with al Qaeda operatives identically situated to the 9/11 hijackers. There is nothing in the language of the AUMF that suggests that Congress intended to limit the military response or the presidential authorization to acts occurring in foreign territories, and it strains reason to believe that Congress, in enacting the AUMF in the wake of those attacks, did *not* intend for it to encompass al Qaeda operatives standing in the exact position as the attackers who brought about its enactment. Furthermore, Congress has not revised or revoked the AUMF since its enactment or since the Supreme Court decided *Hamdi.*

I am also unpersuaded by the claim that because al Qaeda itself is an international terrorist organization instead of a "nation state" or "enemy government," the AUMF cannot apply, consistent with the laws of war and our constitutional guarantees, to such persons. The premise of that claim seems to be that because al Qaeda is not technically in control of an enemy nation or its government, it cannot be considered as anything other than a criminal organization whose members are entitled to all the protections and procedures granted by our constitution. I disagree.

In my view, al Qaeda is much more and much worse than a criminal organization. And while it may be an unconventional enemy force in a historical context, it is an enemy force nonetheless. The fact that it allied itself with an enemy government of a foreign nation only underscores this point, rendering attempts to distinguish its soldiers or operatives as something meaningfully different from military soldiers in service to the Taliban government (or al Qaeda operatives such as Hamdi and Padilla, who fought beside them) equally strained. The President attacked the Taliban in Afghanistan as *retaliation* for al Qaeda's strike upon our nation *because* al Qaeda was centralized there and allied with the Taliban, and it also strains credulity to assert that while we are legitimately at war with the Taliban government, we cannot be at war with al Qaeda. . . .

2.

If the allegations of the Rapp Declaration are true, I am also of the view that al-Marri would fall within the category of persons who may be lawfully detained pursuant to the authority granted by the AUMF. . . .

III. Due Process

While I agree with my colleagues who would hold that the President has the legal authority under the AUMF to detain al-Marri as an enemy combatant for the duration of the hostilities, we part company on the issue of whether the process afforded al-Marri to challenge his detention was sufficient to meet the minimum requirements of due process of law. In my opinion, due process demands more procedural safeguards than those provided to al-Marri in the habeas proceedings below. . . .

C.

The dispute in this appeal is relatively straight-forward, although its resolution is not. Al-Marri contends that he stands in a different posture from Hamdi and that due process demands more rigorous procedural safeguards than those provided by the district court here and by the plurality in *Hamdi.* The government counters that the *Hamdi* plurality's framework provided al-Marri all the process he was due, asserting (1) that the *Hamdi* framework for providing process to a *citizen* enemy combatant captured on a foreign battlefield is, *a fortiori,* constitutionally sufficient for an *alien* enemy combatant seized in the United States; and

(2) that al-Marri failed to take advantage of the process he was provided, making his claim for additional process unpersuasive.

Having carefully considered the plurality's guidance in *Hamdi* and the precedents upon which it relies, I am of the opinion that the district court erred in categorically applying the framework discussed by the *Hamdi* plurality to al-Marri's situation and accepting the Rapp Declaration as sufficient to shift the burden of persuasion to al-Marri without considering the specific circumstances before it. As was the case in *Hamdi,* "the full protections that accompany challenges to detentions in other settings [might] prove unworkable and inappropriate in [al-Marri's] enemy-combatant [proceeding]." *Hamdi*, 542 U.S. at 535. But that remains to be seen because, in my opinion, the district court erred in the initial step of accepting the hearsay affidavit of Rapp "as the most reliable available evidence from the [g]overnment," *id.* at 534, without any inquiry into whether the provision of nonhearsay evidence would unduly burden the government, and erred in failing to then weigh the competing interests of the litigants in light of the factual allegations and burdens placed before it for consideration.

1. . . .

Although I do not rule out the possibility that hearsay evidence might ultimately prove to be the most reliable available evidence from the government in this case, *Hamdi* does not support such a categorical relaxation of the protections due persons who are detained within our borders. . . . The *Hamdi* plurality's acceptance of hearsay evidence from the government in such settings . . . clearly arose from the context of a battlefield detainee, the "exigencies of [such] circumstances," and the "uncommon potential to burden the Executive at a time of ongoing military conflict." *Id.* at 533. The relaxed evidentiary standard was accepted in the balance as appropriate in light of the facts of that case – a person initially detained abroad by our allies on a battlefield in Afghanistan. The plurality rejected an outright disapproval of such hearsay declarations, and described lesser procedures it believed might be sufficient to satisfy the due process rights of such detainees, noting that the normal evidentiary requirements *might* need to be relaxed to account for the governmental interest in military matters. *See id.* at 533-34 (explaining that hearsay "*may* need to be accepted as the most reliable available evidence from the [g]overnment" and "a presumption in favor of the [g]overnment's evidence" would not "offend[ ]" the Constitution in battlefield detainee proceedings). But while the plurality refused to categorically prohibit hearsay declarations, neither did it categorically approve the use of such hearsay declarations in all enemy-combatant proceedings.[13] Hearsay declarations *may* be accepted upon a weighing of the burdens in time of warfare of "providing greater process" against the detainee's liberty interests. *Id.* at 529. But to decide whether a hearsay declaration is acceptable, the court must first take into account "the risk of erroneous deprivation" of the detainee's liberty interest, "the probable value, if any, of any additional or substitute procedural safeguards," and the availability of additional or substitute evidence which might serve the interests of both litigants. . . .

2.

In this case al-Marri's "private interest affected by the official action" is the same as that of Hamdi, *i.e.,* the liberty interest in being free from unlawful seizure and detention. *Hamdi,* 542 U.S. at 529. The risk of an erroneous deprivation of al-Marri's liberty interest, however, is not identical to the risk that was present in *Hamdi.* Al-Marri was not captured on the battlefields of Afghanistan or Iraq, nor even apprehended in a neighboring country where al Qaeda trains its soldiers. He was arrested by civilian federal authorities while residing in Illinois. I am acutely aware of the dangers of detention and imprisonment without compliance with criminal process safeguards, dangers that are even greater when the military detains persons inside the borders of the United States. In my view, the risk of erroneously detaining a civilian or citizen in this country as an enemy combatant is much greater inside the United

---

13. Thus, I do not believe *Hamdi* recognized that the government's burden in enemy-combatant proceedings could always be satisfied by a knowledgeable affiant who summarizes the evidence on which the detention was based. That is not what *Hamdi* said at all. Instead, the plurality merely noted that, in the context of the case before it, the Government had made it clear "that documentation regarding *battlefield detainees* already is kept in the ordinary court of military affairs" and that "[a]ny factfinding imposition created by requiring a knowledgeable affiant to summarize *these* records to an independent tribunal is a minimal one." *Hamdi,* 542 U.S. at 534 (emphasis added). For this reason, the *Hamdi* plurality was unpersuaded by the government's claim that "this basic process [would] have [a] dire impact on the central functions of warmaking." *Id.* I cannot read this language divorced from the context in which it was written and would demand no more than the same benefits/burdens analysis given to Hamdi.

States than in the very different context addressed by the Supreme Court in *Hamdi, i.e.,* a conventional battlefield within the borders of a foreign country in which we are fighting our enemies.

On the other hand, we must consider the government's interest "in detaining those who actually pose an immediate threat to the national security of the United States during ongoing international conflict," *Hamdi,* 542 U.S. at 530, and in "ensuring that those who have in fact fought with the enemy during a war do not return to battle against the United States," *id.* at 531, as well as "the burdens the [g]overnment would face in providing greater process," *id.* at 529.

Here, the government asserts that the Rapp Declaration, which summarizes the intelligence gathered on al-Marri's activities as an al Qaeda operative, is sufficient to meet its initial burden of proving that al-Marri was properly designated an enemy combatant. However, unlike in *Hamdi,* the government has presented *only* the Rapp Declaration. It has made no attempt to show that this hearsay evidence "need[s] to be accepted as the most reliable available evidence from the [g]overnment," *id.* at 533-34, or that additional protections to ensure that the innocent are not detained by our military would be "unworkable and inappropriate in th[is] enemy-combatant setting," *id.* at 535. Nor has there been any consideration of the "probable value, if any, of additional or substitute procedural safeguards" or the availability of more reliable evidence that might be presented by substitute methods which account for the government's weighty interests. *Id.* at 529.

. . . [A]l-Marri argued below that he believed the discovery [he] sought would be primarily from civilian agencies that could produce it without interfering with the war powers and war operations of this government. At a minimum, I believe the government should be required to demonstrate to the district court why this is not the case and why, in balancing the liberty interest of the detainee and the heightened risk of erroneous deprivation, the Rapp Declaration should be accepted as the most reliable available evidence the government can produce without undue burden or serious jeopardy to either its war efforts or its efforts to ensure the national security of this nation.

3. . . .

Al-Marri, like any person accused of being an enemy combatant, is entitled to a fair, meaningful opportunity to contest that designation by requiring the government to demonstrate through "the most reliable available evidence" that he is an enemy combatant, denying the allegations against him, and presenting evidence in support of his contest. *Id.* at 534. As in *Hamdi,* the evidence which will be accepted and the determination of the manner in which due process proceedings must occur will again be left largely to the district courts. *See id.* at 538-39 (noting that "[w]e anticipate that a District Court [will] proceed with the caution that we have indicated is necessary in this setting, engaging in a factfinding process that is both prudent and incremental. We have no reason to doubt that courts faced with these sensitive matters will pay proper heed both to the matters of national security that might arise in an individual case and to the constitutional limitations safeguarding essential liberties that remain vibrant even in times of security concerns"); *accord Boumediene,* 553 U.S. at ----, slip op. at 67-68 ("We make no attempt to anticipate all of the evidentiary and access-to-counsel issues that will arise during the course of the detainees' habeas corpus proceedings. We recognize, however, that the Government has a legitimate interest in protecting sources and methods of intelligence gathering; and we expect that the District Court will use its discretion to accommodate this interest to the greatest extent possible. . . . These and . . . other remaining questions are within the expertise and competence of the District Court to address in the first instance."). In this regard, the district court retains all its normal flexibility to vary the manner in which the presentation of evidence occurs in enemy-combatant proceedings. It is not precluded from accepting the hearsay declaration should it conclude that threats to national security or the war efforts dictate its use. *See Hamdi,* 542 U.S. at 533-34; *see also Boumediene,* 553 U.S. at ----, slip op. at 67 (Habeas corpus courts may not "disregard the dangers the detention in these cases was intended to prevent. . . . Certain accommodations can be made to reduce the burden habeas corpus proceedings will place on the military without impermissibly diluting the protections of the writ."). But, it is not handcuffed by an inflexible procedure that would demand acceptance of a hearsay declaration from the government simply because the government has labeled al-Marri an enemy combatant.

The general rule, therefore, is that al-Marri would be entitled to the normal due process protections available to all within this country, including an opportunity to confront and question witnesses against him. But, if the government can demonstrate to the satisfaction of the district court that this is impractical, outweighed by national security interests, or otherwise unduly burdensome because of the nature of the capture and the potential burdens imposed on the government to produce non-hearsay evidence and accede to discovery requests, then alternatives should be considered and employed. Given the grave national security concerns in matters such as this, and that the Rapp Declaration references not only al-Marri's activities in this country but also those he engaged in abroad prior to his entry here, the Rapp Declaration might conceivably prove to be "the most reliable available evidence" within the meaning of *Hamdi,* at least as to some allegations. However, I am not satisfied to let matters stand as they are when the government has not even been required to demonstrate to the district court why it cannot or should not be required to produce, even for *ex parte* examination, any of the supporting evidence relied upon by Rapp to justify al-Marri's detention. Here, the government has made no showing that "[h]earsay . . . [needs] to be accepted as the most reliable available evidence from the [g]overnment" or that the "exigencies of the circumstances . . . demand . . . [that the] enemy-combatant proceeding[ ] . . . be [otherwise] tailored to alleviate their uncommon potential to burden the Executive at a time of ongoing military conflict." *Hamdi,* 542 U.S. at 533-34; *cf. Boumediene,* slip op. at 64-65 ("Practical considerations and exigent circumstances inform the definition and reach of the law's writs, including habeas corpus. The cases and our tradition reflect this precept.").[16] . . .

---

16. The *Boumediene* Court held that the procedural protections given to enemy combatants under the Military Commissions Act of 2006, Pub. L. No. 109-366, 120 Stat. 2600, fell "well short of the procedures and adversarial mechanisms that would eliminate the need for habeas corpus review," *id.,* 553 U.S. at ----, slip op. at 37, noting in particular that while "[t]he detainee is allowed to present 'reasonably available' evidence, . . . his ability to rebut the Government's evidence against him[, which is accorded a presumption of validity,] is limited by the circumstances of his confinement and his lack of counsel at th[at] stage," *id.,* 553 U.S. at ----, slip op. at 38 (citation omitted). And while the dissent disagreed that the CSRT hearings were an insufficient substitute for habeas, it too pointed out in defense that the CSRT provides "every petitioner . . . the right to present evidence that he has been wrongfully detained," "includ[ing] the right to call witnesses who are reasonably available, question witnesses called by the tribunal, introduce documentary evidence, and testify before the tribunal." *Id.,* 553 U.S. at ----, slip op. at 17 (Roberts, C.J., dissenting). Nowhere, in either *Hamdi* or *Boumediene,* do I find support for the view that a detainee may be wholly deprived of all discovery *and* all rights to cross-examination and confrontation – regardless of the availability of the witnesses and documentary evidence – without any inquiry into whether exigent circumstances or other concerns for national security necessitate such a drastic lessening of the process normally available who challenge their executive detention.

GREGORY, CIRCUIT JUDGE, concurring in the judgment [omitted].

WILLIAMS, CHIEF JUDGE, concurring in part and dissenting in part: . . .

I.

A. . . .

A distillation of [the *Milligan*, *Quirin*, and *Hamdi*] precedents, I believe, yields a definition of an enemy combatant subject to detention pursuant to Congressional authorizations as an individual who meets two criteria: (1) he attempts or engages in belligerent acts against the United States, either domestically or in a foreign combat zone; (2) on behalf of an enemy force.

Given the specific allegations against al-Marri, I have little difficulty concluding that he satisfies the first criterion. First, the allegations set forth in the Rapp Declaration, if true, clearly show that al-Marri was on United States soil to commit acts of belligerency against the United States. *See Quirin,* 317 U.S. at 31 (stating that unlawful combatants include those who commit "hostile acts involving destruction of life or property" on United States soil).

According to the Rapp Declaration, al-Marri also meets what I view as the second requirement of an enemy combatant: that the belligerent acts be carried out on behalf of an enemy force. Unlike the plurality, I cannot accept al-Marri's contention that because he allegedly has ties only to al Qaeda, a terrorist organization that does not control any nation, he does not meet this portion of the definition of enemy combatant.

The plurality opinion may very well be correct that, under the traditional "law of war," persons not affiliated with the military of a *nation-state* may not be considered enemy combatants. And I recognize the respect domestic courts have long afforded the "law of nations." *See* Murray v. Schooner Charming Betsy, 6 U.S. (2 Cranch) 64, 118 (1804) ("[A]n act of Congress ought never to be construed to violate the law of nations if any other possible construction remains."). Here, however, Congress has, through the AUMF, addressed precisely this question by clearly authorizing the President to use force against "organizations," as well as against nation-states. *See* Padilla v. Hanft, 423 F.3d 386, 395-96 (4th Cir. 2005) (noting "the AUMF constitutes . . . a clear statement" in favor of detention). As a specific and targeted congressional directive, the AUMF controls the question of who may be detained, for purposes of domestic law – at least with respect to those individuals that fall within its scope. . . .

I wish to emphasize that by permitting the President to militarily detain al-Marri pursuant to the AUMF I am not being expansive; in al-Marri we are dealing with someone *squarely* within the purposes of the AUMF, which was passed to target organizations, like al Qaeda, responsible for the September 11 attacks and to prevent future terrorist attacks. This case does not present what to me are more difficult issues regarding enemy combatants and the scope of AUMF, such as the status of an individual who joined al Qaeda after September 11, 2001, or an individual who is part of a designated foreign terrorist organization, that played no role in the September 11 attacks. Instead, al-Marri is clearly an "individual[ ] Congress sought to target in passing the AUMF." *Hamdi,* 542 U.S. at 518. In addition, while "indefinite detention" of enemy combatants is not permitted, *see generally Hamdi,* 542 U.S. at 519-20, we remain engaged against the forces of al Qaeda in the border regions of Afghanistan to this day. . . .

B. . . .

. . . I view section 412 of the Patriot Act to refer to the President's power, under Article II §3, to "take Care that the Laws be faithfully executed." U.S. Const., art. II, §3. The statute refers to the Attorney General, the President's agent in implementing the Take Care Clause, and it is found nestled within the immigration code. Fairly read, the Patriot Act does not therefore purport to limit the President's separate Commander-in-Chief power. But the authorization granted in the AUMF, with its explicit reference to military force, relates to the Commander-in-Chief power. Whatever limitations are present in the Patriot Act, therefore, do not restrict the separate and distinct grant of power effected by the AUMF.

C.

I am left with a simple set of facts: the AUMF grants the President, who already has some inherent Article II power to wage war, *see, e.g.,* Chicago & S. Air Lines, Inc. v. Waterman S.S. Corp., 333 U.S. 103, 109 (1948) ("The President . . . possesses in his own right certain powers conferred by the Constitution on him as Commander-in-Chief and as the Nation's organ in foreign affairs."), the power to use necessary and appropriate force against organizations and persons with a role in the September 11 attacks; the Supreme Court has stated that military detention is a "fundamental incident of waging war," *Hamdi,* 542 U.S. at 519; and, the Government alleges that al-Marri has been a member of al Qaeda since at least 1996. I think it clear under these circumstances that al-Marri can be detained as an enemy combatant and agree with the separate opinions of Judge Traxler, Judge Wilkinson, and Judge Niemeyer that so hold. . . .

II.

I do not agree, however, with Judge Traxler's separate concurrence, which concludes that a remand is necessary to permit al-Marri to further challenge his detention. . . .

B.

In *Hamdi,* the Court provided three avenues of guidance for lower courts when considering future enemy combatant cases. First, the Court noted that due process requires that an "enemy combatant must receive notice of the factual basis for his classification, and a fair opportunity to rebut the Government's factual assertions before a neutral decision-maker." *Hamdi,* 542 U.S. at 533. Second, the Court noted that "§2241 and its companion provisions provide at least a skeletal outline of the procedures to be afforded a petitioner in federal habeas review." *Id.* at 525. Thus, "Congress envisioned that habeas petitioners would have some opportunity to present and rebut facts and that courts in cases like this retain some ability to vary the ways in which they do so as mandated by due process." *Id.* at 526. Finally, the Court explained that whatever process is to be utilized, it must be carried out with "caution," and be "both prudent and incremental." *Id.* at 539. . . .

. . . I see nothing in *Hamdi* that forbids a sworn statement – like the Rapp Declaration – from providing sufficient "notice" of the allegations against al-Marri. Moreover. . . the magistrate judge required the Government to provide al-Marri the declaration in response to his request.

With respect to the Supreme Court's guidance that the process resemble customary habeas review, the procedures the magistrate judge proposed for handling the initial stage of the proceedings – which the district court later adopted in substantial part – in many ways mirrored traditional habeas practice under 28 U.S.C.A. §2254 and §2255 by requiring both parties to put forth affidavits and other materials for an initial determination of which party's presentation was more persuasive. . . .

Finally, and most importantly, *Hamdi* stressed the need for a "prudent" and "incremental" process. The magistrate judge proposed just that, outlining an iterative process in which al-Marri failed to participate "in any meaningful way." Indeed, as the magistrate judge noted, al-Marri refused to deny allegations in the Rapp Declaration that were peculiarly within al-Marri's knowledge. He failed to dispute even the assertion that he was performing poorly in school. It is simply beyond the pale for al-Marri to contend that he was unable, without further discovery from the Government, to put forth evidence that he did or did not attend class. By failing to participate, Al-Marri simply short-circuited the entire "incremental" process. . . .

Judge Duncan has authorized me to indicate that she joins in this opinion.

WILKINSON, CIRCUIT JUDGE, concurring in part and dissenting in part [omitted].

NIEMEYER, CIRCUIT JUDGE, concurring in the judgment in part and dissenting in part, as indicated herein [omitted].

DUNCAN, CIRCUIT JUDGE, concurring in part and dissenting in part [omitted].

* * *

29

Secret Evidence

B. CLASSIFIED INFORMATION PROCEDURES ACT

Page 866. Insert the following two cases after Note 10.

United States v. Abu Ali

United States Court of Appeals, Fourth Circuit, 2008
528 F.3d 210

WILKINSON, MOTZ and TRAXLER, Circuit Judges: [Ahmed Omar Abu Ali was born in the United States of Saudi parents. He was sent to Saudi Arabia for college education. While attending school there, he became affiliated with an Al Qaeda cell. In the course of meetings with Al Qaeda operatives in Saudi Arabia, Abu Ali suggested "assassinations or kidnappings of members of the U.S. Senate, the U.S. Army, and the Bush administration, a plan to rescue the prisoners at Guantánamo Bay, and plans to blow up American warplanes on U.S. bases and at U.S. ports, similar to the USS Cole operation." The cell began his training to reenter the United States as a "sleeper," for purposes of conducting later terrorist acts.

However, the Saudi counterterrorist agency Mabahith arrested Abu Ali before his training was completed and interrogated him. It also notified the FBI, which suggested questions for the interrogation. Eventually, the Saudi authorities surrendered Abu Ali to the United States, where he was tried for providing material support to a foreign terrorist organization, among several counts, partly on the basis of statements he made during the Saudi interrogation. When he challenged the admissibility of this evidence on the grounds that he had been tortured, the Saudi authorities made two Mabahith agents available for depositions in Saudi Arabia. Abu Ali's counsel attended the depositions and questioned the witnesses, but Abu Ali was not permitted to attend. At trial, the court also admitted unredacted versions of classified evidence that his defense team had only seen in redacted form before trial. He was convicted, and this appeal followed.] . . .

Unlike some others suspected of terrorist acts and designs upon the United States, Abu Ali was formally charged and tried according to the customary processes of the criminal justice system. Persons of good will may disagree over the precise extent to which the formal criminal justice process must be utilized when those suspected of participation in terrorist cells and networks are involved. There should be no disagreement, however, that the criminal justice system does retain an important place in the ongoing effort to deter and punish terrorist acts without the sacrifice of American constitutional norms and bedrock values. As will be apparent herein, the criminal justice system is not without those attributes of adaptation that will permit it to function in the post-9/11 world. These adaptations, however, need not and must not come at the expense of the requirement that an accused receive a fundamentally fair trial. In this case, we are satisfied that Abu Ali received a fair trial, though not a perfect one, and that the criminal justice system performed those functions which the Constitution envisioned for it. The three of us unanimously express our conviction that this is so in this opinion, which we have jointly authored.

Some differences do exist, however, among the panel members. Judge Wilkinson and Judge Traxler join in the opinion in its entirety. Judge Motz dissents [in parts not here relevant.] . . .

IV.

We next address Abu Ali's claim that the taking of the depositions of the Saudi Mabahith officials in Riyadh violated his Sixth Amendment Confrontation Clause rights. We hold that the procedures developed by the district court to meet the extraordinary circumstances of this case adequately protected Abu Ali's Sixth Amendment rights. We therefore reject his claim.

A.

We briefly summarize the facts relevant to his Confrontation Clause claim here. On June 8, 2003, the Mabahith arrested Abu Ali on suspicion that he was a member of the al-Faq'asi terrorist cell. Soon after his detention, Abu Ali confessed to his involvement with the cell when confronted with the fact that several other detained cell members had identified him. On July 18, 2003, while still in Saudi custody, Abu Ali wrote a handwritten confession which he was videotaped reading on July 24, 2003. The government offered both Abu Ali's handwritten and videotaped confessions as evidence at trial.

Abu Ali argued that he was tortured by the Mabahith and that his confessions were therefore involuntary. In depositions taken pursuant to Rule 15 of the Federal Rules of Criminal Procedure, Abu Ali's two principal interrogators both denied that they had ever tortured Abu Ali or were aware of any other Saudi government official engaging in such behavior. Transcripts of this testimony were made part of the record in the district court's hearing on Abu Ali's motion to suppress his confession and a videotape of the deposition (as redacted pursuant to the court's order) was played at trial and made part of the trial record.

B.

Abu Ali claims that his Sixth Amendment Confrontation Clause right was violated because he was not physically present when the Rule 15 depositions of the Mabahith officers were taken. Since the government planned to introduce the depositions at trial, Abu Ali claims that he should have been physically present when the Mabahith officers were deposed. This argument is premised on the well-accepted notion that "eye-to-eye" contact between the accused and his accuser is more likely to lead to the truth. *See* Coy v. Iowa, 487 U.S. 1012 (1988) ("It is always more difficult to tell a lie about a person 'to his face' than 'behind his back.'").

Abu Ali's absence at the Rule 15 deposition was the result of the logistical arrangements the trial court made to deal with the practical difficulties of securing testimony from the Mabahith officers. As Saudi citizens who reside in Saudi Arabia, the Mabahith officers were beyond the subpoena power of the district court. Given this limitation, the United States government officially inquired into whether the Saudi Arabian government would allow the officers to testify at trial in the United States. The Saudi government denied this request, but permitted the officers to sit for depositions in Riyadh. As represented by counsel for the United States, this was a first in Saudi-American relations: the Saudi government had never before allowed such foreign access to a Mabahith officer.

Given the possibility of taking the deposition in Riyadh, the district court found it impractical for Abu Ali to travel to Saudi Arabia for two reasons. First, it would have been difficult for United States Marshals to maintain custody of Abu Ali while in Saudi Arabia. Second, the fact that Abu Ali committed his offenses in Saudi Arabia might subject him to prosecution overseas, complicating – if not precluding – his return to the United States to face trial. In fact, the government represented at oral argument that Abu Ali never asked the district court to allow him to travel to Saudi Arabia for the depositions, and we find no evidence in the record to dispute this claim.

Given these practical difficulties – witnesses who could only testify in Saudi Arabia and a defendant unable to go to Saudi Arabia – the trial court attempted to fashion deposition procedures that would best preserve Abu Ali's Confrontation Clause right. At the court's directive, two defense attorneys, including Abu Ali's lead attorney, attended the depositions in Saudi Arabia, while a third attorney sat with Abu Ali in Virginia. Two attorneys for the government and a translator were also present in the room in Saudi Arabia while the Mabahith officers were being deposed.

A live, two-way video link was used to transmit the proceedings to a courtroom in Alexandria. This permitted Abu Ali and one of his attorneys to see and hear the testimony contemporaneously; it also allowed the Mabahith officers to see and hear Abu Ali as they testified. A court reporter in Alexandria transcribed the testimony in real time, and both the witnesses and Abu Ali were videotaped during the depositions, so that the jury could see their reactions. The trial court presided over the deposition testimony of the Mabahith officials from the courtroom in Alexandria, ruling on objections as they arose. Furthermore, Abu Ali was able to communicate via cell phone with his defense counsel in Saudi Arabia during the frequent breaks in the proceedings. In addition, the court was willing to stop the depositions if Abu Ali's counsel in Saudi Arabia wanted to consult with their client.

Having fashioned these procedures, the district court presided over seven days of deposition testimony from several Saudi Mabahith officers involved in the arrest, detention, and interrogation of Abu Ali. The subject matter of the depositions encompassed all aspects of Abu Ali's experience with the Saudi criminal justice system, including the manner of his arrest, the length of his interrogation, the conditions of his confinement, the Mabahith's methods of questioning, and the circumstances surrounding his confessions.

Of critical importance was the testimony of two Saudi government officials, a Brigadier General and a Captain in the Mabahith, who presided over the interrogation of Abu Ali. These officers stated that Abu Ali was not blindfolded, handcuffed, or shackled in any way during his interrogation, and that he was provided with food, water, and access to a bathroom during breaks in questioning. Both the Brigadier General and the Captain adamantly denied that they directed, participated in, or were aware of any government official using physical force or psychological coercion against Abu Ali.

Abu Ali's counsel actively participated throughout these depositions, objecting frequently during the government's direct examination and cross-examining each of the witnesses at length. In particular, Abu Ali's counsel were able to question the interrogating officers about Abu Ali's claims that he was tortured and beaten; deprived of sleep, food, and water; and denied use of a bathroom and mattress.

C.

The Confrontation Clause of the Sixth Amendment provides that "[i]n all criminal prosecutions, the accused shall enjoy the right . . . to be confronted with the witnesses against him." U.S. Const. amend. VI. This clause traditionally affords "the defendant a face-to-face meeting with witnesses appearing before the trier of fact." *Coy,* 487 U.S. at 1016. However, the right of the defendant to physically confront the witnesses against him is not absolute.

In Maryland v. Craig, 497 U.S. 836 (1990), the Supreme Court held that a district court may constitutionally admit testimony taken in the physical absence of the defendant so long as two conditions are met. *Id.* at 850. First, the denial of "face-to-face confrontation" must be "necessary to further an important public policy." *Id.* Second, the district court must ensure that protections are put in place so that "the reliability of the testimony is otherwise assured." *Id.* We find that both of *Craig*'s conditions are satisfied in this case.

First, the Supreme Court has long acknowledged that "no governmental interest is more compelling than the security of the Nation." Haig v. Agee, 453 U.S. 280, 307 (1981). . . . This case – in which the defendant is charged with crimes targeting American civilians and the President of the United States – plainly implicates this vital interest. This is not to suggest that a generalized interest in law enforcement is sufficient to satisfy the first prong of *Craig*. *Craig* plainly requires a public interest more substantial than convicting someone of a criminal offense. The prosecution of those bent on inflicting mass civilian casualties or assassinating high public officials is, however, just the kind of important public interest contemplated by the *Craig* decision.

Insistence on face-to-face confrontation may in some circumstances limit the ability of the United States to further its fundamental interest in preventing terrorist attacks. It is unquestionable that the struggle against terrorism is one of global dimension and that the United States depends upon its allies for logistical support and intelligence in this endeavor. This cooperation can result in foreign officials possessing information vital to prosecutions occurring in American courts. If the government is flatly prohibited from deposing foreign officials anywhere but in the United States, this would jeopardize the government's ability to prosecute terrorists using the domestic criminal justice system.

Thus, the district court reasonably determined that it was necessary in this case for the Mabahith officers to testify without the defendant physically present. Given the Saudi government's insistence that the Mabahith officers could only testify in Saudi Arabia and given that the defendant, for reasons of security or personal volition, could not travel overseas, requiring face-to-face confrontation here would have precluded the government from relying on the Saudi officers' important testimony. This would, to put it mildly, have greatly hindered efforts to prosecute the defendant, because the circumstances surrounding the confession bore crucially on any jury assessment of its voluntariness. The Sixth Amendment is not so inflexible as to require this outcome. *See* Mattox v. United States, 156 U.S. 237, 243 (1895) (noting that "[t]he law in its wisdom declares that the rights of the public shall not be wholly sacrificed in order that an incidental benefit may be preserved to the accused").

The second prong of the *Craig* test requires a district court to make certain that, absent face-to-face confrontation, "the reliability of the testimony is otherwise assured." *Craig,* 497 U.S. at 850. In *Craig,* the Court provided a blueprint on how to satisfy this requirement when it noted that "the presence of [the] other elements of confrontation – oath, cross-examination, and observation of the witness'[s] demeanor – adequately ensures that the testimony is both reliable and subject to rigorous adversarial testing in a manner functionally equivalent to that accorded live, in-person testimony." *Id.* at 851.

These "other elements" are present here. First, the Saudi witnesses testified under oath. While the oath used in this case, at the suggestion of defense counsel, was apparently an oath used in the Saudi criminal justice system, we cannot conclude, without more, that such an oath failed to serve its intended purpose of encouraging truth through solemnity. The oath used here was similar in most respects to the oath used in American judicial proceedings, and the appellant raised no objection to the oath in his briefs. Second, as discussed earlier, defense counsel was able to cross-examine the Mabahith witnesses extensively. Finally, the defendant, judge, and jury were all able to observe the demeanor of the witnesses. Both the defendant and the judge were able to view the witnesses as they testified via two-way video link, and the jury watched a videotape of the deposition at trial. This videotape presented side-by-side footage of the Mabahith officers testifying and the defendant's simultaneous reactions to the testimony.

In fact, the procedures used in this case were in some ways more protective of the defendant's interests than those used in *Craig*. While the Court in *Craig* approved the use of one-way video testimony, *see Craig,* 497 U.S. at 860, the depositions in this case were taken via a two-way video link. This two-way link meant that the witnesses were able to view the defendant as they testified, a protection not present in *Craig*.

. . . There is simply no evidence in the record that would lead this court to conclude that the defendant did not have a constitutionally sufficient chance to cross-examine the Mabahith witnesses. . . .

We thus find there to be no violation of the Confrontation Clause under *Craig*. The district court properly found that logistical and international necessities required the Mabahith officials to testify without the defendant present in order to further the government's undoubted national security interests. Furthermore, the procedures designed by the district court to replicate the "rigorous adversarial testing" present in a face-to-face confrontation plainly meet the reliability prong of *Craig*. . . .

VI.

Abu Ali also challenges the district court's handling of certain classified information under the provisions of the Classified Information Procedures Act ("CIPA"), 18 U.S.C. App. 3, §§1-16 (West 2000 & Supp. 2007).[13] Abu Ali's primary contention is that the district court violated his Sixth Amendment Confrontation Clause rights by admitting as evidence unredacted versions of two classified documents that Abu

13. These issues were separately raised via classified briefs and argued in closed proceedings before this panel.

Ali had only been permitted to view in a redacted form, and by refusing to allow Abu Ali and his lead trial counsel to attend and participate in the hearings conducted under CIPA to discuss the classified evidence. . . .

A.

The Sixth Amendment guarantees that "[i]n all criminal prosecutions, the accused shall enjoy . . . the right to be confronted with the witnesses against him." U.S. Const. amend. VI. Its "main and essential purpose . . . is to secure for the opponent the opportunity of cross-examination." Delaware v. Van Arsdall, 475 U.S. 673, 678 (1986). However, the right "means more than being allowed to confront the witness physically." *Id.* "[T]he principal evil at which the Confrontation Clause was directed was the civil-law mode of criminal procedure, and particularly its use of *ex parte* examinations as evidence against the accused." Crawford v. Washington, 541 U.S. 36, 54 (2004). Thus, while this is not the ordinary case, we think the criminal defendant's right to confront witnesses necessarily encompasses his right to also see any documentary evidence that such witnesses offer at trial as evidence to support a conviction. *Cf.* Abourezk v. Reagan, 785 F.2d 1043, 1060 (D.C. Cir. 1986) ("It is a hallmark of our adversary system that we safeguard party access to evidence tendered in support of a requested court judgment. The openness of judicial proceedings serves to preserve both the appearance and the reality of fairness in the adjudications of United States courts. It is therefore the firmly held main rule that a court may not dispose of the merits of a case on the basis of *ex parte, in camera* submissions.").

A defendant's right to see the evidence that is tendered against him *during* trial, however, does not necessarily equate to a right to have classified information disclosed to him *prior* to trial. Evidentiary privileges may serve as valid bases to block the disclosure of certain types of evidence, and the validity of such privileges may be tested by in camera and ex parte proceedings before the court "for the limited purpose of determining whether the asserted privilege is genuinely applicable." *Id.* As a general rule, "[i]f the court finds that the claimed privilege does not apply, then the other side must be given access to the information." *Id.* If the court finds that the privilege does apply, then it may preclude access to the information. But neither scenario results in the conviction of a defendant "based upon evidence he was never permitted to see and to rebut." *Id.*

In the area of national security and the government's privilege to protect classified information from public disclosure, we look to CIPA for appropriate procedures. . . .

C.

With these principles in mind, we turn first to Abu Ali's Confrontation Clause challenge to the government's introduction at trial of two unredacted, classified documents that memorialized communications between Sultan Jubran [an Al Qaeda operative] and Abu Ali in the days following the May 2003 safe house raids conducted by the Saudi officials in Medina, as well as to his exclusion from the CIPA proceedings in which these communications were discussed.

1. . . .

[Only one of Abu Ali's lawyers obtained a security clearance. The government disclosed to the security-cleared lawyer unredacted copies of evidence it intended to declassify and introduce at trial, but explained that it would take some precautions to prevent public disclosure of the unredacted documents. It also afforded Abu Ali's non-cleared lawyers only redacted versions of the same documents.]

. . . The first declassified document was dated May 27, 2003, and read as follows:

> Peace, How are you and how is your family? I hope they are good. I heard the news about the children's sickness. I wish them a speedy recovery, God willing. Anyway, please keep in touch. Greetings to the group, Hani.

The government intended to demonstrate that "Hani" was a known alias of Abu Ali and that "news about the children's sickness" was a coded reference to the raids conducted by the Mabahith and the arrest of the Medina cell members. The second declassified document was dated June 6, 2003, and read as follows:

> To my brother, Peace to you with God's mercy and blessings. Thank God, I am fine. I was saved from the accident by a great miracle. I ask God that I would be thankful to Him. I have no idea about the others. However, according to what one doctor mentioned, 'Adil was not with them, thank God. The important thing is to get yourself ready for the medical checkup because you may have an appointment soon. Therefore, you must keep yourself ready by refraining from eating high fat meals and otherwise.

With regard to this communication, the government intended to demonstrate that the term "accident" was also a coded reference to the safe house raids. According to the government's theory, Sultan Jubran was advising Abu Ali that he did not know which cell members had escaped and which were captured, but that he and al-Faq'asi (a/k/a "Adil"), had escaped, and warning that Abu Ali might also be at risk.

A comparison of the classified and unclassified documents reveals that the declassified versions provided the dates, the opening salutations, the entire substance of the communications, and the closings, and had only been lightly redacted to omit certain identifying and forensic information.

On October 19, 2005, the government filed an in camera, ex parte motion pursuant to §4 of CIPA, seeking a protective order prohibiting testimony and lines of questioning that would lead to the disclosure of the classified information during the trial. *See* 18 U.S.C. App. 3 §4. The government advised that the classified portions of the communications could not be provided to Abu Ali and his uncleared counsel because they contained highly sensitive information which, if confirmed in a public setting, would divulge information detrimental to national security interests. The district court granted the government's motion by in camera, ex parte, sealed order. However, the district court ruled that the United States could use the "silent witness rule" to disclose the classified information to the jury at trial.[18] . . .

---

18. The "silent witness" rule was described in United States v. Zettl, 835 F.2d 1059, 1063 (4th Cir. 1987), as follows.

> [T]he witness would not disclose the information from the classified document in open court. Instead, the witness would have a copy of the classified document before him. The court, counsel and the jury would also have copies of the classified document. The witness would refer to specific places in the document in response to questioning. The jury would then refer to the particular part of the document as the witness answered. By this method, the classified information would not be made public at trial but the defense would be able to present that classified information to the jury.

Id.

3.

Having carefully considered the circumstances and evidence below, we conclude that the district court's determination that the redacted classified information need not be disclosed to the defendant, his uncleared counsel, and the public was not an abuse of discretion. Nor do we think that the district court's exclusion of Abu Ali and his uncleared counsel from the CIPA proceedings ran afoul of the Confrontation Clause. The district court's admission of the classified versions of the documents as evidence for consideration by the jury without disclosing the same versions to Abu Ali, however, was clearly contrary to the rights guaranteed to Abu Ali by the Confrontation Clause.

We begin with the district court's exclusion of Abu Ali and his uncleared counsel from the CIPA proceedings. The district court was presented with a §4 motion by the government to protect the classified information and a §5 motion, made at a later date, by Abu Ali that he be allowed to disclose that information. Initially, the district court found the redacted, unclassified version of the communications to be adequate to meet the defendant's need for information. CIPA expressly provides for such redactions of classified information from documents sought or required to be produced to the defendant, and the determination may be based upon an ex parte showing that the disclosure would jeopardize national security interests. The district court appropriately balanced the interests and made a reasonable determination that disclosure of the redacted information was not necessary to a fair trial.

There was likewise no abuse of discretion in the district court's decision to preclude Abu Ali's uncleared counsel from cross-examining the government's witnesses about the redacted information, which would have effectively disclosed the classified information that the court had already ruled need not be disclosed. A defendant and his counsel, if lacking in the requisite security clearance, must be excluded from hearings that determine what classified information is material and whether substitutions crafted by the government suffice to provide the defendant adequate means of presenting a defense and obtaining a fair trial. Thus, the mere exclusion of Abu Ali and his uncleared counsel from the CIPA hearings did not run afoul of CIPA or Abu Ali's Confrontation Clause rights.

We also conclude that the district court struck an appropriate balance between the government's national security interests and the defendant's right to explore the manner in which the communications were obtained and handled. Abu Ali and his uncleared counsel were provided with the substance of the communications, the dates, and the parties involved, and CIPA-cleared defense counsel was provided with the classified versions and afforded unfettered opportunity to cross-examine the government's witnesses concerning these matters. At the conclusion of the examinations, defense counsel pointed to no specific problem with the issues explored. The district court also expressly considered Abu Ali's rights under the Confrontation Clause and determined that public examination of these witnesses was not necessary to prevent infringement of them. Having fully considered the record and the classified information ourselves, we agree. Uncleared defense counsel were not entitled to disclose the classified information via their questioning of the witnesses about their roles in extracting, sharing, transferring, and handling the communications, and Abu Ali, who was ably represented by counsel at the hearing on this issue, was not deprived of his right to confrontation or to a fair trial merely because he and his uncleared counsel were not also allowed to attend.

The error in the case, which appears to have originated in the October 2005 CIPA proceeding, was that CIPA was taken one step too far. The district court did not abuse its discretion in protecting the classified information from disclosure to Abu Ali and his uncleared counsel, in approving a suitable substitute, or in determining that Abu Ali would receive a fair trial in the absence of such disclosure. But, for reasons that remain somewhat unclear to us, the district court granted the government's request that the complete, unredacted classified document could be presented to the jury via the "silent witness" procedure. The end result, therefore, was that the jury was privy to the information that was withheld from Abu Ali.

As noted above, CIPA contemplates and authorizes district courts to prevent the disclosure of classified information, as was done in this case, so long as it does not deprive the defendant of a fair trial. CIPA also authorizes restrictions upon the questioning of the witnesses to ensure that classified information remains classified. Indeed, even the "silent witness" procedure contemplates situations in which the jury is provided classified information that is withheld from the public, but not from the defendant. In addition, CIPA provides district courts wide discretion to evaluate and approve suitable substitutions to be presented to the jury. CIPA does not, however, authorize courts to provide classified documents to the jury when only such substitutions are provided to the defendant. Nor could it. There is a stark difference between ex parte submissions from prosecutors which protect the disclosure of irrelevant, nonexculpatory, or privileged information, and situations in which the government seeks to use *ex parte* information in court as evidence to obtain a conviction. And, the notion that such "safeguards against wide-ranging discovery . . . would be sufficient to justify a conviction on secret evidence is patently absurd." *Id.*; *see also* United States v. Innamorati, 996 F.2d 456, 488 (1st Cir. 1993) (finding no error in prosecutor's ex parte submission of information for consideration as to whether it must be disclosed to the defendant, but noting that "there [was] no question . . . of convictions based upon secret evidence furnished to the factfinder but withheld from the defendants").

The same can be said for the evidence here. If classified information is to be relied upon as evidence of guilt, the district court may consider steps to protect some or all of the information from unnecessary public disclosure in the interest of national security and in accordance with CIPA, which specifically contemplates such methods as redactions and substitutions so long as these alternatives do not deprive the defendant of a fair trial. However, the government must at a minimum provide the same version of the evidence to the defendant that is submitted to the jury. We do not balance a criminal defendant's right to see the evidence which will be used to convict him against the government's interest in protecting that evidence from public disclosure. If the government does not want the defendant to be privy to information that is classified, it may either declassify the document, seek approval of an effective substitute, or forego its use altogether. What the government cannot do is hide the evidence from the defendant, but give it to the jury. Such plainly violates the Confrontation Clause.

D.

Having determined that submission of the classified documents to the jury ran afoul of Abu Ali's Confrontation Clause rights, we turn now to consider whether that error was harmless. We conclude that it was. . . .

VIII. . . .

For the foregoing reasons, the judgment is affirmed in part, reversed in part, and remanded for further proceedings consistent with this decision.

Affirmed in Part, Reversed in Part, and Remanded.

[Dissenting opinion of DIANA GRIBBON MOTZ, Circuit Judge, omitted.]

United States v. Rosen

United States District Court, Eastern District of Virginia, 2007
487 F. Supp. 2d 703

ELLIS, District Judge. This Espionage Act (18 U.S.C. §793) prosecution involves a substantial amount of classified information the government contends is information relating to the national defense ("NDI")[19] and for this reason the government seeks to avoid public disclosure of this material in the course of the trial. To this end, the government, by motion pursuant to §6 of the Classified Information Procedures Act ("CIPA"),[20] has proposed utilizing a procedure at trial whereby substantial quantities of classified information would be disclosed to the Court, the jury, and counsel, but withheld from the public. This novel proposal, if allowed, would effectively close a substantial portion of the trial. Accordingly, defendants challenge this proposed procedure on the grounds that it is neither authorized by CIPA nor constitutionally permissible.

I.

Both defendants are charged with conspiracy to communicate NDI to persons not authorized to receive it, in violation of 18 U.S.C. §793(g), (e). Rosen is additionally charged with aiding and abetting alleged co-conspirator Lawrence Franklin's unauthorized communication of NDI to persons not authorized to receive it, in violation of 18 U.S.C. §§793(d) and 2. The superceding indictment generally alleges that over a course of several years, defendants cultivated various sources of information within the United States government, obtained NDI from those sources, and then disseminated that NDI to others not authorized to receive it, including co-workers, journalists, and foreign government officials. For a more complete recitation of the facts alleged in the superceding indictment, as well as a more precise delineation of the government's burden of proof, see United States v. Rosen, 445 F. Supp. 2d. 602 (E.D. Va. 2006) [*infra* p. 281] . . . .

---

19. It is important to recognize that NDI and classified material may not be coextensive sets. . . . While classified status may be probative of information's NDI status, it is not conclusive.

20. 18 U.S.C. App. 3.

III.

[After defendants proposed to offer classified information in their defense at trial and objected to the government's proposed substitutions pursuant to CIPA], "[t]he government . . . proposed a procedure for handling this material at trial and it is this proposal that is at issue here. The government's proposal is novel; no published opinion has been found or cited in which the precise procedure proposed here was judicially approved or used. Simply put, the government proposes that while the jury, the Court, and counsel will, for the most part, have access to the unredacted classified material, the public will not. Instead, the public, in the course of the trial, will see and hear only the substitutions that have passed through the CIPA §6(c) process. In other words, and putting to one side the not insubstantial practical problems inherent in conducting a trial pursuant to the government's proposed procedure, its use would surely exclude the public from substantial and critical parts of the trial. This result is evident from a more detailed description of the proposed procedure.

The government's proposal is, in effect, a variant and a substantial expansion of the so-called "silent witness rule," a rule that has been used and judicially approved in certain, but not all circumstances. . . . As noted, the effect of using the procedure in this case would be the exclusion of the public from substantial portions of the trial.

The proposed procedure would work as follows: for each classified document discussed at trial, the Court, the witness, counsel, and the jurors would have the unredacted classified document in front of them, either in paper form or via computer screens viewable only by those persons. The public, however, would see only a redacted version. When counsel or a witness wishes to direct the jury to a classified portion of the document, counsel and the witness would refer to the page, paragraph and line numbers, with the Court, opposing counsel, and the jury following along, but members of the public could not follow along because they would be unaware of the specific information referenced by counsel or the witness. And, the witness answering the questions about the document would not be permitted to refer to specific language or information in the document, except by use of certain codes. For example, to rebut the government's contention that certain material is NDI, defendants will likely wish to call witnesses to compare various public source documents with the alleged NDI. To do so effectively may well require the witness to refer to specific language or contents of both the public source document and the alleged NDI. Anticipating this, the government proposes that the witness would not speak the names of certain specific countries, foreign persons, etc., but would instead use a code (e.g., "Country A," "Report X," "Foreign Person Y," "Foreign Person Z," etc.) provided also to counsel, the Court, and the jury. Moreover, this code would change with respect to different alleged overt acts, presumably to prevent the public from inferring the meaning of the generic designations or otherwise breaking the code. For example, if a witness discussing a particular alleged disclosure is instructed to refer to Monaco as Country A, a different witness (or even the same witness) discussing another alleged disclosure might use Country B or C to refer to Monaco.

Likewise, when recordings discussing classified information are played, the government proposes that the Court, counsel, witness, and jury listen on special headphones to the entire recording. The public, however, would not hear the full recording; instead, the recorded conversations would be played aloud in the courtroom, but where classified information is discussed in the recording, the public version would revert to static. Also, the public would receive only a redacted transcript of the conversations.

In sum, the novel and distinctive feature of the government's proposed procedure is that the public is walled off from seeing and hearing everything the jury, the Court, the attorneys and the witnesses see and hear. What the public does not see or hear is the heart of the case, namely the classified material the government claims is the NDI that the defendants allegedly received and distributed without authorization. A further, related novel and distinctive feature of the government's proposal relates to the jury. Although jurors will see and hear classified material, they, of course, will not have received security clearances for this purpose. Nor has this ever been otherwise in cases involving classified material, for a variety of reasons including the substantial time and effort typically required for such clearances to be completed and the substantial question whether it is constitutionally permissible to exclude jurors because they could not pass a security clearance investigation. The government's remedy for this anomaly is simply to have the jurors instructed that they cannot disclose to anyone the classified material they will see and hear during the trial.

With this description in mind, the analysis now proceeds to address the following questions:

(i) Whether the government's proposed procedure is explicitly or implicitly authorized by CIPA.

(ii) Whether the government's proposed procedure violates the right to a public trial, guaranteed to defendants by the Sixth Amendment and to the public by the First Amendment.

IV.

A.

The government urges that the use of the silent witness rule, codes, and redacted recordings are "substitutions" authorized by CIPA. Defendants disagree, noting the government's proposed procedure is nowhere authorized by CIPA, either explicitly or implicitly. Defendants are correct, a conclusion that follows from CIPA's plain language, but also from the fact that the government's proposed procedure simply cannot fit within CIPA's confines even assuming the statute's plain language would not otherwise preclude it.

Analysis of this statutory argument properly focuses on CIPA §6(c) and §8(b) . . . . As noted, CIPA §6(c) allows the government to move that in lieu of disclosing classified information at trial, a "substitution" be used, which could take the form of a summary of the information or a presumably sanitized statement of facts the classified statement would tend to prove. Importantly, no substitutions can be used unless there is a judicial finding that the substitution provides defendants with "substantially the same ability to make his defense as would disclosure of the specific classified information." Consistent with this, CIPA §8(b) also permits introduction and use at trial of redacted versions of classified materials unless "the whole ought in fairness to be considered."

Significantly, neither §6(c) nor §8(b) explicitly authorize[s] or state[s] that "substitutions" may be made available to the public and the jury on different terms. CIPA is at best silent on this issue. Yet, this silence should not be construed as implicitly authorizing the government's proposal. To the contrary, it seems clear that CIPA envisions that "substitutions," if not unfair to defendants, will be used at a public trial in identical form for both the jury and the public. While it is true, as reflected in CIPA's legislative history, that "Congress expected trial judges to fashion creative solutions in the interests of justice for classified information problems,"[9] there is no evidence that Congress expected this creativity to extend to adopting procedures that effectively

---

9. United States v. North, 713 F. Supp. 1452 (D.D.C. 1989) (citing H. Rep. No. 96-1436, 1980 U.S.C.C.A.N. 4294).

close the trial to the public. Indeed, given the strong presumption in the law that trials will be open and that evidence will be fully aired in public, CIPA's silence about whether "substitutions" and "excisions" can be made available to the public and jury on different terms should be interpreted as a prohibition on doing so. Closing a trial, even partially, is a highly unusual result disfavored by the law. A statute, even one regulating the use of classified information, should not be construed as authorizing a trial closure based on Congress' mere silence or use of ambiguous language. Rather, because a trial closure implicates important constitutional rights, CIPA should not be read to authorize closure absent a clear and explicit statement by Congress in the statutory language.

In short, CIPA only authorizes the use of substitutions to avoid disclosure of classified information *to the public and the jury,* provided defendant's right to present a defense is not impaired; this authority is not the authority to close a trial to the public.

B.

Even assuming, *arguendo,* that the CIPA provision allowing "substitutions" might be stretched to encompass the government's proposed procedure, there is no doubt that the procedure would not pass muster under CIPA's fairness requirements. Where, as here, a central issue in the case is whether the government's alleged NDI is indeed genuinely NDI, and the proposed procedure would amount to a wholesale use of the silent witness rule to cover all of the alleged NDI, it cannot be said that the procedure affords defendants "substantially the same ability to make [their] defense as would disclosure of the specific classified information." CIPA §6(c). A few examples vividly illustrate this point.

As noted, the government in this case has the burden of proving beyond a reasonable doubt that the alleged NDI is indeed NDI. To this end, the government will likely invite witnesses to compare the substance of certain of defendants' emails, telephone conversations, or faxes with certain alleged NDI to show that defendants had obtained NDI and were disseminating it without authorization. Defendants, of course, may wish to show, and indeed to emphasize, the dissimilarities between the alleged NDI and the information they obtained. Plainly, they would be significantly hobbled in doing so by use of the government's proposed procedure, inasmuch as the specific information could not be used in open court. The silent comparison of paragraphs or sentences, even where supplemented by codes, would effectively preclude defense counsel from driving home important points to the jury.

Similarly, it is apparent that defendants intend at trial to rebut the government's claim that certain material is NDI by having witnesses compare the alleged NDI to contemporaneous public domain material. Once again, the proposed procedure would unfairly impact defendants' ability to establish this defense. In this context, the silent witness rule, applied across the board as the government proposes here, essentially robs defendants of the chance to make vivid and drive home to the jury their view that the alleged NDI is no such thing, as essentially similar material was abundant in the public domain. Importantly in this respect, it is hard to see how defendants could effectively show, via the silent witness rule, that the details of differences between public source material and the alleged NDI are neither minor nor trivial. . . .

. . . In short, the use of codes would render virtually impossible an effective line of cross-examination vital to the defense. . . .

Yet another fatal defect in the fairness of the proposed procedure is apparent from the way in which it would hamper defendants should they choose to testify. Clearly, the proposed procedure would unfairly hinder defendants in their effort to explain why they believed any information they sought to obtain, the information they received, and the information they disclosed to others was not NDI. In this regard, defendants must be able to explain precisely what they knew and when, and from whom or what they learned it, and why they did not believe the material was NDI they were not authorized to have, or otherwise lacked the requisite *mens rea*. Yet, the proposed procedure would unfairly hinder defendants from doing so. For example, statements like "I heard from Foreign Person C the fact about Country X, reflected at Exhibit A page 3 paragraph 4 line 2 – well, except for the last clause – and so when I asked Franklin for confirmation of that fact, I thought I was asking for a matter of public record," may provide some exculpatory description of defendants' state of mind, assuming the jury could decode the statement quickly enough to follow the questioning. Yet, it would be difficult, if not impossible, for defendants to explain fully why they believed the information they sought or had was in the public domain without revealing details about the information, the identity and reliability of Person C, etc. Because the proposed procedure shackles defendants in this way, it cannot pass muster under CIPA.

Finally, it must be noted that the government's proposed frequently-changing system of coded references not only invites juror confusion, but virtually guarantees it. Given the sheer number of substitutions and the proliferation of coded phrases, varying from witness to witness and overt act to overt act, the likelihood of juror confusion would be a sufficient ground, by itself, for rejecting the wholesale proposed substitutions under CIPA §6(c). . . .

V.

Defendants' challenge to the government's proposed procedure rests on constitutional as well as statutory grounds. Specifically, defendants argue that even if CIPA's language can be stretched to cover the government's proposed procedure, that procedure nonetheless fails as a violation of defendants' Sixth Amendment right to a public trial and the public's First Amendment right to a trial open to public scrutiny. Thus, even if the procedure passed muster under CIPA, constitutional analysis is nonetheless required. This follows, defendants argue, because the proposed procedure effectively excludes the public from essential portions of the trial.[20]

Nor is there any doubt that the portions of the trial that would be closed to the public are critical portions of the trial. It is clear that the government's proposal precludes the public from hearing and evaluating the evidence on a crucial and contested element of the case, namely, whether the information at issue is NDI and whether defendants knew it to be such. Moreover, the quality and quantity of material the government proposes to exclude from public view is significant. Testimony about the putative NDI at issue in seven of the alleged nine disclosures would be partially closed to the public, as would the recordings and documents corresponding to this NDI. Notably, the government's proposed procedure would treat even certain related public domain documents, including news reports, as if they were classified documents. In short, in the circumstances of this case, the government's proposal is clearly equivalent to sealing essential aspects of the trial.

---

20. It is noteworthy in this respect that the government sensibly appears to have abandoned its original position that the proposed use of the silent witness rule, coded testimony, and redacted recordings does not close the trial because the public would be present in the courtroom. This argument, if credited, leads to the absurd result that a trial unintelligible to the public is still "open" to the public simply because the public is physically present to see and hear what they cannot understand. The public's physical presence, by itself, does not guarantee that a trial is public; it is also necessary that the trial be reasonably comprehensible to the physically present public.

The analysis of defendants' constitutional argument properly begins with the recognition that defendants and the public have a fundamental right to a trial open to the public. The right to a public trial contributes to just adjudication, stimulates public confidence in the judicial system, and ensures that the public is fairly apprised of the proceedings in cases of public concern. A public trial contributes to just adjudication in several ways: (i) requiring witness[es]' testimony to be public deters perjury; (ii) requiring a judge's rulings to be made in public deters partiality and bias; and (iii) requiring prosecutors to present their charges and evidence publicly deters prosecutorial vindictiveness and abuse of power. In these ways, the presence of the public encourages accurate factfinding and wise use of judicial and prosecutorial discretion, thereby contributing to public confidence that justice has prevailed at trial. In short, justice must not only be done, it must be seen to be done.

Given the important interests at stake, it is now well-settled that defendants in criminal cases and the public both have a right to a trial open to public scrutiny. *See* Press-Enterprise Co. v. Superior Court of California, 464 U.S. 501, 510 (1984) (public's First Amendment right); Waller v. Georgia, 467 U.S. 39, 44-45 (1984) (defendant's Sixth Amendment right). It is also well-settled that the standard governing whether the public trial right has been infringed is the same whether the right is asserted by the press under the First Amendment or by a defendant under the Sixth Amendment. *Waller,* 467 U.S. at 46-47. Under this constitutional standard, a trial is presumptively open, and may be closed only if certain criteria are met. These criteria are set forth in *Press-Enterprise* and its progeny, as follows:

> (1) an "overriding interest" must exist to close the trial,
> (2) the closure is no broader than necessary to protect that interest,
> (3) the court considers reasonable alternatives to closure, and
> (4) the court makes specific findings on the record concerning the existence of the overriding interest, the breadth of the closure, and the unavailability of alternatives to facilitate appellate review.

Press-Enterprise, 464 U.S. at 510. As the proponent of closing the proceedings, the government bears a "weighty" burden to establish that closure is permissible. *Press-Enterprise,* 464 U.S. at 509-10. Decisions to close trials must be made on a case by case basis, with attention to the facts and circumstances of each case; statutes *per se* requiring closure in certain circumstances are impermissible. Globe Newspaper Co. v. Superior Court, 457 U.S. 596, 611 n.27 (1982). Finally, before trials may be closed, the public must be given notice and an opportunity to be heard. In re Knight Publishing Co., 743 F.2d 231, 234-35 (4th Cir. 1984). An erroneous denial of a public trial is a structural error not amenable to harmless error analysis. *Bell,* 236 F.3d at 165 (citing cases).

Each of the four *Press-Enterprise* elements is separately considered.

1. Overriding Interest

The government claims that its interest in protecting classified information is a compelling and overriding one, and has cited numerous cases in support of this claim. While it is true, as an abstract proposition, that the government's interest in protecting classified information can be a qualifying compelling and overriding interest, it is also true that the government must make a specific showing of harm to national security in specific cases to carry its burden in this regard. The government's *ipse dixit* that information is damaging to national security is not sufficient to close the courtroom doors nor to obtain the functional equivalent, namely trial by code. *Press-Enterprise* and *In re Washington Post* require more; they require a judicial inquiry into the legitimacy of the asserted national security interest, and specific findings, sealed if necessary, about the harm to national security that would ensue if the request to close the trial is not granted. *See Press-Enterprise,* 464 U.S. at 510; In re Washington Post, 807 F.2d 383, 391-92 (4th Cir. 1986) (rejecting the government's argument that courts should defer to Executive Branch assertions that trial closures are necessary for national security reasons, and stating that a proceeding cannot be closed merely because the case implicated CIPA at an earlier stage). Moreover, the government's *ipse dixit* is insufficient whether it appears by way of classified status, or the bald assertion of counsel that information is damaging to national security. Thus, granting that national security concerns can justify appropriately tailored trial closures, the government nonetheless bears the burden of demonstrating, as a factual matter, that harm to national security would result from failing to close the trial.

Here, the government has not met its burden; instead, it has done no more than to invoke "national security" broadly and in a conclusory fashion, as to all the classified information in the case. Of course, classification decisions are for the Executive Branch, and the information's classified status must inform an assessment of the government's asserted interests under *Press-Enterprise.* But ultimately, trial judges must make their own judgment about whether the government's asserted interest in partially closing the trial is compelling or overriding. As noted, a generalized assertion of "national security interests," whether by virtue of the information's classified status or upon representation of counsel, is not alone sufficient to overcome the presumption in favor of open trials. Here, the government has not proffered any evidence about danger to national security from airing the evidence publicly, let alone an item-by-item description of the harm to national security that will result from disclosure at trial of each specific piece of information as to which closure is sought, as required by *Press-Enterprise*.

Moreover, quite aside from the government's failure to provide any evidence of harm to national security from an open trial, the government's assertion of an overriding interest justifying a trial closure is undermined by the substance of the proposed procedure, to wit, that the jury and uncleared witnesses will be permitted to receive unredacted classified information. Given that the government appears willing to trust its confidential information to jurors, alternates, and uncleared witnesses, including (potentially) defendants, it is difficult to credit fully the government's claim that the classified information at issue is deserving of rigorous protection.

The government urges that this proposed disclosure to the jury does not reflect any inconsistency on its part, because the jurors could be instructed never to disclose the classified information they received at trial. Yet such an instruction appears patently unfair here, because it would suggest to the jury that the information at issue is NDI. Nor is this a minor consideration given that the status of the information as NDI is a central issue in the case, and indeed an element of the charged crime as to which the government bears the burden of proof beyond a reasonable doubt. An instruction that the jurors must treat the information they receive as a closely-held government secret is not easily reconciled with the instruction that the jury is the sole judge of the facts of the case and that it alone determines whether the information at issue is NDI, *i.e.*, whether it is closely held and potentially damaging to national security if revealed. While the two instructions are not flatly contradictory, they would be beyond the capacity of most jurors to reconcile . . . .

In short, the government's asserted overriding interest is not treated as such by the government itself, given that the putative NDI will be disclosed to uncleared jurors and witnesses. And while the government's cited cases support the notion that national security interests *can be* sufficiently compelling to justify a partial closure of the trial, they also require that the government satisfy *Press-Enterprise* by adequately supporting its motion with a description of the specific harm to national security that would ensue from disclosure. The government has not done so here. Accordingly, its motion fails under the first prong of *Press-Enterprise.*

2. Narrowly Tailored

For the same reasons, there is no basis to conclude that the government's proposal is narrowly tailored to protect any national security interests. Since the government has not identified with specificity which of the classified information to be kept from public view would harm national security if disclosed to the broader public, or how the national security would be affected, it is impossible to evaluate whether the proposed closure is as narrowly tailored as possible to protect that asserted interest.

3. Alternatives

Likewise, assuming that an overriding interest exists here because disclosure of some or all of the classified information at issue would damage national security, it is evident that reasonable alternatives to closure exist here. To wit, the government could propose conventional CIPA §6(c) substitutions that would be given to the jury and the public in the same form. Whether these substitutions would pass CIPA §6(c) fairness standards is another question not here presented.

4. Findings

Although the conclusions concerning the other *Press-Enterprise* factors obviate the need for factual findings, the absence of any affidavit describing the ensuing harms to national security should the trial not be closed is noteworthy. A highly detailed explanation of the ensuing harms to national security is especially necessary to make the thorough factual findings required for a closure when, as here, much of the classified information at issue is not self-evidently damaging to national security. . . .

VI.

To summarize, the wholesale use of the silent witness rule, coded testimony, and redacted recordings effectively closes the trial. This procedure is not a "substitution" authorized by CIPA, and even if it were, it would not afford defendants substantially the same opportunity to present their defense as the specific classified information. Moreover, even if the procedure passed muster under CIPA, it nonetheless would have to satisfy the *Press-Enterprise* test because it effectively closes portions of the trial. The proposed procedure does not; the government's showing of an overriding interest in protecting sensitive national security information has been insufficient to this point, and the government's claim that the information at issue is damaging to the national security if publicly disclosed is belied by its own proposal to release the information to uncleared persons. This opinion does not foreclose the government from proposing specific §6(c) substitutions that pass CIPA muster. Nor does this opinion foreclose consideration of or narrowly limited use of the silent witness rule where the government provides a specific factual basis for a claim that public disclosure would damage the national security.

For these reasons, defendants' motion to strike must be granted, and the government's motion to close the trial, styled a CIPA §6(c) motion, must be denied. At the government's request and with no objection from defendants, entry of an appropriate Order will be delayed to afford the government time to consider how to proceed with respect to the CIPA process.

* * *

30

Trial by Military Commission

B. TRIAL BY MILITARY COMMISSION AFTER 9/11

Page 906. Add the following material at the end of Note 8.

Military Commissions Act of 2006

Pub. L. No. 109-366, 120 Stat. 2636
(codified in scattered sections of 10 U.S.C.)

Section 1. Short Title . . .

(a) Short Title – This Act may be cited as the Military Commissions Act of 2006. . . .

Sec. 2. Construction of Presidential Authority to Establish Military Commissions.

The authority to establish military commissions under chapter 47A of title 10, United States Code, as added by section 3(a), may not be construed to alter or limit the authority of the President under the Constitution of the United States and laws of the United States to establish military commissions for areas declared to be under martial law or in occupied territories should circumstances so require.

Sec. 3. Military Commissions. [Amending Subtitle A of 10 U.S.C. to insert after Chapter 47 a new Chapter 47A, Military Commissions.]

Chapter 47A – Military Commissions

Subchapter I – General Provisions

§948a. Definitions

In this chapter:

(1) Unlawful enemy combatant. –

(A) The term "unlawful enemy combatant" means –

(i) a person who has engaged in hostilities or who has purposefully and materially supported hostilities against the United States or its co-belligerents who is not a lawful enemy combatant (including a person who is part of the Taliban, al Qaeda, or associated forces); or

(ii) a person who, before, on, or after the date of the enactment of the Military Commissions Act of 2006, has been determined to be an unlawful enemy combatant by a Combatant Status Review Tribunal or another competent tribunal established under the authority of the President or the Secretary of Defense.

(B) Co-belligerent. – In this paragraph, the term "co-belligerent," with respect to the United States, means any State or armed force joining and directly engaged with the United States in hostilities or directly supporting hostilities against a common enemy.

(2) Lawful enemy combatant. – The term "lawful enemy combatant" means a person who is –

(A) a member of the regular forces of a State party engaged in hostilities against the United States;

(B) a member of a militia, volunteer corps, or organized resistance movement belonging to a State party engaged in such hostilities, which are under responsible command, wear a fixed distinctive sign recognizable at a distance, carry their arms openly, and abide by the law of war; or

(C) a member of a regular armed force who professes allegiance to a government engaged in such hostilities, but not recognized by the United States.

(3) Alien. – The term "alien" means a person who is not a citizen of the United States. . . .

§948b. Military commissions generally

(a) Purpose. – This chapter establishes procedures governing the use of military commissions to try alien unlawful enemy combatants engaged in hostilities against the United States for violations of the law of war and other offenses triable by military commission.

(b) Authority for Military Commissions under This Chapter. – The President is authorized to establish military commissions under this chapter for offenses triable by military commission as provided in this chapter[1]. . . .

(f) Status of Commissions under Common Article 3. – A military commission established under this chapter is a regularly constituted court, affording all the necessary "judicial guarantees which are recognized as indispensable by civilized peoples" for purposes of common Article 3 of the Geneva Conventions.

(g) Geneva Conventions Not Establishing Source of Rights. – No alien unlawful enemy combatant subject to trial by military commission under this chapter may invoke the Geneva Conventions as a source of rights.

§948c. Persons subject to military commissions

Any alien unlawful enemy combatant is subject to trial by military commission under this chapter.

§948d. Jurisdiction of military commissions

(a) Jurisdiction. – A military commission under this chapter shall have jurisdiction to try any offense made punishable by this chapter or the law of war when committed by an alien unlawful enemy combatant before, on, or after September 11, 2001.

(b) Lawful Enemy Combatants. – Military commissions under this chapter shall not have jurisdiction over lawful enemy combatants. . . .

(c) Determination of Unlawful Enemy Combatant Status Dispositive. – A finding, whether before, on, or after the date of the enactment of the

---

[1. The President exercised this authority by Exec. Order No. 13,425, *Trial of Alien Unlawful Enemy Combatants by Military Commission*, 72 Fed. Reg. 7737 (Feb. 14, 2007), superseding the provisions of the Military Order of Nov. 13, 2001, that relate to military commissions.]

Military Commissions Act of 2006, by a Combatant Status Review Tribunal or another competent tribunal established under the authority of the President or the Secretary of Defense that a person is an unlawful enemy combatant is dispositive for purposes of jurisdiction for trial by military commission under this chapter. . . .

Subchapter III – Pre-Trial Procedure . . .

§948r. Compulsory self-incrimination prohibited; treatment of statements obtained by torture and other statements

(a) In General. – No person shall be required to testify against himself at a proceeding of a military commission under this chapter.

(b) Exclusion of Statements Obtained by Torture. – A statement obtained by use of torture shall not be admissible in a military commission under this chapter, except against a person accused of torture as evidence that the statement was made.

(c) Statements Obtained before Enactment of Detainee Treatment Act of 2005. – A statement obtained before December 30, 2005 (the date of the enactment of the Defense [*sic*] Treatment Act of 2005) in which the degree of coercion is disputed may be admitted only if the military judge finds that –

(1) the totality of the circumstances renders the statement reliable and possessing sufficient probative value; and

(2) the interests of justice would best be served by admission of the statement into evidence.

(d) Statements Obtained after Enactment of Detainee Treatment Act of 2005. – A statement obtained on or after December 30, 2005 (the date of the enactment of the Defense [*sic*] Treatment Act of 2005) in which the degree of coercion is disputed may be admitted only if the military judge finds that –

(1) the totality of the circumstances renders the statement reliable and possessing sufficient probative value;

(2) the interests of justice would best be served by admission of the statement into evidence; and

(3) the interrogation methods used to obtain the statement do not amount to cruel, inhuman, or degrading treatment prohibited by section 1003 of the Detainee Treatment Act of 2005. . . .

Subchapter IV – Trial Procedure

§ 949a. Rules

(a) Procedures and Rules of Evidence. – Pretrial, trial, and post-trial procedures, including elements and modes of proof, for cases triable by military commission under this chapter may be prescribed by the Secretary of Defense, in consultation with the Attorney General. Such procedures shall, so far as the Secretary considers practicable or consistent with military or intelligence activities, apply the principles of law and the rules of evidence in trial by general courts-martial. Such procedures and rules of evidence may not be contrary to or inconsistent with this chapter.

(b) Rules for Military Commission. –

(1) Notwithstanding any departures from the law and the rules of evidence in trial by general courts-martial authorized by subsection (a), the procedures and rules of evidence in trials by military commission under this chapter shall include the following:

(A) The accused shall be permitted to present evidence in his defense, to cross-examine the witnesses who testify against him, and to examine and respond to evidence admitted against him on the issue of guilt or innocence and for sentencing, as provided for by this chapter.

(B) The accused shall be present at all sessions of the military commission (other than those for deliberations or voting), except when excluded under section 949d of this title.

(C) The accused shall receive the assistance of counsel . . . .

(D) The accused shall be permitted to represent himself . . . .

(2) In establishing procedures and rules of evidence for military commission proceedings, the Secretary of Defense may prescribe the following provisions:

(A) Evidence shall be admissible if the military judge determines that the evidence would have probative value to a reasonable person.

(B) Evidence shall not be excluded from trial by military commission on the grounds that the evidence was not seized pursuant to a search warrant or other authorization.

(C) A statement of the accused that is otherwise admissible shall not be excluded from trial by military commission on grounds of alleged coercion or compulsory self-incrimination so long as the evidence complies with the provisions of section 948r of this title. . . .

(E) (i) Except as provided in clause (ii), hearsay evidence not otherwise admissible under the rules of evidence applicable in trial by general courts-martial may be admitted in a trial by military commission if the proponent of the evidence makes known to the adverse party, sufficiently in advance to provide the adverse party with a fair opportunity to meet the evidence, the intention of the proponent to offer the evidence, and the particulars of the evidence (including information on the general circumstances under which the evidence was obtained). The disclosure of evidence under the preceding sentence is subject to the requirements and limitations applicable to the disclosure of classified information in section 949j(c) of this title. . . .

(ii) Hearsay evidence not otherwise admissible under the rules of evidence applicable in trial by general courts-martial shall not be admitted in a trial by military commission if the party opposing the admission of the evidence demonstrates that the evidence is unreliable or lacking in probative value.

(F) The military judge shall exclude any evidence the probative value of which is substantially outweighed –

(i) by the danger of unfair prejudice, confusion of the issues, or misleading the commission; or

(ii) by considerations of undue delay, waste of time, or needless presentation of cumulative evidence. . . .

§949d. Sessions . . .

(d) Closure of Proceedings. –

(1) The military judge may close to the public all or part of the proceedings of a military commission under this chapter, but only in accordance with this subsection.

(2) The military judge may close to the public all or a portion of the proceedings under paragraph (1) only upon making a specific finding that such closure is necessary to –

(A) protect information the disclosure of which could reasonably be expected to cause damage to the national security, including intelligence or law enforcement sources, methods, or activities; or

(B) ensure the physical safety of individuals.

(3) A finding under paragraph (2) may be based upon a

presentation, including a presentation ex parte or in camera, by either trial counsel or defense counsel.

(e) Exclusion of Accused from Certain Proceedings. – The military judge may exclude the accused from any portion of a proceeding upon a determination that, after being warned by the military judge, the accused persists in conduct that justifies exclusion from the courtroom –

(1) to ensure the physical safety of individuals; or

(2) to prevent disruption of the proceedings by the accused.

(f) Protection of Classified Information. –

(1) National security privilege. –

(A) Classified information shall be protected and is privileged from disclosure if disclosure would be detrimental to the national security. The rule in the preceding sentence applies to all stages of the proceedings of military commissions under this chapter.

(B) The privilege referred to in subparagraph (A) may be claimed by the head of the executive or military department or government agency concerned based on a finding by the head of that department or agency that –

(i) the information is properly classified; and

(ii) disclosure of the information would be detrimental to the national security. . . .

(2) Introduction of classified information. –

(A) Alternatives to disclosure. – To protect classified information from disclosure, the military judge, upon motion of trial counsel, shall authorize, to the extent practicable –

(i) the deletion of specified items of classified information from documents to be introduced as evidence before the military commission;

(ii) the substitution of a portion or summary of the information for such classified documents; or

(iii) the substitution of a statement of relevant facts that the classified information would tend to prove.

(B) Protection of sources, methods, or activities. – The military judge, upon motion of trial counsel, shall permit trial counsel to introduce otherwise admissible evidence before the military commission, while protecting from disclosure the sources, methods, or activities by which the United States acquired the evidence if the military judge finds that (i) the sources, methods, or activities by which the United States acquired the evidence are classified, and (ii) the evidence is reliable. The military judge may require trial counsel to present to the military commission and the defense, to the extent practicable and consistent with national security, an unclassified summary of the sources, methods, or activities by which the United States acquired the evidence.

(C) Assertion of National security privilege at trial. – During the examination of any witness, trial counsel may object to any question, line of inquiry, or motion to admit evidence that would require the disclosure of classified information. Following such an objection, the military judge shall take suitable action to safeguard such classified information. Such action may include the review of trial counsel's claim of privilege by the military judge in camera and on an ex parte basis, and the delay of proceedings to permit trial counsel to consult with the department or agency concerned as to whether the national security privilege should be asserted.

(3) Consideration of privilege and related materials. – A claim of privilege under this subsection, and any materials submitted in support thereof, shall, upon request of the Government, be considered by the military judge in camera and shall not be disclosed to the accused. . . .

§949j. Opportunity to obtain witnesses and other evidence

(a) Right of Defense Counsel. – Defense counsel in a military commission under this chapter shall have a reasonable opportunity to obtain witnesses and other evidence as provided in regulations prescribed by the Secretary of Defense.

(b) Process for Compulsion. – Process issued in a military commission under this chapter to compel witnesses to appear and testify and to compel the production of other evidence –

(1) shall be similar to that which courts of the United States having criminal jurisdiction may lawfully issue; and

(2) shall run to any place where the United States shall have jurisdiction thereof.

(c) Protection of Classified Information. –

(1) With respect to the discovery obligations of trial counsel under this section, the military judge, upon motion of trial counsel, shall authorize, to the extent practicable –

(A) the deletion of specified items of classified information from documents to be made available to the accused;

(B) the substitution of a portion or summary of the information for such classified documents; or

(C) the substitution of a statement admitting relevant facts that the classified information would tend to prove.

(2) The military judge, upon motion of trial counsel, shall authorize trial counsel, in the course of complying with discovery obligations under this section, to protect from disclosure the sources, methods, or activities by which the United States acquired evidence if the military judge finds that the sources, methods, or activities by which the United States acquired such evidence are classified. The military judge may require trial counsel to provide, to the extent practicable, an unclassified summary of the sources, methods, or activities by which the United States acquired such evidence.

(d) Exculpatory Evidence. –

(1) As soon as practicable, trial counsel shall disclose to the defense the existence of any evidence known to trial counsel that reasonably tends to exculpate the accused. Where exculpatory evidence is classified, the accused shall be provided with an adequate substitute in accordance with the procedures under subsection (c).

(2) In this subsection, the term "evidence known to trial counsel," in the case of exculpatory evidence, means exculpatory evidence that the prosecution would be required to disclose in a trial by general court-martial under chapter 47 of this title. . . .

Subchapter VI – Post-Trial Procedure and Review of Military Commissions . . .

§950b. Review by the convening authority . . .

[The MCA authorizes the convening authority to reconsider the findings and sentence of the military commission, but prohibits it from reconsidering findings of not guilty or increasing the severity of a sentence.]

§950c. Appellate referral; waiver or withdrawal of appeal

(a) Automatic Referral for Appellate Review. – Except as provided under subsection (b), in each case in which the final decision of a military commission (as approved by the convening authority) includes a finding of guilty, the convening authority shall refer the case to the Court of Military Commission Review. Any such referral shall be made in accordance with procedures prescribed under regulations of the Secretary. . . .

§950f. Review by Court of Military Commission Review

(a) Establishment. – The Secretary of Defense shall establish a Court of Military Commission Review which shall be composed of one or more panels, and each such panel shall be composed of not less than three appellate military judges. For the purpose of reviewing military commission decisions under this chapter, the court may sit in panels or as a whole in accordance with rules prescribed by the Secretary. . . .

(c) Cases To Be Reviewed. – The Court of Military Commission Review, in accordance with procedures prescribed under regulations of the Secretary, shall review the record in each case that is referred to the Court by the convening authority under section 950c of this title with respect to any matter of law raised by the accused.

(d) Scope of Review. – In a case reviewed by the Court of Military Commission Review under this section, the Court may act only with respect to matters of law.

§950g. Review by the United States Court of Appeals for the District of Columbia Circuit and the Supreme Court

(a) Exclusive Appellate Jurisdiction. –

(1) (A) Except as provided in subparagraph (B), the United States Court of Appeals for the District of Columbia Circuit shall have exclusive jurisdiction to determine the validity of a final judgment rendered by a military commission (as approved by the convening authority) under this chapter. . . .

(b) Standard for Review. – In a case reviewed by it under this section, the Court of Appeals may act only with respect to matters of law.

(c) Scope of Review. – The jurisdiction of the Court of Appeals on an appeal under subsection (a) shall be limited to the consideration of –

(1) whether the final decision was consistent with the standards and procedures specified in this chapter; and

(2) to the extent applicable, the Constitution and the laws of the United States.

(d) Supreme Court. – The Supreme Court may review by writ of certiorari the final judgment of the Court of Appeals pursuant to section 1257 of title 28. . . .

§950j. Finality or proceedings, findings, and sentences . . .

(b) Provisions of Chapter Sole Basis for Review of Military Commission Procedures and Actions. – Except as otherwise provided in this chapter and notwithstanding any other provision of law (including section 2241 of title 28 or any other habeas corpus provision), no court, justice, or judge shall have jurisdiction to hear or consider any claim or cause of action whatsoever, including any action pending on or filed after the date of the enactment of the Military Commissions Act of 2006, relating to the prosecution, trial, or judgment of a military commission under this chapter, including challenges to the lawfulness of procedures of military commissions under this chapter.

Subchapter VII. Punitive Matters

§950p. Statement of substantive offenses

(a) Purpose. – The provisions of this subchapter codify offenses that have traditionally been triable by military commissions. This chapter does not establish new crimes that did not exist before its enactment, but rather codifies those crimes for trial by military commission. . . .

§950v. Crimes triable by military commissions . . .

(b) Offenses. – The following offenses shall be triable by military commission under this chapter at any time without limitation: . . .

(2) Attacking civilians. – Any person subject to this chapter who intentionally engages in an attack upon a civilian population as such, or individual civilians not taking active part in hostilities, shall be punished, if death results to one or more of the victims, by death or such other punishment as a military commission under this chapter may direct, and, if death does not result to any of the victims, by such punishment, other than death, as a military commission under this chapter may direct.

(3) Attacking civilian objects. – Any person subject to this chapter who intentionally engages in an attack upon a civilian object that is not a military objective shall be punished as a military commission under this chapter may direct. . . .

(24) Terrorism. – Any person subject to this chapter who intentionally kills or inflicts great bodily harm on one or more protected persons, or intentionally engages in an act that evinces a

wanton disregard for human life, in a manner calculated to influence or affect the conduct of government or civilian population by intimidation or coercion, or to retaliate against government conduct, shall be punished, if death results to one or more of the victims, by death or such other punishment as a military commission under this chapter may direct, and, if death does not result to any of the victims, by such punishment, other than death, as a military commission under this chapter may direct.

(25) Providing material support for terrorism. –

(A) Offense. – Any person subject to this chapter who provides material support or resources, knowing or intending that they are to be used in preparation for, or in carrying out, an act of terrorism (as set forth in paragraph (24)), or who intentionally provides material support or resources to an international terrorist organization engaged in hostilities against the United States, knowing that such organization has engaged or engages in terrorism (as so set forth), shall be punished as a military commission under this chapter may direct.

(B) Material support or resources defined. – In this paragraph, the term "material support or resources" has the meaning given that term in section 2339A(b) of title 18. . . .

(28) Conspiracy. – Any person subject to this chapter who conspires to commit one or more substantive offenses triable by military commission under this chapter, and who knowingly does any overt act to effect the object of the conspiracy, shall be punished, if death results to one or more of the victims, by death or such other punishment as a military commission under this chapter may direct, and, if death does not result to any of the victims, by such punishment, other than death, as a military commission under this chapter may direct. . . .

Sec. 5. Treaty Obligations Not Establishing Grounds for Certain Claims.

(a) In General – No person may invoke the Geneva Conventions or any protocols thereto in any habeas corpus or other civil action or proceeding to which the United States, or a current or former officer, employee, member of the Armed Forces, or other agent of the United States is a party as a source of rights in any court of the United States or its States or territories. . . .

Sec. 6. Implementation of Treaty Obligations.

(a) Implementation of Treaty Obligations. –

(1) In general. – The acts enumerated in subsection (d) of section 2441 of title 18, United States Code, as added by subsection (b) of this section, and in subsection (c) of this section, constitute violations of common Article 3 of the Geneva Conventions prohibited by United States law.

(2) Prohibition on grave breaches. – The provisions of section 2441 of title 18, United States Code, as amended by this section, fully satisfy the obligation under Article 129 of the Third Geneva Convention for the United States to provide effective penal sanctions for grave breaches which are encompassed in common Article 3 in the context of an armed conflict not of an international character. No foreign or international source of law shall supply a basis for a rule of decision in the courts of the United States in interpreting the prohibitions enumerated in subsection (d) of such section 2441.

(3) Interpretation by the President. –

(A) As provided by the Constitution and by this section, the President has the authority for the United States to interpret the meaning and application of the Geneva Conventions and to promulgate higher standards and administrative regulations for violations of treaty obligations which are not grave breaches of the Geneva Conventions.

(B) The President shall issue interpretations described by subparagraph (A) by Executive Order published in the Federal Register.

(C) Any Executive Order published under this paragraph shall be authoritative (except as to grave breaches of common Article 3) as a matter of United States law, in the same manner as other administrative regulations.

(D) Nothing in this section shall be construed to affect the constitutional functions and responsibilities of Congress and the judicial branch of the United States. . . .

Sec. 7. Habeas Corpus Matters.

(a) In General. – Section 2241 of title 28, United States Code, is amended by striking both the subsection (e) added by section 1005(e)(1) of Public Law 109-148 (119 Stat. 2742) and the subsection (e) added by section 1405(e)(1) of Public Law 109-163 (119 Stat. 3477) and inserting the following new subsection (e):

> "(e)(1) No court, justice, or judge shall have jurisdiction to hear or consider an application for a writ of habeas corpus filed by or on behalf of an alien detained by the United States who has been determined by the United States to have been properly detained as an enemy combatant or is awaiting such determination.
>
> "(2) Except as provided in paragraphs (2) and (3) of section 1005(e) of the Detainee Treatment Act of 2005 (10 U.S.C. 801 note), no court, justice, or judge shall have jurisdiction to hear or consider any other action against the United States or its agents relating to any aspect of the detention, transfer, treatment, trial, or conditions of confinement of an alien who is or was detained by the United States and has been determined by the United States to have been properly detained as an enemy combatant or is awaiting such determination.".

(b) Effective Date. – The amendment made by subsection (a) shall take effect on the date of the enactment of this Act, and shall apply to all cases, without exception, pending on or after the date of the enactment of this Act which relate to any aspect of the detention, transfer, treatment, trial, or conditions of detention of an alien detained by the United States since September 11, 2001. . . .

34

Statutory Access to National Security Information

A. THE FREEDOM OF INFORMATION ACT

1. The Statutory Text

Page 997. Add the following Note at the end of Note 10.

11. *Amendments to FOIA.* On December 31, 2007, Congress amended FOIA by enacting the Open Government Act of 2007, Pub. L. No. 110-175, 121 Stat. 2524. Highlights are described in a Senate Judiciary Committee Report, S. Rep. No. 110-59 (2007):

> III. SECTION-BY-SECTION SUMMARY OF THE BILL . . .
>
> *Sec. 3. Protection of fee status for news media*
>
> This section amends 5 U.S.C. 552(a)(4)(A)(ii) to make clear that independent journalists are not barred from obtaining fee waivers solely because they lack an institutional affiliation with a recognized news media entity. In determining whether to grant a fee waiver, an agency shall consider the prior publication history of the requestor. If the requestor has no prior publication history and no current affiliation with a news organization, the agency shall review the requestor's plans for disseminating the requested material and whether those plans include distributing the material to a reasonably broad audience.

Sec. 4. Recovery of attorney fees and litigation costs

This section, the so-called *Buckhannon* fix, amends 5 U.S.C. 552(a)(4)(E) to clarify that a complainant has substantially prevailed in a FOIA lawsuit, and is eligible to recover attorney fees, if the complainant has obtained relief through a judicial or administrative order or if the pursuit of a claim was the catalyst for the voluntary or unilateral change in position by the opposing party. The section responds to the Supreme Court's ruling in Buckhannon Board and Care Home, Inc. v. West Virginia Dep't of Health and Human Resources, 532 U.S. 598 (2001), which eliminated the "catalyst theory" of attorney fee recovery under certain Federal civil rights laws. Requestors have raised concerns that the holding in Buckhannon could be extended to FOIA cases. This section clarifies that *Buckhannon*'s holding does not and should not apply to FOIA litigation. . . .

Sec. 6. Time limits for agencies to act on requests

The section clarifies that the 20-day time limit on responding to a FOIA request commences on the date on which the request is first received by the agency. Further, the section states that if the agency fails to respond within the 20-day limit, the agency may not then [assess search fees, except under "unusual or exceptional" circumstances].

Sec. 7. Individualized tracking numbers for requests and status information

Requires agencies to establish tracking systems by assigning a tracking number to each FOIA request; notifying a requestor of the tracking number within ten days of receiving a request; and establishing a telephone or Internet tracking system to allow requesters to easily obtain information on the status of their individual requests, including an estimated date on which the agency will complete action on the request. . . .

Sec. [9.] Openness of agency records maintained by a private entity

This section clarifies that agency records kept by private contractors licensed by the government to undertake record keeping functions remain subject to FOIA just as if those records were maintained by the relevant government agency. . . .

B. OTHER OPEN GOVERNMENT LAWS

1. Presidential Records Act

Page 1016. Add this case at the bottom of the page.

American Historical Association v. National Archives and Records Administration

United States District Court, District of Columbia, 2007
516 F. Supp. 2d 90

COLLEEN KOLLAR-KOTELLY, United States District Judge. Plaintiffs filed suit against the National Archives and Records Administration ("NARA") and the Archivist of the United States (collectively, "the Government" or "Defendants"), seeking injunctive and declaratory relief related to Executive Order 13,233, signed by President George W. Bush on November 1, 2001, which purported to "further implemen[t]" the Presidential Records Act ("PRA") of 1978, 44 U.S.C. §§2201-2207 (1991). . . . In Count II of their Complaint, Plaintiffs asked the Court to order the release of specific documents that had been withheld, initially under the terms of the Executive Order, but later under the incumbent president's independent invocation of constitutional privilege. . . .

. . . On September 24, 2005, the Court . . . granted summary judgment for Defendants with respect to Count II of Plaintiffs' Complaint, finding that Plaintiffs were required to show some "demonstrated, specific need" for the records they sought in order to overcome the president's assertion of constitutional privilege, but that Plaintiffs had conceded that they could make no such required showing of need. [402 F. Supp. 2d 171.] . . .

I. BACKGROUND . . .

B. Procedural History

. . . In Count I of Plaintiffs' Complaint, Plaintiffs allege that the following terms of the Bush Order are contrary to law:

- "[T]hat access to materials may be delayed for an unlimited period of time after the expiration of the 12-year restriction period while a former president and the incumbent president 'review' materials proposed for release[.]" [Exec. Order §3(b).]

• "[T]hat when a former president makes a claim of executive privilege . . . , the incumbent president 'will concur' in that claim absent 'compelling circumstances,' . . . ." [Exec. Order §4.]

• "[T]hat, regardless of whether the incumbent president 'concurs' in a former president's claim of privilege under the 'compelling circumstances' standard, the Archivist 'shall not permit access to the records' unless and until the former president agrees, or a court orders that materials be released, even if the claim of privilege is legally improper or unfounded[.]" [Exec. Order §3(d).]

• "[T]hat the constitutional privileges of the executive branch may be asserted by a surrogate who has never held the office of the presidency, if the surrogate has been 'designated' to do so by a former president who is deceased or disabled or by the family of a deceased or disabled former president, even though the Constitution does not allow for assertion of a claim of executive privilege by someone who has not held the office of president[.]" [Exec. Order §10.]

• "[T]hat a former vice president may assert a claim of executive privilege independent of the privilege of the former or incumbent president, . . . even though there is no constitutional basis for a vice presidential executive privilege." [Exec. Order §11.]

Plaintiffs allege that "[i]mplementation of the Bush Order by the Archivist constitutes agency action that is arbitrary, capricious, an abuse of discretion, not in accordance with law, and in excess of statutory authority and limitations within the meaning of the APA [Administrative Procedure Act] (5 U.S.C. §706(2)(A) & (C))." "In the alternative," Plaintiffs argue that "regardless of whether there has yet been agency action with respect to the Bush Order, plaintiffs have a nonstatutory right to obtain judicial review of the lawfulness of the Bush Order's restrictions on the defendants' ability to comply with their legal obligations. Because the Bush Order is contrary to the terms of the PRA and lacks a valid constitutional basis, plaintiffs are entitled to a declaration under 28 U.S.C. §2201 that the Order is unlawful and an injunction providing that the defendants may not implement it."

. . . Defendants argue that after the Court dismissed Count II of Plaintiffs' Amended Complaint, "[n]o other documents are now subject to the assertion of executive privilege by either President Bush or by a former President or his representatives." Plaintiffs as a result "cannot demonstrate that they are subject to any real or immediate harm arising from those provisions in E.O. §3 that deny access to presidential records in the event that a former or incumbent President or their representative assert privilege." Furthermore, Defendants argue that "Plaintiffs just as clearly cannot demonstrate that they are subject to any real or immediate injury arising from E.O. §4, which provides that the incumbent President will 'concur' in the privilege decision of a former President absent 'compelling circumstances.'" With respect to provisions of the Bush Order governing the *review* of records by former presidents or their representatives or former vice presidents that occurs prior to any assertion of privilege, Defendants acknowledge that this review process delays Plaintiffs' access to records, but argue that it is beyond dispute that the President and former Presidents have the *constitutional* right to invoke privilege over presidential communications, which in turn necessarily contemplates that these officials or their representatives be given the time and opportunity to review records for privilege. Owing to the unavoidable and necessary "delay" that is required for this process, it is impossible for plaintiffs to demonstrate that Section 3 of the E.O. gives rise on its face to a legally cognizable injury-in-fact that is redressable by the Court. Defendants also argue that Plaintiffs' review claims can be dismissed on the merits if found to be justiciable, because "[t]he PRA . . . does not impose any temporal limitations on a President's or former President's authority to invoke constitutional privilege, and instead makes clear that its provisions cannot be construed to 'limit' such privileges[,]" as well as that a Court-imposed limitation on the time period within which an incumbent or former President could review documents "would unquestionably trench upon separation-of-powers principles." . . .

III. DISCUSSION

A. Most of Plaintiffs' claims are not ripe for adjudication . . .

. . . Plaintiffs do not allege that an incumbent or former president or incumbent or former vice president has actually asserted a privilege with respect to any document requests presently at issue. . . . It is not certain or even likely that privilege shall be asserted by a former president or his representatives or by a former vice president with respect to any of Plaintiffs' pending document requests such that Plaintiffs' challenges to the *assertion* provisions of the Bush Order are purely speculative and not ripe at this time. . . .

As the Court concludes that Plaintiffs' claims pursuant to §§3(d), 4, 10, and 11 of the Bush Order – which relate to the assertion of executive privilege – are not ripe for review, the Court shall dismiss without prejudice Plaintiffs' challenges to these provisions of the Bush Order. . . .

B. Plaintiffs have standing to pursue their challenge to the Archivist's reliance on Section 3(b) of Executive Order 13,233, which is ripe for review

1. Standing . . .

Defendants argue that "plaintiffs [ ] cannot demonstrate standing/ ripeness to challenge E.O. §3(b) on the ground that it delays access to presidential records pending the review for privilege by a *former* President," or pending the review by representatives of a former president, because "the incumbent President retains the constitutional authority to take into account the privilege views of a deceased President's representatives – or, for that matter, anyone else – as part of his *own* review process." In short, Defendants argue that because it is "the practice of the incumbent President to wait for comments on privilege" from the former presidents' representatives, the delay is not "caused" by E.O. §3(b), nor would it be redressed by its undoing in light of the current president's practice.

The Court rejects Defendants' standing arguments in light of the posture of at least one of Plaintiffs' document requests. Plaintiff National Security Archive has FOIA requests for documents "currently pending for review by the representatives of former President Reagan," and accordingly has been harmed by the delay created by E.O. §3(b). The *average* delay caused by a former president's review of a document request is 170 days, or nearly six months. Denial of "timely access" constitutes "informational injury," thereby precluding any "serious challenge" to the injury element of the standing analysis. Byrd v. EPA, 174 F.3d 239, 243 (D.C. Cir. 1999), *cert. denied,* 120 S. Ct. 1418 (2000). The Archivist's reliance on §3(b) has "caused" the delay, because in relying on §3(b), the Archivist is not permitted to release the requested documents prior to review by a former president. *See* Bush Order §3(b) ("After receiving the records he requests, the former President shall review those records as expeditiously as possible, and for no longer than *90 days* for requests that are not unduly burdensome. The Archivist *shall* not permit access to the records by a requester during this period of review or when requested by the former President to extend the time for review.") (emphasis added). Under the PRA and its implementing regulations as relied upon by the Archivist prior to his reliance on the Bush Order in his interpretation thereof, it is within the Archivist's discretion to release documents pending review by a former president after a former president has had notice of said document request for at least 30 days.

. . . [T]he Court concludes that Plaintiffs have standing to pursue their claim that the delay created by §3(b) of the Bush Order violates the APA.

2. Ripeness

The Court finds that in this case, the question involves statutory and other legal interpretation "that would not benefit from further factual development of the issues presented[,]" "[n]or will our review inappropriately interfere with further administrative action" since the Archivist has determined that he will implement the PRA in compliance with the Bush Order. Plaintiffs (who have an interest in accessing historical presidential and vice presidential records in a timely fashion for academic and other purposes) and the NARA (and Archivist) itself have an interest in the Court's making a conclusive finding as to whether the Archivist's reliance on §3(b) is proper such that documents pending review by former presidents and their representatives can be released at the Archivist's discretion after the 30-day period set forth in the PRA's implementing regulations.

Defendants argue that Plaintiffs' claim pursuant to §3(b) is not ripe, citing "very significant reasons . . . for withholding consideration of plaintiffs' claims, every one of which touches upon sensitive separation-of-powers principles concerning the invocation of executive privilege by past Presidents and the incumbent." Defendants further argue that the Court should avoid addressing constitutional questions when possible . . . . [T]he Court need not decide this case on purely constitutional grounds, as the Court shall assess in the first and final instance whether the Archivist's reliance on the Bush Order violates the APA . . . .

C. The Archivist's reliance on §3(b) of Executive Order 13,233 is arbitrary, capricious, an abuse of discretion, and not in accordance with law and accordingly in violation of the APA

Plaintiffs argue that "[i]mplementation of the Bush Order by the Archivist constitutes agency action that is arbitrary, capricious, an abuse of discretion, not in accordance with law, and in excess of statutory authority and limitations within the meaning of the APA." . . .

Pursuant to 44 U.S.C. §2203(f)(1):

> Upon the conclusion of a President's term of office, or if a President serves consecutive terms upon the conclusion of the last term, the Archivist of the United States shall assume responsibility for the custody, control, and preservation of, and access to, the Presidential records of that President. The Archivist shall have an affirmative duty to make such records available to the public as rapidly and completely as possible consistent with the provisions of this Act.

44 U.S.C. §2203(f)(1). The PRA clarifies that "[n]othing in this Act shall be construed to confirm, limit, or expand any constitutionally-based privilege which may be available to an incumbent or former President." *Id.* §2204(c)(2). The PRA also explicitly charges the Archivist with promulgating regulations to carry out the PRA. *Id.* §2206.

In order to carry out the provisions of the PRA, regulations were created to "implement the provisions of the [PRA]" . . . . Pursuant to 36 C.F.R. §1270.46, "[t]he Archivist shall not disclose any records covered by any notice [given by the Archivist to a former president] required by paragraphs (a) or (c) of this section for at least 30 calendar days from receipt of the notice by the former President. . . ." *Id.* The Bush Order, on the other hand, states that "[a]fter receiving the records he requests, the former President shall review those records as expeditiously as possible, and for no longer than 90 days for requests that are not unduly burdensome. The Archivist shall not permit access to the records by a requester during this period of review or when requested by the former President to extend the time for review." E.O. §3(b). . . .

. . . Plaintiffs' argument prevails. The Bush Order effectively eliminates the Archivist's discretion to release a former president's documents while such documents are pending a former president's review, which can be extended – presumably indefinitely – upon the former president's request. Furthermore, the Bush Order provides a 90-day floor for a former president's review of documents. While Defendants are correct that 36 C.F.R. §1270.46(d) does not specify a "maximum" time for review, Defendants seem to miss that after 30 days from a former president's receipt of notice of documents to be disclosed, the Archivist may make a discretionary decision with respect to the release of such documents though they are pending the former president's review. Accordingly, in relying on §3(b) of the Bush Order, the Archivist effectively denies himself the discretion (and accordingly the need to make reasoned, discretionary decisions with respect to the appropriate length of review) to release documents still under a former president's review as he is permitted to do pursuant to 36 C.F.R. §1270.46(d).

As the PRA clarifies that "[n]othing in this Act shall be construed to confirm, limit, or expand any constitutionally-based privilege which may be available to an incumbent or former President," 44 U.S.C. §2204(c)(2), the Archivist's reliance on §3(b) would not be construed to violate the Act or its implementing regulations if §3(b) is necessary to preserve a constitutionally-based privilege available to an incumbent or former president. "Unless, therefore, the delays attributable to the Order are either necessary to protect constitutionally based privileges . . . or otherwise necessary to serve some statutory purpose (which the government does not assert), they cannot be squared with the Act's requirements." In examining whether the delay created by the Bush Order is required to protect any constitutionally-based privilege, the Court shall assume without deciding that a former president and/or his representatives and a former vice president have some authority to invoke executive privilege. The Court nonetheless concludes that the Archivist's reliance on §3(b) of the Bush Order is not necessary to preserve any constitutionally-based privilege. . . .

. . . [N]one of the pertinent cases touching on a former president's executive privilege holds that the *length* of time for review has constitutional implications.

. . . [T]he Constitution does not require the Archivist to permit a former president an unlimited amount of time to review materials for privilege. While presumably a former president must have *some* time to review documents for privilege, as a former president may at very least be heard to assert claims of executive privilege, *see Nixon v. Administrator* [of General Serv., 433 U.S. 425 (1977),] at 439, the Court does not find any support for the proposition that removing discretion from the Archivist with respect to what constitutes a reasonable time for said review after 30 days has expired would somehow threaten a former president's ability to make privilege determinations.

As the Court finds that the Archivist's reliance on §3(b) of Executive Order 13,233 violates the APA, the Court need not reach Plaintiffs' alternative argument that Plaintiffs have a nonstatutory right to judicial review and a declaration under 28 U.S.C. §2201 because Executive Order 13,233 is contrary to the terms of the PRA and lacks a valid constitutional basis.

IV. CONCLUSION

Based on the aforementioned reasoning, the Court shall . . . dismiss without prejudice for lack of justiciability Plaintiffs' challenges to §§3(d), 4, 10, and 11 of Executive Order 13,233; declare that the Archivist's reliance on §3(b) of Executive Order 13,233 is arbitrary, capricious, an abuse of discretion, and not in accordance with law in violation of the APA; enjoin the Archivist from further relying on §3(b) of Executive Order 13,233; and DISMISS the instant case. . . .

35

Access to National Security Information in Civil Litigation

C. PROTECTING "STATE SECRETS" IN CIVIL LITIGATION

Page 1050. Add this case after Note 5.

El-Masri v. United States

United States Court of Appeals, Fourth Circuit, 2007
479 F.3d 296, *cert. denied*, 128 S. Ct. 373

KING, Circuit Judge. Khaled El-Masri appeals from the dismissal of his civil action against former Director of Central Intelligence George Tenet, three corporate defendants, ten unnamed employees of the Central Intelligence Agency (the "CIA"), and ten unnamed employees of the defendant corporations. In his Complaint in the Eastern District of Virginia, El-Masri alleged that the defendants were involved in a CIA operation in which he was detained and interrogated in violation of his rights under the Constitution and international law. The United States intervened as a defendant in the district court, asserting that El-Masri's civil action could not proceed because it posed an unreasonable risk that privileged state secrets would be disclosed. By its Order of May 12, 2006, the district court agreed with the position of the United States and dismissed El-Masri's Complaint. *See* El-Masri v. Tenet, 437 F. Supp. 2d 530, 541 (E.D. Va. 2006) (the "Order"). On appeal, El-Masri contends that the district court misapplied the state secrets doctrine and erred in dismissing his Complaint. As explained below, we affirm.

I.

A.

On December 6, 2005, El-Masri, a German citizen of Lebanese descent, filed his Complaint in this case, alleging, in substance, as follows: on December 31, 2003, while travelling in Macedonia, he was detained by Macedonian law enforcement officials; after twenty-three days in Macedonian custody, he was handed over to CIA operatives, who flew him to a CIA-operated detention facility near Kabul, Afghanistan; he was held in this CIA facility until May 28, 2004, when he was transported to Albania and released in a remote area; and Albanian officials then picked him up and took him to an airport in Tirana, Albania, from which he travelled to his home in Germany. The Complaint asserted that El-Masri had not only been held against his will, but had also been mistreated in a number of other ways during his detention, including being beaten, drugged, bound, and blindfolded during transport; confined in a small, unsanitary cell; interrogated several times; and consistently prevented from communicating with anyone outside the detention facility, including his family or the German government. El-Masri alleged that his detention and interrogation were

> carried out pursuant to an unlawful policy and practice devised and implemented by defendant Tenet known as "extraordinary rendition": the clandestine abduction and detention outside the United States of persons suspected of involvement in terrorist activities, and their subsequent interrogation using methods impermissible under U.S. and international laws.

Complaint ¶3.

According to the Complaint, the corporate defendants provided the CIA with an aircraft and crew to transport El-Masri to Afghanistan, pursuant to an agreement with Director Tenet, and they either knew or reasonably should have known that "Mr. El-Masri would be subjected to prolonged arbitrary detention, torture and cruel, inhuman, or degrading treatment in violation of federal and international laws during his transport to Afghanistan and while he was detained and interrogated there." Complaint ¶61. El-Masri also alleges that CIA officials "believed early on that they had the wrong person," and that Director Tenet was notified in April 2004 that "the CIA had detained the wrong person" in El-Masri. *Id.* ¶43.

The Complaint alleged three separate causes of action. The first claim was against Director Tenet and the unknown CIA employees, pursuant to Bivens v. Six Unknown Named Agents of Federal Bureau of Narcotics, 403 U.S. 388 (1971), for violations of El-Masri's Fifth Amendment right to due process. Specifically, El-Masri contends that Tenet and the defendant CIA employees contravened the Due Process Clause's prohibition against subjecting anyone held in United States custody to treatment that shocks the conscience or depriving a person of liberty in the absence of legal process. El-Masri's second cause of action was initiated pursuant to the Alien Tort Statute (the "ATS"), and alleged that each of the defendants had contravened the international legal norm against prolonged arbitrary detention. The third cause of action was also asserted under the ATS, and maintained that each defendant had violated international legal norms prohibiting cruel, inhuman, or degrading treatment.

On March 8, 2006, the United States filed a Statement of Interest in the underlying proceedings, pursuant to 28 U.S.C. §517, and interposed a claim of the state secrets privilege. The then Director of the CIA, Porter Goss, submitted two sworn declarations to the district court in support of the state secrets privilege claim. The first declaration was unclassified, and explained in general terms the reasons for the United States' assertion of privilege. The other declaration was classified; it detailed the information that the United States sought to protect, explained why further court proceedings would unreasonably risk that information's disclosure, and spelled out why such disclosure would be detrimental to the national security (the "Classified Declaration"). . . . On March 13, 2006, the United States formally moved to intervene as a defendant in the district court proceedings. Contemporaneous with seeking to intervene as a defendant, the United States moved to dismiss the Complaint, contending that its interposition of the state secrets privilege precluded the litigation of El-Masri's causes of action.

El-Masri responded that the state secrets doctrine did not necessitate dismissal of his Complaint, primarily because CIA rendition operations, including El-Masri's alleged rendition, had been widely discussed in public forums. In support of this contention, Steven Macpherson Watt, a human rights adviser to the American Civil Liberties Union, filed a sworn declaration in the district court, dated April 7, 2006, in which he asserted that United States officials – including Secretary of State Condoleezza Rice, White House Press Secretary Scott McClellan, and Directors Tenet and Goss – had publicly acknowledged that the United States had conducted renditions. Watt also observed that international human rights organizations had issued statements on various United

States rendition operations, including El-Masri's alleged rendition, and that at least one such release had described the use of privately owned aircraft in the renditions of El-Masri and others. Additionally, according to Watt, the European Parliament and the Council of Europe had commenced investigations into possible European cooperation in United States renditions, and similar inquiries were pending in eighteen European countries.

Watt further asserted that "[m]edia reports on the rendition program generally, and Mr. El-Masri's rendition specifically, are too numerous to assemble." Watt Declaration ¶26. According to Watt, these media reports revealed the existence of secret CIA detention facilities where some rendition subjects were held, as well as the United States' "modus operandi" for conducting renditions: "masked men in an unmarked jet seize their target, cut off his clothes, put him in a blindfold and jumpsuit, tranquilize him and fly him away." *Id.* ¶26(vi). And, Watt represented, the news media had documented some of the details of El-Masri's alleged rendition, including the underlying "decision-making process" and the roles of the German and Macedonian governments. *Id.* ¶26(viii).

On May 12, 2006, . . . the district court concluded that the claim of the state secrets privilege was valid, and that, "given the application of the privilege to this case, the United States' motion to dismiss must be . . . granted." *See* Order, 437 F. Supp. 2d at 541. El-Masri has appealed from the Order and corresponding judgment of dismissal . . . .

II.

El-Masri maintains on appeal that the district court misapplied the state secrets doctrine in dismissing his Complaint without requiring any responsive pleadings from the defendants or permitting any discovery to be conducted. Importantly, El-Masri does not contend that the state secrets privilege has no role in these proceedings. To the contrary, he acknowledges that at least some information important to his claims is likely to be privileged, and thus beyond his reach. But he challenges the court's determination that state secrets are so central to this matter that any attempt at further litigation would threaten their disclosure. As explained below, we conclude that the district court correctly assessed the centrality of state secrets in this dispute. We therefore affirm its Order and the dismissal of El-Masri's Complaint.

A.

1.

[Here the court reviews the holdings of the Supreme Court in United States v. Reynolds, 345 U.S. 1, 10 (1953), and Totten v. United States, 92 U.S. 105 (1875), and related matters.]

2.

A court faced with a state secrets privilege question is obliged to resolve the matter by use of a three-part analysis. At the outset, the court must ascertain that the procedural requirements for invoking the state secrets privilege have been satisfied. Second, the court must decide whether the information sought to be protected qualifies as privileged under the state secrets doctrine. Finally, if the subject information is determined to be privileged, the ultimate question to be resolved is how the matter should proceed in light of the successful privilege claim.

a.

The procedural requirements for invoking the state secrets privilege are set forth in *Reynolds* . . . .

b.

After a court has confirmed that the *Reynolds* procedural prerequisites are satisfied, it must determine whether the information that the United States seeks to shield is a state secret, and thus privileged from disclosure. This inquiry is a difficult one, for it pits the judiciary's search for truth against the Executive's duty to maintain the nation's security. The *Reynolds* Court recognized this tension, observing that "[j]udicial control over the evidence in a case cannot be abdicated to the caprice of executive officers" – no matter how great the interest in national security – but that the President's ability to preserve state secrets likewise cannot be placed entirely at the mercy of the courts. 345 U.S. at 9-10. Moreover, a court evaluating a claim of privilege must "do so without forcing a disclosure of the very thing the privilege is designed to protect."

The *Reynolds* Court balanced those concerns by leaving the judiciary firmly in control of deciding whether an executive assertion of the state secrets privilege is valid, but subject to a standard mandating restraint in the exercise of its authority. A court is obliged to honor the Executive's assertion of the privilege if it is satisfied, "from all the circumstances of the case, that there is a reasonable danger that compulsion of the evidence will expose military matters which, in the interest of national security, should not be divulged." *Reynolds,* 345 U.S. at 10. In assessing the risk that such a disclosure might pose to national security, a court is obliged to accord the "utmost deference" to the responsibilities of the executive branch. [United States v. Nixon, 418 U.S. 683 (1974)], at 710. Such deference is appropriate not only for constitutional reasons, but also practical ones: the Executive and the intelligence agencies under his control occupy a position superior to that of the courts in evaluating the consequences of a release of sensitive information. In the related context of confidentiality classification decisions, we have observed that "[t]he courts, of course, are ill-equipped to become sufficiently steeped in foreign intelligence matters to serve effectively in the review of secrecy classifications in that area." United States v. Marchetti, 466 F.2d 1309, 1318 (4th Cir. 1972). The executive branch's expertise in predicting the potential consequences of intelligence disclosures is particularly important given the sophisticated nature of modern intelligence analysis, in which "[t]he significance of one item of information may frequently depend upon knowledge of many other items of information," and "[w]hat may seem trivial to the uninformed, may appear of great moment to one who has a broad view of the scene and may put the questioned item of information in its proper context." *Id.* In the same vein, in those situations where the state secrets privilege has been invoked because disclosure risks impairing our foreign relations, the President's assessment of the diplomatic situation is entitled to great weight.

The Executive bears the burden of satisfying a reviewing court that the *Reynolds* reasonable-danger standard is met. A court considering the Executive's assertion of the state secrets privilege, however, must take care not to "forc[e] a disclosure of the very thing the privilege is designed to protect" by demanding more information than is necessary. *Reynolds,* 345 U.S. at 8. Frequently, the explanation of the department head who has lodged the formal privilege claim, provided in an affidavit or personal declaration, is sufficient to carry the Executive's burden. *See, e.g.,* Sterling v. Tenet, 416 F.3d 338, 345 (4th Cir. 2005) (relying on declarations of CIA Director); *Reynolds,* 345 U.S. at 5 (relying on Claim of Privilege by Secretary of Air Force and affidavit of Air Force Judge Advocate General). In some situations, a court may conduct an in camera examination of the actual information sought to be protected, in order to ascertain that the criteria set forth in *Reynolds* are fulfilled. *See Sterling,* 416 F.3d at 345. The degree to which such a reviewing court should probe depends in part on the importance of the assertedly privileged information to the position of the party seeking it. *See Reynolds,* 345 U.S. at 11. "Where there is a strong showing of necessity, the claim of privilege should not be lightly accepted. . . ." *Id.* On the other hand, "even the most compelling necessity cannot overcome the claim of privilege if the court is ultimately satisfied that military secrets are at stake." *Id.* Indeed, in certain circumstances a court may conclude that an explanation by the Executive of why a question cannot be answered would itself create an unacceptable danger of injurious disclosure. *See id.* at 9. In such a situation, a court is obliged to accept the executive branch's claim of privilege without further demand. *See id.*

After information has been determined to be privileged under the state secrets doctrine, it is absolutely protected from disclosure – even for the purpose of in camera examination by the court. On this point, *Reynolds* could not be more specific: "When . . . the occasion for the privilege is appropriate, . . . the court should not jeopardize the security which the privilege is meant to protect by insisting upon an examination of the evidence, even by the judge alone, in chambers." 345 U.S. at 10. Moreover, no attempt is made to balance the need for secrecy of the privileged information against a party's need for the information's disclosure; a court's determination that a piece of evidence is a privileged state secret removes it from the proceedings entirely. *See id.* at 11.

c.

The effect of a successful interposition of the state secrets privilege by the United States will vary from case to case. If a proceeding involving state secrets can be fairly litigated without resort to the privileged information, it may continue. But if "'the circumstances make clear that sensitive military secrets will be so central to the subject matter of the litigation that any attempt to proceed will threaten disclosure of the privileged matters,' dismissal is the proper remedy." *Sterling,* 416 F.3d at 348 (quoting DTM Research, LLC v. AT & T Corp., 245 F.3d 327, 334 (4th Cir. 2001)). The Supreme Court has recognized that some matters are so pervaded by state secrets as to be incapable of judicial resolution once the privilege has been invoked. *See Totten,* 92 U.S. at 107; *Reynolds,* 345 U.S. at 11 n.26. Although *Totten* has come to primarily represent a somewhat narrower principle – a categorical bar on actions to enforce secret contracts for espionage – it rested, as we have already observed, on the proposition that a cause cannot be maintained if its trial would inevitably lead to the disclosure of privileged information. *See* 92 U.S. at 107. And in *Reynolds,* while concluding that dismissal was unnecessary because the privileged information was peripheral to the plaintiffs' action, the Court made clear that where state secrets form the very subject matter of a court proceeding, as in *Totten,* dismissal at the pleading stage – "without ever reaching the question of evidence" – is appropriate. *See* 345 U.S. at 11 n.26. In a recent decision unanimously reaffirming *Totten*'s validity, the Supreme Court approvingly quoted *Reynolds*'s discussion of *Totten* as a matter in which dismissal on the pleadings was appropriate because the very subject matter of the action was a state secret. *See* Tenet v. Doe, 544 U.S. 1, 9 (2005).

Our own decisions applying the state secrets privilege have also recognized that, in certain proceedings, the unavailability of privileged state secrets as evidence will necessarily lead to dismissal. In Farnsworth Cannon, Inc. v. Grimes, an action alleging tortious interference with a classified contract to perform services for the Navy, our en banc Court affirmed the district court's dismissal on state secrets grounds. *See* 635 F.2d 268 (4th Cir. 1980). We reasoned that privileged secrets were so central to the dispute that "[i]n an attempt to make out a prima facie case during an actual trial, the plaintiff and its lawyers would have every incentive to probe as close to the core secrets as the trial judge would permit." *Id.* at 281. "Such probing in open court," we concluded, "would inevitably be revealing," and dismissal was therefore warranted. *Id.*

In *Fitzgerald v. Penthouse International, Ltd.,* in 1985, we affirmed the district court's dismissal, under the state secrets doctrine, of an action alleging that a magazine article on the Navy's classified marine mammal program had libelously accused the plaintiff of espionage. *See* 776 F.2d 1236, 1237-38 (4th Cir. 1985). There, the Secretary of the Navy had filed a public declaration asserting that the plaintiff's plan to call witnesses with knowledge of the Navy's classified program risked the disclosure of military secrets, since those witnesses could be questioned about the secret information to which they were privy. *See id.* at 1242. In addition, the Secretary filed a separate, classified declaration that elaborated on his reasons for asserting the state secrets privilege in the case. *See id.* at 1243 n.9. From all the circumstances, we concluded that "there was simply no way this particular case could be tried without compromising sensitive military secrets," and ruled that the district court had not erred in dismissing it. *Id.* at 1243.

More recently, in our 2005 *Sterling* decision, we affirmed the dismissal of a Title VII action initiated by an African-American CIA officer alleging unlawful discriminatory practices by CIA management. *See* 416 F.3d at 341. We concluded that state secrets were so central to that proceeding that it could not be litigated given the Executive's invocation of the privilege. *Id.* at 346-48. The evidence in the dispute would have consisted primarily of documents and testimony regarding the assignments and performance evaluations of CIA operatives, and many of the necessary witnesses were individuals whose very identities were state secrets. *Id.* at 347-48. Indeed, as Judge Wilkinson explained, "the whole object of the suit and of the discovery [was] to establish a fact that is a state secret – namely, the methods and operations of the Central Intelligence Agency." *Id.* at 348 (internal quotation marks and citation omitted). In those circumstances, dismissal was deemed appropriate.

Our sister circuits have likewise recognized that the unavailability of privileged information may, in some instances, necessarily lead to dismissal. *See* Kasza v. Browner, 133 F.3d 1159, 1170 (9th Cir. 1998) (affirming dismissal, on state secrets grounds, of action alleging that Air Force had unlawfully handled hazardous waste in classified operating area); Black v. United States, 62 F.3d 1115, 1118-19 (8th Cir. 1995) (affirming dismissal, on state secrets grounds, of action alleging that executive branch officials had engaged in "campaign of harassment and psychological attacks" against plaintiff); Bareford v. Gen. Dynamics Corp., 973 F.2d 1138, 1140 (5th Cir. 1992) (affirming dismissal, on state secrets grounds, of action alleging manufacturing and design defects in military weapons system); Halkin v. Helms, 690 F.2d 977, 981 (D.C. Cir. 1982) (affirming dismissal, on state secrets grounds, of action alleging unlawful CIA surveillance); *cf.* Tenenbaum v. Simonini, 372 F.3d 776, 777-78 (6th Cir. 2004) (affirming summary judgment because no defense was available without resort to privileged state secrets).

3.

To summarize, our analysis of the Executive's interposition of the state secrets privilege is governed primarily by two standards. First, evidence is privileged pursuant to the state secrets doctrine if, under all the circumstances of the case, there is a reasonable danger that its disclosure will expose military (or diplomatic or intelligence) matters which, in the interest of national security, should not be divulged. *See Reynolds,* 345 U.S. at 10. Second, a proceeding in which the state secrets privilege is successfully interposed must be dismissed if the circumstances make clear that privileged information will be so central to the litigation that any attempt to proceed will threaten that information's disclosure. *See Sterling,* 416 F.3d at 348; *see also Reynolds,* 345 U.S. at 11 n.26; *Totten,* 92 U.S. at 107. With these controlling principles in mind, and being cognizant of the delicate balance to be struck in applying the state secrets doctrine, we proceed to our analysis of El-Masri's contentions.

B.

1. . . .

a.

The heart of El-Masri's appeal is his assertion that the facts essential to his Complaint have largely been made public, either in statements by United States officials or in reports by media outlets and foreign governmental entities. He maintains that the subject of this action is simply "a rendition and its consequences," and that its critical facts – the CIA's operation of a rendition program targeted at terrorism suspects, plus the tactics employed therein – have been so widely discussed that litigation concerning them could do no harm to national security. As a result, El-Masri contends that the district court should have allowed his case to move forward with discovery, perhaps with special procedures imposed to protect sensitive information.

El-Masri's contention in that regard, however, misapprehends the nature of our assessment of a dismissal on state secrets grounds. The controlling inquiry is not whether the general subject matter of an action can be described without resort to state secrets. Rather, we must ascertain whether an action can be *litigated* without threatening the disclosure of such state secrets. Thus, for purposes of the state secrets analysis, the "central facts" and "very subject matter" of an action are those facts that are essential to prosecuting the action or defending against it.

El-Masri is therefore incorrect in contending that the central facts of this proceeding are his allegations that he was detained and interrogated under abusive conditions, or that the CIA conducted the rendition program that has been acknowledged by United States officials. Facts such as those furnish the general terms in which El-Masri has related his story to the press, but advancing a case in the court of public opinion, against the United States at large, is an undertaking quite different from prevailing against specific defendants in a court of law. If El-Masri's civil action were to proceed, the facts central to its resolution would be the roles, if any, that the defendants played in the events he alleges. To establish a prima facie case, he would be obliged to produce admissible evidence not only that he was detained and interrogated, but that the defendants were involved in his detention and interrogation in a manner that renders them personally liable to him. Such a showing could be made only with evidence that exposes how the CIA organizes, staffs, and supervises its most sensitive intelligence operations. With regard to Director Tenet, for example, El-Masri would be obliged to show in detail how the head of the CIA participates in such operations, and how information concerning their progress is relayed to him. With respect to the defendant corporations and their unnamed employees, El-Masri would have to demonstrate the existence and details of CIA espionage contracts, an endeavor practically indistinguishable from that categorically barred by *Totten* and *Tenet v. Doe. See* Totten v. United States, 92 U.S. 105, 107 (1875) (establishing absolute bar to enforcement of confidential agreements to conduct espionage, on ground that "public policy forbids the maintenance of any suit in a court of justice, the trial of which would inevitably lead to the disclosure of matters which the law itself regards as confidential"); Tenet v. Doe, 544 U.S. 1, 10-11 (2005) (reaffirming *Totten* in unanimous decision). Even marshalling the evidence necessary to make the requisite showings would implicate privileged state secrets, because El-Masri would need to rely on witnesses whose identities, and evidence the very existence of which, must remain confidential in the interest of national security. *See Sterling,* 416 F.3d at 347 ("[T]he very methods by which evidence would be gathered in this case are themselves problematic.").

b.

Furthermore, if El-Masri were somehow able to make out a prima facie case despite the unavailability of state secrets, the defendants could not properly defend themselves without using privileged evidence. The main avenues of defense available in this matter are to show that El-Masri was not subject to the treatment that he alleges; that, if he was subject to such treatment, the defendants were not involved in it; or that, if they were involved, the nature of their involvement does not give rise to liability. Any of those three showings would require disclosure of information regarding the means and methods by which the CIA gathers intelligence. If, for example, the truth is that El-Masri was detained by the CIA but his description of his treatment is inaccurate, that fact could be established only by disclosure of the actual circumstances of his detention, and its proof would require testimony by the personnel involved. Or, if El-Masri was in fact detained as he describes, but the operation was conducted by some governmental entity other than the CIA, or another government entirely, that information would be privileged. Alternatively, if the CIA detained El-Masri, but did so without Director Tenet's active involvement, effective proof thereof would require a detailed explanation of how CIA operations are supervised. Similarly, although an individual CIA officer might demonstrate his lack of involvement in a given operation by disclosing that he was actually performing some other function at the time in question, establishing his alibi would likely require him to reveal privileged information.

Moreover, proof of the involvement – or lack thereof – of particular CIA officers in a given operation would provide significant information on how the CIA makes its personnel assignments. Similar concerns would attach to evidence produced in defense of the corporate defendants and their unnamed employees. And, like El-Masri's prima facie case, any of the possible defenses suggested above would require the production of witnesses whose identities are confidential and evidence the very existence of which is a state secret. We do not, of course, mean to suggest that any of these hypothetical defenses represents the true state of affairs in this matter, but they illustrate that virtually any conceivable response to El-Masri's allegations would disclose privileged information.

c.

It is clear from precedent that the "central facts" or "very subject matter" of a civil proceeding, for purposes of our dismissal analysis, are those facts necessary to litigate it – not merely to discuss it in general terms. In *Bareford v. General Dynamics Corp.,* several plaintiffs who had been injured or whose decedents had died in the 1987 missile attack on the U.S.S. Stark in the Persian Gulf initiated an action against the manufacturers of the vessel's weapons system, alleging that the system had been defectively manufactured and designed. *See* 973 F.2d 1138, 1140 (5th Cir. 1992). Those allegations, like El-Masri's, could be set forth without revealing state secrets; the plaintiffs' assertion that a Navy weapons system was defective was not, in itself, detrimental to national security. The facts central to the resolution of the proceeding, however, were whether the weapons system was intended to destroy the missile that struck the Stark and, if so, why it failed. Those critical factual questions could not be answered, the Fifth Circuit concluded, without threatening disclosure of privileged state secrets, and thus dismissal was appropriate. *See id.* at 1143-44. . . .

[Here the court reviews other similar Court of Appeals decisions.]

In light of these decisions, we must reject El-Masri's view that the existence of public reports concerning his alleged rendition (and the CIA's rendition program in general) should have saved his Complaint from dismissal. Even if we assume, arguendo, that the state secrets privilege does not apply to the information that media outlets have published concerning those topics, dismissal of his Complaint would nonetheless be proper because the public information does not include the facts that are central to litigating his action. Rather, those central facts – the CIA means and methods that form the subject matter of El-Masri's claim – remain state secrets. Consequently, pursuant to the standards that El-Masri has acknowledged as controlling, the district court did not err in dismissing his Complaint at the pleading stage.

2.

El-Masri also contends that, instead of dismissing his Complaint, the district court should have employed some procedure under which state secrets would have been revealed to him, his counsel, and the court, but withheld from the public. Specifically, he suggests that the court ought to have received all the state secrets evidence in camera and under seal, provided his counsel access to it pursuant to a nondisclosure agreement (after arranging for necessary security clearances), and then conducted an in camera trial. We need not dwell long on El-Masri's proposal in this regard, for it is expressly foreclosed by *Reynolds,* the Supreme Court decision that controls this entire field of inquiry. *Reynolds* plainly held that when "the occasion for the privilege is appropriate, . . . the court should not jeopardize the security which the privilege is meant to protect by insisting upon an examination of the evidence, even by the judge alone, in chambers." 345 U.S. at 10. El-Masri's assertion that the district court erred in not compelling the disclosure of state secrets to him and his lawyers is thus without merit.

C.

In addition to his analysis under the controlling legal principles, El-Masri presents a sharp attack on what he views as the dire constitutional and policy consequences of dismissing his Complaint. He maintains that the district court's ruling, if affirmed, would enable the Executive to unilaterally avoid judicial scrutiny merely by asserting that state secrets are at stake in a given matter. More broadly, he questions the very application of the state secrets doctrine in matters where "egregious executive misconduct" is alleged, contending that, in such circumstances, the courts' "constitutional duty to review executive action" should trump the procedural protections traditionally accorded state secrets.

Contrary to El-Masri's assertion, the state secrets doctrine does not represent a surrender of judicial control over access to the courts. As we have explained, it is the court, not the Executive, that determines whether the state secrets privilege has been properly invoked. In order to successfully claim the state secrets privilege, the Executive must satisfy the court that disclosure of the information sought to be protected would expose matters that, in the interest of national security, ought to remain secret. Similarly, in order to win dismissal of an action on state secrets grounds, the Executive must persuade the court that state secrets are so central to the action that it cannot be fairly litigated without threatening their disclosure. The state secrets privilege cannot be successfully interposed, nor can it lead to dismissal of an action, based merely on the Executive's assertion that the pertinent standard has been met.

In this matter, the reasons for the United States' claim of the state secrets privilege and its motion to dismiss were explained largely in the Classified Declaration, which sets forth in detail the nature of the information that the Executive seeks to protect and explains why its disclosure would be detrimental to national security. We have reviewed the Classified Declaration, as did the district court, and the extensive information it contains is crucial to our decision in this matter. El-Masri's contention that his Complaint was dismissed based on the Executive's "unilateral assert[ion] of a need for secrecy" is entirely unfounded. It is no doubt frustrating to El-Masri that many of the specific reasons for the dismissal of his Complaint are classified. An inherent feature of the state secrets privilege, however, is that the party against whom it is asserted will often not be privy to the information that the Executive seeks to protect. That El-Masri is unfamiliar with the Classified Declaration's explanation for the privilege claim does not imply, as he would have it, that no such explanation was required, or that the district court's ruling was simply an unthinking ratification of a conclusory demand by the executive branch.

We also reject El-Masri's view that we are obliged to jettison procedural restrictions – including the law of privilege – that might impede our ability to act as a check on the Executive. Indeed, El-Masri's position in that regard fundamentally misunderstands the nature of our relationship to the executive branch. El-Masri envisions a judiciary that possesses a roving writ to ferret out and strike down executive excess. Article III, however, assigns the courts a more modest role: we simply decide cases and controversies. Thus, when an executive officer's liability for official action can be established in a properly conducted judicial proceeding, we will not hesitate to enter judgment accordingly. But we would be guilty of excess in our own right if we were to disregard settled legal principles in order to reach the merits of an executive action that would not otherwise be before us – especially when the challenged action pertains to military or foreign policy. We decline to follow such a course, and thus reject El-Masri's invitation to rule that the state secrets doctrine can be brushed aside on the ground that the President's foreign policy has gotten out of line.

D.

As we have observed in the past, the successful interposition of the state secrets privilege imposes a heavy burden on the party against whom the privilege is asserted. *See Sterling,* 416 F.3d at 348 ("We recognize that our decision places, on behalf of the entire country, a burden on Sterling that he alone must bear."). That party loses access to evidence that he needs to prosecute his action and, if privileged state secrets are sufficiently central to the matter, may lose his cause of action altogether. Moreover, a plaintiff suffers this reversal not through any fault of his own, but because his personal interest in pursuing his civil claim is subordinated to the collective interest in national security. *See id.* ("[T]here can be no doubt that, in limited circumstances like these, the fundamental principle of access to court must bow to the fact that a nation without sound intelligence is a nation at risk."); *Fitzgerald,* 776 F.2d at 1238 n.3 ("When the state secrets privilege is validly asserted, the result is unfairness to individual litigants – through the loss of important evidence or dismissal of a case – in order to protect a greater public value"). In view of these considerations, we recognize the gravity of our conclusion that El-Masri must be denied a judicial forum for his Complaint, and reiterate our past observations that dismissal on state secrets grounds is appropriate only in a narrow category of disputes. *See Sterling,* 416 F.3d at 348; *Fitzgerald,* 776 F.2d at 1241-42. Nonetheless, we think it plain that the matter before us falls squarely within that narrow class, and we are unable to find merit in El-Masri's assertion to the contrary. . . .

Affirmed.

36

Restraining Unauthorized Disclosures of National Security Information

B. RESTRAINING LEAKS BY ESPIONAGE PROSECUTIONS

Page 1077. Add the following case after Note 7.

United States v. Rosen

United States District Court, Eastern District of Virginia, 2006
445 F. Supp. 2d 602

ELLIS, District Judge. In this Espionage Act prosecution, defendants Steven Rosen and Keith Weissman have been charged in Count I of a superseding indictment with conspiring to transmit information relating to the national defense[1] to those not entitled to receive it, in violation of 18 U.S.C. §793(g) [providing criminal liability for co-conspirators]. Defendants, by pretrial motion, attack the constitutionality of §793 in three ways. First, they argue that the statute, as applied to them, is unconstitutionally vague in violation of the Due Process Clause of the Fifth Amendment. Second, they argue that the statute, as applied to them, abridges their First Amendment right to free speech and their First Amendment right to petition the government. Third, defendants assert

1. The phrase "information relating to the national defense" will sometimes be referred to herein as NDI.

the First Amendment rights of others by attacking the statute as facially overbroad. In the alternative, defendants urge the Court to avoid these constitutional issues by interpreting the statute as applying only to the transmission of tangible items, *i.e.*, documents, tapes, discs, maps and the like.

In addition, defendant Rosen has been charged in Count III of the superseding indictment with aiding and abetting the transmission of information relating to the national defense to one not entitled to receive it, in violation of 18 U.S.C. §793(d) and 2. He seeks dismissal of this count on the ground that the facts alleged in the superseding indictment in support of this count are legally insufficient.

I.

During the period of the conspiracy alleged in Count I, defendants Rosen and Weissman were employed by the American Israel Public Affairs Committee (AIPAC) in Washington, D.C. AIPAC is a pro-Israel organization that lobbies the United States executive and legislative branches on issues of interest to Israel, especially U.S. foreign policy with respect to the Middle East. Rosen was AIPAC's Director of Foreign Policy Issues . . . . Rosen did not have a security clearance during the period of the alleged conspiracy . . . . Defendant Weissman was AIPAC's Senior Middle East Analyst . . . . Alleged co-conspirator Lawrence Franklin worked on the Iran desk in the Office of the Secretary of the Department of Defense (DOD) and held a top secret security clearance during the alleged conspiracy.[3]

In general, the superseding indictment alleges that in furtherance of their lobbying activities, defendants (i) cultivated relationships with government officials with access to sensitive U.S. government information, including NDI, (ii) obtained the information from these officials, and (iii) transmitted the information to persons not otherwise entitled to receive it, including members of the media, foreign policy analysts, and officials of a foreign government.

The government's recitation of the acts constituting the conspiracy begins on April 13, 1999, when Rosen told an unnamed foreign official

---

3. On October 5, 2005, Franklin pled guilty to one count of conspiracy to communicate national defense information to one not entitled to receive it, in violation of 18 U.S.C. §§793(d) and (g), and to one count of conspiracy to communicate classified information to an agent of a foreign government in violation of 50 U.S.C. §783 and 18 U.S.C. §371.

(FO-1) that he had "picked up an extremely sensitive piece of intelligence" which he described as "codeword protected intelligence." Rosen proceeded to relate this piece of intelligence, which concerned terrorist activities in Central Asia, to the foreign official. . . . The superseding indictment alleges further that Weissman's role in the conspiracy became apparent on June 11, 1999, when Weissman told the same foreign official that he had obtained a "secret FBI, classified FBI report" relating to the Khobar Towers bombing from three different sources, including a member of the United States government. Later that day, Weissman told FO-1 that he had interested a member of the media in the report.

According to the superseding indictment, roughly eighteen months later, on December 12, 2000, Rosen and Weissman met with a United States government official (USGO-1) who had access to classified information relating to U.S. strategy pertaining to a certain Middle East country. Following this meeting, Rosen allegedly had a conversation with a member of the media in which he communicated classified information relating to the U.S. government's deliberations on its strategy towards that particular Middle Eastern country. . . .

In August 2002, Rosen was introduced to Franklin through a contact at the DOD. Rosen, Weissman, Franklin and another DOD employee finally met nearly six months later, on February 12, 2003. At this meeting, Franklin disclosed to Rosen and Weissman information relating to a classified draft internal United States government policy document concerning a certain Middle Eastern country. . . . Rosen met with FO-2 and discussed the same draft internal policy document that Franklin had discussed with Rosen and Weissman. . . .

[The court goes on to describe in some detail a number of other instances in which Rosen and Weissman allegedly knowingly received classified information and passed it on to other AIPAC employees, foreign officials, and journalists.]

The superseding indictment also charges Rosen with aiding and abetting Franklin in the latter's violation of 18 U.S.C. §793(d). Specifically, Rosen is alleged to have aided and abetted Franklin's March 17, 2003 transmission by fax of the document he had created from the classified draft internal policy document related to a certain Middle Eastern country.

Rosen and Weissman have challenged the constitutionality of Count I of the superseding indictment on three separate but related grounds. First, the defendants argue that the government's application of 18 U.S.C. §793(e) in this prosecution violates the Fifth Amendment's Due Process Clause under the vagueness doctrine because the statute's indeterminate language failed to provide these defendants with adequate warning that their conduct was proscribed. In addition to this as-applied vagueness claim, defendants make two arguments based on the guarantees of the First Amendment. First, they argue that their conduct, as alleged in the superseding indictment, may not be proscribed without transgressing the First Amendment's guarantees of free speech and the right to petition the government. Second, even assuming the statute's constitutional application here, they raise a facial challenge to the statute pursuant to the First Amendment's well-recognized overbreadth doctrine. Finally, in a separate motion to dismiss, Rosen challenges the sufficiency of the allegation that he aided and abetted Franklin's violation of §793(d). Each of these contentions is separately addressed.

II.

The operative statute at issue in defendant's constitutional challenge is codified at 18 U.S.C. §793 and provides, in pertinent part, as follows:

> [Subsections (d) and (e) are set forth in the casebook at p. 1067.]
>
> (g) If two or more persons conspire to violate any of the foregoing provisions of this section, and one or more of such persons do any act to effect the object of the conspiracy, each of the parties to such conspiracy shall be subject to the punishment provided for the offense which is the object of the conspiracy.

18 U.S.C. §793. A brief history of this statute provides necessary context and helps illuminate the analysis of the questions presented. . . .

[After a lengthy discussion, the court ruled that §793 applies to information transmitted in oral, as well as tangible, form.]

Defendants' first constitutional challenge to the statute is based on the principle that the Due Process clause of the Fifth Amendment prohibits punishment pursuant to a statute so vague that "men of common intelligence must necessarily guess at its meaning and differ as to its application." United States v. Lanier, 520 U.S. 259, 266 (1997) (quoting Connally v. General Constr. Co., 269 U.S. 385, 391 (1926)). . . .

IV. . . .

C.

. . . [A]ny inherent vagueness in the terms "relating to the national defense" or "entitled to receive" as used in §§793(d) and (e) is cured through the judicial glosses that have been added to these phrases. To the extent that oral transmission of information relating to the national defense makes it more difficult for defendants to know whether they are violating the statute, the statute is not thereby rendered unconstitutionally vague because the statute permits conviction only of those who "willfully" commit the prohibited acts and do so with bad faith. So construed, both phrases pass Fifth Amendment muster; they are not unconstitutionally vague as applied to these defendants.

D.

Seeking to avoid this conclusion, defendants argue that notwithstanding the clarity of the statute's language, the application of the statute to these defendants is so novel and unprecedented that it violates the fair warning prong of the vagueness doctrine. As explained *supra*, the constitutionally required clarity of a statute may be provided through the gloss of judicial interpretation, and it is precisely the judicial glosses on §793 that save the statute from defendants' vagueness challenge. The corollary of this principle is that "due process bars courts from applying a novel construction of a criminal statute to conduct that neither the statute nor any prior judicial decision has fairly disclosed to be within its scope." *Lanier*, 520 U.S. at 266. . . . [T]he test . . . is whether the language and application of the statute has provided defendants adequate warning that their conduct was proscribed. Section 793, as applied here, meets this test; its language and history provided adequate warning to these defendants that the statute proscribed the alleged conduct.

Defendants argue that the present prosecution represents a novel construction of the statute which they could not have anticipated because "leaks" of classified information by non-governmental persons have never been prosecuted under this statute. The statute's plain language rebuts this argument.[38] It is clear from this plain language that defendants' conduct, as alleged in the superseding indictment is within the sweep of the statute. . . . [T]he defendants here cannot argue persuasively that the result reached here amounts to an unforeseeable judicial enlargement of §793.

And, it is useful in this regard to address defendants' frequent use of

---

38. In amending the statute in 1950, Congress made it quite clear that the statute was intended to apply to the transmission of national defense information by non-government employees by adding subsection (e). . . .

the term "leak" in advancing their argument that there was not constitutionally adequate notice that the statute reached the alleged conduct. The term "leak," at bottom, connotes in this context, an unpermitted or unauthorized transmission or transfer of information, which of course, is an act plainly within §793, assuming all the other requirements are met. So, labeling an event a "leak" does not remove the event from the statute's scope. At best, the term "leak" is a euphemism used to imply or suggest to a careless reader that the transmission of the information was somehow authorized. Whether the "leaks" or transmissions of information in this case were authorized is likely to be a sharply controverted issue in this case and if the government does not carry its burden of showing that the transfers of information were unauthorized, the prosecution fails. But the analysis here proceeds, as it must, on the superseding indictment's allegations, including the allegation that all transmissions of NDI were unauthorized. At this point, therefore, defendants frequent use of "leak" as a characterization of what occurred is unavailing.

Also unsuccessful is defendants' claim that past applications of the statute fail to provide fair warning that the statute could be applied to the facts alleged in the superseding indictment. *Morison* itself rebuts this claim. Notably, in *Morison* the Fourth Circuit considered the very similar argument that the statute was intended to apply only to classic espionage cases and therefore did not apply to Morison's "leak" to a news publication. In rejecting this argument, the Fourth Circuit noted the rarity of prosecutions under §793(e), but stated

> that the rarity of prosecution under the statutes does not indicate that the statutes were not to be enforced as written. We think in any event, the rarity of use of the statute as a basis for prosecution is at best a questionable basis for nullifying the clear language of the statute, and we think the revision of 1950 and its reenactment of section 793(d) demonstrate that Congress did not consider such statute meaningless or intend that the statute and its prohibitions were to be abandoned.

Morison, 844 F.2d at 1067. The Fourth Circuit's reasoning in rejecting Morison's challenge is equally applicable to the defendants here, and therefore, for the same reasons, defendants' vagueness challenge based on the novelty of this prosecution fails as well.

V.

The defendants' next constitutional challenge rests on the First Amendment's guarantees of free speech and the right to petition the government for grievances. . . . Defendants' First Amendment challenge exposes the inherent tension between the government transparency so essential to a democratic society and the government's equally compelling need to protect from disclosure information that could be used by those who wish this nation harm. In addressing this tension, it is important to bear in mind that the question to be resolved here is not whether §793 is the optimal resolution of this tension, but whether Congress, in passing this statute, has struck a balance between these competing interests that falls within the range of constitutionally permissible outcomes.

As an initial matter, it is necessary to confront the government's proposed categorical rule that espionage statutes cannot implicate the First Amendment. This contention overreaches. In the broadest terms, the conduct at issue – collecting information about United States' foreign policy and discussing that information with government officials (both United States and foreign), journalists, and other participants in the foreign policy establishment – is at the core of the First Amendment's guarantees. *See* Mills v. Alabama, 384 U.S. 214, 218 (1966) ("[T]here is practically universal agreement that a major purpose of [the First] Amendment was to protect the free discussion of governmental affairs."). And, even under a more precise description of the conduct – the passing of government secrets relating to the national defense to those not entitled to receive them in an attempt to influence United States foreign policy – the application of §793 to the defendants is unquestionably still deserving of First Amendment scrutiny. . . .

Given that the application of the statute to these defendants warrants First Amendment scrutiny, the question then becomes whether Congress may nonetheless penalize the conduct alleged in the superseding indictment, for while the invocation of "national security" does not free Congress from the restraints of the First Amendment, it is equally well established that the invocation of the First Amendment does not "provide immunity for every possible use of language," Frohwerk v. U.S., 249 U.S. 204, 206 (1919), and that "the societal value of speech must, on occasion, be subordinated to other values and considerations." Dennis v. United States, 341 U.S. 494, 503 (1951). As Justice Frankfurter aptly put it in *Dennis:*

> The demands of free speech in a democratic society as well as the interest in national security are better served by a candid and informed weighing of the competing interests, within the confines of the judicial process, than by announcing dogmas too inflexible for the non-Euclidian problems to be solved.

Dennis, 341 U.S. at 524-25 (Frankfurter, J., concurring). Thus, to determine, on any given occasion, whether the government's interest prevails over the First Amendment, courts must begin with "an assessment of the competing societal interests" at stake, *Morison,* 844 F.2d at 1082, and proceed to the "delicate and difficult task" of weighing those interests "to determine whether the resulting restriction on freedom can be tolerated." United States v. Robel, 389 U.S. 258, 264 (1967).

As already noted, the defendants' First Amendment interests at stake in this prosecution, and those of the third parties raised by defendants, are significant and implicate the core values the First Amendment was designed to protect. The collection and discussion of information about the conduct of government by defendants and others in the body politic is indispensable to the healthy functioning of a representative government, for "[a]s James Madison put it in 1822: 'A popular Government, without popular information, or a means of acquiring it, is but a Prologue to a Farce or a Tragedy; or, perhaps both.'" *Morison,* 844 F.2d at 1081 (Wilkinson, J., concurring) (quoting 9 Writings of James Madison 103 (G. Hunt ed., 1910)). This is especially so in the context of foreign policy because, as Justice Stewart observed in the Pentagon Papers case:

> In the absence of the government checks and balances present in other areas of our national life, the only effective restraint upon executive policy and power in the areas of national defense and international affairs may lie in an enlightened citizenry-in an informed and critical public opinion which alone can here protect the values of democratic government.

New York Times v. United States, 403 U.S. 713, 728 (1971) (Stewart J., concurring). . . .

But importantly, the defendants here are not accused merely of disclosing government secrets, they are accused of disclosing NDI, *i.e.*, government secrets the disclosure of which could threaten the security of the nation. And, however vital an informed public may be, it is well established that disclosure of certain information may be restricted in service of the nation's security, for "[i]t is 'obvious and unarguable' that no governmental interest is more compelling than the security of the Nation." Haig v. Agee, 453 U.S. 280, 307 (1981). And, as the Supreme

Court has repeatedly noted, one aspect of the government's paramount interest in protecting the nation's security is the government's "compelling interest in protecting both the secrecy of information important to our national security and the appearance of confidentiality so essential to the effective operation of our foreign intelligence service." *Snepp,* 444 U.S. at 509 n.3. Thus, the right to free speech and the value of an informed citizenry is not absolute and must yield to the government's legitimate efforts to ensure "the environment of physical security which a functioning democracy requires." *Morison,* 844 F.2d at 1082. This point is best expressed in the Supreme Court's pithy phrase that "while the Constitution protects against the invasion of individual rights, it is not a suicide pact." *Aptheker,* 378 U.S. at 509.

Of course, the abstract proposition that the rights protected by the First Amendment must at times yield to the need for national security does not address the concrete issue of whether the §793, as applied here, violates the First Amendment. This determination depends on whether §793 is narrowly drawn to apply only to those instances in which the government's need for secrecy is legitimate, or whether it is too indiscriminate in its sweep, seeking in effect, to excise the cancer of espionage with a chainsaw instead of a scalpel. In this respect, the first clause of §793(e) implicates only the defendants' right to disclose, willfully, information the government has sought to keep confidential due to the potential harm its disclosure poses to the national security in situations in which the defendants have reason to believe that such disclosure could be used to injure the United States or aid a foreign government. Likewise, §793(d), which defendants are charged with conspiring to violate, implicates the same interests, but is limited to those people – generally government employees or contractors – with authorized possession of the information. Thus, it seems fair to say that §793, taken together with its judicial glosses, is more the result of a legislative scalpel and not a chainsaw. This, however, does not end the analysis.

As defendants correctly argue, the analysis of the First Amendment interests implicated by §§793(d) and (e) depends on the relationship to the government of the person whose First Amendment rights are implicated. In this respect, there are two classes of people roughly correlating to those subject to prosecution under §793(d) and those subject to prosecution under §793(e). The first class consists of persons who have access to the information by virtue of their official position. These people are most often government employees or military personnel with access to classified information, or defense contractors with access to classified information, and are often bound by contractual agreements whereby they agree not to disclose classified information. As such, they are in a position of trust with the government. The second class of persons are those who have no employment or contractual relationship with the government, and therefore have not exploited a relationship of trust to obtain the national defense information they are charged with disclosing, but instead generally obtained the information from one who has violated such a trust.

There can be little doubt, as defendants readily concede, that the Constitution permits the government to prosecute the first class of persons for the disclosure of information relating to the national defense when that person knew that the information is the type which could be used to threaten the nation's security, and that person acted in bad faith, *i.e.*, with reason to believe the disclosure could harm the United States or aid a foreign government. Indeed, the relevant precedent teaches that the Constitution permits even more drastic restraints on the free speech rights of this class of persons. . . .

. . . For this reason, the government may constitutionally punish government employees like Franklin for the willful disclosure of national defense information, and if the government proves the defendants conspired with Franklin in his commission of that offense, they may be subject to prosecution, as well. 18 U.S.C. §793(g).

But the analysis must go beyond this because the defendants are also charged with conspiring to violate §793(e) for their own disclosures of NDI to those not entitled to receive it. In this regard, they belong in the second class of those subject to prosecution under §793 – namely, those who have not violated a position of trust with the government to obtain and disclose information, but have obtained the information from one who has. The defendants argue that unlike Morison, Marchetti or Snepp, they did not agree to restrain their speech as part of their employment, and accordingly their First Amendment interests are more robust. . . .

One possible implication . . . is that a special relationship with the government is necessary before the government may constitutionally punish the disclosure of information relating to the national defense. Seizing upon this possible implication, defendants here contend that the First Amendment bars Congress from punishing those persons, like defendants, without a special relationship to the government for the disclosure of NDI. In essence, their position is that once a government secret has been leaked to the general public and the first line of defense thereby breached, the government has no recourse but to sit back and watch as the threat to the national security caused by the first disclosure multiplies with every subsequent disclosure. This position cannot be sustained. Although the question whether the government's interest in preserving its national defense secrets is sufficient to trump the First Amendment rights of those not in a position of trust with the government is a more difficult question, and although the authority addressing this issue is sparse, both common sense and the relevant precedent point persuasively to the conclusion that the government can punish those outside of the government for the unauthorized receipt and deliberate retransmission of information relating to the national defense.

Of course, in some instances the government's interest is so compelling, and the defendant's purpose so patently unrelated to the values of the First Amendment, that a constitutional challenge is easily dismissed. The obvious example is the unauthorized disclosure of troop movements or military technology to hostile foreign powers by non-governmental persons, conduct typically prosecuted under §794. But this is not such a case; the government has not charged the defendants under §794(a), and therefore the most relevant precedent, although it dealt with the freedom of press, is the Supreme Court's decision in New York Times Co. v. United States, 403 U.S. 713 (1971) (per curiam). . . . [A] close reading of [the concurring] opinions indicates that the result may have been different had the government sought to prosecute the newspapers under §793(e) subsequent to the publication of the Pentagon Papers. [Here the court analyzed these opinions. *See also* casebook pp. 1090-1093.] While the Supreme Court's discussion of the application of §793(e) to the newspapers is clearly *dicta,* lower courts "are bound by the Supreme Court's considered *dicta* almost as firmly as by the Court's outright holdings, particularly when, as here, a *dictum* is of recent vintage and not enfeebled by any subsequent statement." McCoy v. Massachusetts Institute of Technology, 950 F.2d 13, 19 (1st Cir. 1991). In sum, Congress's attempt to provide for the nation's security by extending punishment for the disclosure of national security secrets beyond the first category of persons within its trust to the general populace is a reasonable, and therefore constitutional[,] exercise of its power. . . .

. . . [E]ven when a person is charged with the transmission of intangible "information" the person had "reason to believe could be used to the injury of the United States," the application of the statute without the requirement that disclosure of the information be potentially harmful to the United States would subject non-governmental employees to prosecution for the innocent, albeit negligent, disclosure of information relating to the national defense. Punishing defendants engaged in public debate for unwittingly harming a legitimate government interest is inconsistent with the Supreme Court's First Amendment jurisprudence. Limiting the set of information relating to the national defense to that information which the defendant *knows,* if disclosed, is potentially harmful to the United States, by virtue of the statute's willfulness requirement, avoids this problem. Thus, for these reasons, information relating to the national defense, whether tangible or intangible, must necessarily be information which if disclosed, is potentially harmful to the United States, and the defendant must know that disclosure of the information is potentially harmful to the United States. The alternative construction simply is not sustainable. So limited, the statute does not violate the defendants' First Amendment guarantee of free speech.

For essentially the same reasons, §793, as applied to these defendants, does not violate the defendants' First Amendment right to petition the government for grievances. The Supreme Court has stated that "[t]he right to petition is cut from the same cloth as the other guarantees of [the First] Amendment, and is an assurance of a particular expression of freedom." McDonald v. Smith, 472 U.S. 479, 482 (1985). Indeed, "this right is implicit in 'the very idea of government, republican in form.'" *Id.* . . . For this reason, defendants contend that §793 cannot constitutionally be applied to their alleged conduct.

This argument suffers the same fatal flaws as defendants' argument under the First Amendment's free speech guarantee. Like the First Amendment's guarantee of free speech, the right to petition the government for grievances is not absolute, and may be validly regulated. *See* California Motor Transport v. Trucking Unlimited, 404 U.S. 508, 514-15 (1972) ("First Amendment rights may not be used as the means or pretext for achieving 'substantive evils'") (citing NAACP v. Button, 371 U.S. 415, 444 (1963)). . . . [T]he right to petition the government is validly restrained if the government does so for a legitimate purpose. And because the government's vital and legitimate national security interest is validly served through these statutes, the defendants' right to petition the government, like their right to free speech, must yield. . . .

[The court then rejected the defendants' challenge based on the overbreadth doctrine.]

VII.

In the end, it must be said that this is a hard case, and not solely because the parties' positions and arguments are both substantial and complex. It is also a hard case because it requires an evaluation of whether Congress has violated our Constitution's most sacred values, enshrined in the First and the Fifth Amendment, when it passed legislation in furtherance of our nation's security. The conclusion here is that the balance struck by §793 between these competing interests is constitutionally permissible because (1) it limits the breadth of the term "related to the national defense" to matters closely held by the government for the legitimate reason that their disclosure could threaten our collective security; and (2) it imposes rigorous scienter requirements as a condition for finding criminal liability.

The conclusion that the statute is constitutionally permissible does not reflect a judgment about whether Congress could strike a more appropriate balance between these competing interests, or whether a more carefully drawn statute could better serve both the national security and the value of public debate. Indeed, the basic terms and structure of this statute have remained largely unchanged since the administration of William Howard Taft. The intervening years have witnessed dramatic changes in the position of the United States in world affairs and the nature of threats to our national security. The increasing importance of the United States in world affairs has caused a significant increase in the size and complexity of the United States' military and foreign policy establishments, and in the importance of our nation's foreign policy decision making. Finally, in the nearly one hundred years since the passage of the Defense Secrets Act mankind has made great technological advances affecting not only the nature and potential devastation of modern warfare, but also the very nature of information and communication. These changes should suggest to even the most casual observer that the time is ripe for Congress to engage in a thorough review and revision of these provisions to ensure that they reflect both these changes, and contemporary views about the appropriate balance between our nation's security and our citizens' ability to engage in public debate about the United States' conduct in the society of nations.

An appropriate Order will issue.

* * *

37

Restraints on Publication of National Security Information

A. CASE STUDY: THE PENTAGON PAPERS LITIGATION

2. The Threat of Criminal Prosecution

Page 1091. Add the following case after Note 7.

United States v. Rosen

United States District Court, Eastern District of Virginia, 2006
445 F. Supp. 2d 602

[The opinion is set forth *supra* p. 281.]

* * *